Nationalism & Antisemitism in Modern Europe 1815–1945

by

SHMUEL ALMOG

Published for the

Vidal Sassoon International Center for
the Study of Antisemitism (SICSA),
The Hebrew University of Jerusalem

in cooperation with

The Zalman Shazar Center
for Jewish History
The Historical Society of Israel

by

PERGAMON PRESS
Member of Maxwell Macmillan Pergamon Publishing Corporation

OXFORD · NEW YORK · BEIJING · FRANKFURT
SÃO PAULO · SYDNEY · TOKYO · TORONTO

U.K.	Pergamon Press plc, Headington Hill Hall, Oxford OX3 0BW, England
U.S.A.	Pergamon Press Inc., Maxwell House, Fairview Park, Elmsford, New York 10523, U.S.A.
PEOPLE'S REPUBLIC OF CHINA	Pergamon Press, Room 4037, Qianmen Hotel, Beijing, People's Republic of China
FEDERAL REPUBLIC OF GERMANY	Pergamon Press GmbH, Hammerweg 6, D-6242 Kronberg, Federal Republic of Germany
BRAZIL	Pergamon Editora Ltda, Rua Eça de Queiros 346, CEP 04011, Paraiso, São Paulo, Brazil
AUSTRALIA	Pergamon Press Australia Pty Ltd., P.O. Box 544, Potts Point, N.S.W. 2011, Australia
JAPAN	Pergamon Press, 5th Floor, Matsuoka Central Building, 1-7-1 Nishishinjuku, Shinjuku-ku, Tokyo 160, Japan
CANADA	Pergamon Press Canada Ltd., Suite No. 271, 253 College Street, Toronto, Ontario, Canada M5T 1R5

English edition © 1990 Pergamon Press plc
First published in Hebrew by the Zalman Shazar Center for Jewish History, Jerusalem

Translation by Ralph Mendel.
Picture editor: Yael Maman.

First edition 1990

Library of Congress Cataloging in Publication Data
Almog, S.
[Le 'umiyut ve-anṭishemiyut be-Eropah ha-modernit, 1815–1945. English]
Nationalism and antisemitism in modern Europe, 1815–1945 / by Shmuel Almog. — 1st ed.
p. cm. — (Studies in antisemitism)
Translation of : Le 'umiyut ve-anṭishemiyut be-Eropah ha-modernit, 1815–1945.
Bibliography: p.
Includes index.
1. Antisemitism—Europe—History. 2. Nationalism—Europe—History. 3. Jews—Europe—History. 4. Europe—Ethnic relations.
I. Title. II. Series.
DS146.E85A4613 1989 940'.04924—dc20 89-16157

British Library Cataloguing in Publication Data
Almog, Shmuel
Nationalism and antisemitism in modern Europe, 1815–1945, – (Studies in antisemitism)
1. Europe. Jews. Racial discrimination by Society, history
I. Title II. Vidal Sassoon International Center for the Study of Antisemitism III. Zalman Shazar Center for Jewish History IV. Historical Society of Israel V. Series
805.8'924'04
ISBN 0-08-037254-6 Hardcover
ISBN 0-08-037774-2 Flexicover

Typeset, printed and bound in Great Britain by BPCC Hazell Books, Aylesbury, Bucks, England Member of BPCC Ltd

Contents

Preface

SHMUEL ALMOG

This book seeks to fill a lacuna in an area which has generated growing public interest in recent years—the study of antisemitism. Almost half a century after the Holocaust, the world seems to be more aware of the implications of this catastrophe than ever before. Paradoxically, even the revisionist denial that the Holocaust ever occurred, or the attempt to diminish its magnitude, testify to an ever-growing preoccupation with this event. Nor has the period since the Second World War overshadowed the singularity of the Holocaust phenomenon. There is today a greater sensitivity to, and a growing willingness to face, the questions raised by the Holocaust, especially as historical research has brought to light many important facts about Nazi rule and has provided a detailed record of the murder of European Jewry.

The attempt to discover why Hitler chose the Jews as his prime target leads one to study the historical record of Jewish victimization. The focal point of such study is the relationship between Jews and Gentiles, not merely in the recent past but throughout history. Similarly, the Jews' millennia-long historical tradition and their dispersal across most of the globe are of primary importance in the study of antisemitism. Research therefore should not be confined to one particular area or seek to answer a given set of questions but must spread out in many directions, both in time and in space.

Antisemitism is not a matter of the past. It is still very much alive and in recent years has often reared its ugly head, evoking a striking sense of interplay between past and present. The reverberations of the Holocaust and the awakening of a new antisemitism, whether parading openly or cloaked as anti-Zionism, obligate us to probe the history of Jew-hatred. The persistence of this phenomenon, after all that the world and the Jews have experienced in the past half century, underscores the need to study and understand it.

Within the complex web of Jew-hatred, one must try to single out those strands which can be traced across the generations: the old versus the new, the permanent alongside the ephemeral, the characteristic as opposed to the marginal, and so forth. Modern antisemitism is a hybrid of religious and racial, economic and cultural, ideological and political components: it is an international protean phenomenon woven into a fabric of complex human relations.

It is no easy task to unravel a single thread from this fabric and follow its convoluted trail. Let us consider, for example, nationalism, which is the point of departure for my present discussion. Without doubt nationalism is a major phenomenon of modern history, and its impact on recent European history has been immense. It has also played a crucial role in the forging of relations between the Jews and their surroundings, so much so that modern antisemitism is incomprehensible without reference to nationalism. Thus, consideration of nationalism is integral to any treatment of modern antisemitism, particularly in the European context. Nevertheless, one cannot isolate the element of nationalism and portray it in its ostensibly pristine form as either favorable, hostile or merely indifferent to the Jews. Nationalism usually appears against a diverse backdrop, and great caution must be exercised in delineating its precise boundaries *vis-à-vis* the shifting historical setting.

In this book an attempt is made to describe the interaction between nationalism and antisemitism in post-Napoleonic Europe. A more or less chronological order is followed, and while the focus is naturally on the significant points of interface between the two phenomena, these are considered in terms of major historical events. Notwithstanding the apparent similarities between different national movements and the almost unvarying recurrence of antisemitic motifs, considerable differences still exist between each region and country, (as well as between the historical actors and the successive generations). To illustrate the diversity of these phenomena, annotated passages from representative sources are provided. Structurally, however, the book follows the thrust of

historical continuity and addresses itself to the use which nationalism made of antisemitism for its own purposes.

Finally, I would like to express my heartfelt thanks to the many
friends who helped to turn the manuscript into a readable book:
Ina Friedman, Yohai Goell, Moshe Goodman, Rony Lipovetsky,
Yael Maman, Sarah Hinde Nathansen, Mimi Berman Schneider-
man, Irit Sivan and, last but not least, to the SICSA staff headed
by Sue Fox.

Foreword

SHMUEL ETTINGER*

SHMUEL ALMOG's book is the first in a series of planned monographs
[forming an historical subseries to the Studies in Antisemitism
Series] devoted to the history and characteristics of Jew-hatred over
the centuries. The term "antisemitism," which was coined in the
1870s, was consonant with the worldview of many educated Europeans of the era. Using the achievements of biology, anthropology and
linguistics as their base, they sought an objective scientific foundation, as it were, to classify and grade various human groups.
Though some of them—such as the French linguist and historian
Ernest Renan, who spoke of the superiority of a group of peoples
termed "Aryans" (or Indo-Europeans) over the "Semitic" peoples—
referred to speakers of *all* the Semitic languages, the term "antisemitism," which soon became commonplace in the writings of the
time, was meant to convey hatred and opposition toward Jews and
Judaism alone.

Manifestations of this hatred, or fear of the Jews' ostensibly
predatory influence, first appeared as early as Hellenistic-Roman
times, and perhaps even earlier, and intensified after the triumph
of Christianity in Europe and the spread of Islam in the Near East
and North Africa. Thus, observing the history of the Jews and their
relations with the peoples around them, the persistence of a hostile
attitude toward them on the part of non-Jews is discernible throughout the Middle Ages and in the modern era as well. True, every anti-
Jewish outburst was rooted in specific conditions of time and place,
but the perpetrators' mind-set was preconditioned by theological,
social and cultural arguments from earlier periods. These had a

* We mourn the untimely death of our editor-in-chief, Professor Shmuel Ettinger.

cumulative effect, thus supporting the view of those researchers who find within the variety of antisemitic manifestations the continuity of human consciousness. The negative stereotype of the Jew was forged in theological debates, preachers' sermons, popular traditions, and through works of literature, painting and sculpture. So profoundly did this negative stereotype penetrate the mentality and culture of the European peoples in particular, that its main features survived the waning of the Church's influence among enlightened circles and the rise of critical-rationalist currents and scientific thinking.

Accordingly, the editors have seen fit to include in this series studies describing manifestations of enmity toward Jews and Judaism throughout history, and the interrelation between these and intellectual, political, social and cultural trends that prevailed in the countries where Jews were living. A series of such studies should contribute to the understanding of this phenomenon, which has affected the history of the Jews for centuries and which, moreover, from the end of the nineteenth into our own century, has had an impact on political and social struggles in many European countries. The Nazis used antisemitism as a highly influential factor in the attainment of their political goals among European nations demonstrating how pervasive and deep-rooted Jew-hatred was there. And who can deny the close connection between antisemitism and the Holocaust of European Jewry?

Nevertheless, the nineteenth century and the first decades of the twentieth witnessed an accelerated integration of the majority of European Jews into the economic, cultural, scientific, and subsequently even the political life of their respective countries, as well as the attainment of equal rights before the law, which they and the advocates of their integration called "emancipation." Without the support of important sectors within European society, such advanced integration would have been impossible. This support emanated from forces that were pushing for modernization in European societies—large sections of the bourgeoisie and the liberal and radical parties, which had acquired strength as a result of the democratization of political regimes, as well as of education and the ascendancy of their principles. From an historical perspective, the integration of the Jews into European life can be described as an impressive success story: a process in which large numbers of Jews moved from remote areas of Eastern Europe and the Ottoman Empire, having been engaged in fringe occupations mostly within a backward rural economy, to the major European centers, where they achieved eminence in the economy, the press, science, and the arts.

There is no doubt that the pace and scope of the Jews' integration into mainstream European life and their growing presence in various domains were factors contributing to a hostile backlash and increasing friction with diverse population groups. The Jews' competitors in these new endeavors now joined those who had previously hated and feared them on religious and traditional grounds—the clergy, large sections of the nobility, merchants, guild craftsmen, and the bulk of the peasantry. However, had it not been for the negative stereotype of the Jew, which was retained even by would-be modernizers and the liberal and radical intelligentsia, many among these groups would probably not have attributed collective characteristics to persons of Jewish extraction who were no different from them in terms of education and lifestyle, especially at a time when religious differences had begun to lose importance for them. The result was that the modernization processes which expedited the Jews' integration into the surrounding society fuelled modern antisemitism as an ideology and a social and political movement.

This duality is also discernible in the attitude toward the Jews of the thinkers and ideologues of nationalism, as well as the leaders and activists of the national movements in Europe. The modern national ideas that inspired the leaders of these movements evolved out of opposition to the rulers' claim that they be considered the keepers of political sovereignty and of the common will. Sovereignty belonged not to the ruler but to the "people"—according to the spokesmen of the national idea—and only this factor was entitled to determine the nation's goals and needs. Hence also their objections to the privileges of particular classes—especially the nobility and the Church—typical of the state structure during the feudal and absolutist periods.

Though the term "people" comprises many citizens with divergent views, the spokesmen of nationalism maintained that expression could be given to the "general will" of the people (Jean Jacques Rousseau, the coiner of this phrase, was not fortuitously considered a progenitor of modern national thought). Many nationalists took exception to or rejected the "consensual" or "contractual" principle of the modern political theorists, preferring instead to revert to the organic concepts of the ancient and medieval periods. Such concepts saw in the state the incarnation of a "people spirit" (*Volksgeist*) to which one was affiliated naturally through birth ("nation" from the Latin *natio*, meaning "birth," seems to affirm this). In this view, a nation grows and develops like any other organism.

At first the national ideologies and movements combined universal and humanistic elements together with an emphasis on the uniqueness of the nation; but as these movements grew, the sense in each of the particular and different intensified and came to the fore. As long as the primary aim of a national movement was to develop the nation's language and culture and preserve its distinctive way of life, no acute friction ensued with its neighbors, or even with the imperial polity of which it was part. However, once the spiritual and cultural aspirations of the national movement began to materialize, many started calling for political autonomy based on a specific historical territory (where other ethnic groups had settled as well). When demands were made for independence and political sovereignty, the discord between nations grew sharper, and national particularity, genuine or illusory, took centerstage.

This development left its mark on the attitude of most national movements towards the Jews. As early as the French Revolution, the spokesmen for the French and Batavian (Dutch) nations were divided on whether Jews constituted a religious group within the "nation" or—because of their special laws (the *Halakhah*) and hopes for a national restoration in the messianic age—they constituted a separate nation, a nation unto themselves. Those who stressed the character of the nation as an organic unity, particularly when regarding Christianity as a central component of that entity, spurned the Jews as alien and even harmful to the nation. Similarly, the appeal to the historical past as a unifying element dredged up from time immemorial "creations of the people"—customs, proverbs, passion plays, folk tales and ballads—which were permeated with hatred towards the Jews. This, in turn, served the nationalist ideologues as a prime argument in support of their view.

There were others, however, who demanded appropriate expression for public opinion and wished to create a political structure befitting the nation according to law (*Rechtsstaat*) composed of equal citizens, not a hierarchical "Christian state." They opposed discrimination within the state, including anti-Jewish discrimination, yet they nonetheless urged the Jews to modify their religion and customs which were deemed a barrier to full citizenship for the Jews. This was urged by the liberals in Baden, Germany, in the 1820s and 1830s, and by the Hungarian national leader Lajos Kossuth in the 1840s. Overall, many advocates of national ideas emphasized, in their nascent stages, the rights of the individual; they manifested a liberal approach to economic issues and a democratic attitude toward the running of the state. Such elements, far from desiring to remove the Jews from the national state, even tried to enlist their support for the national struggle and were resolute in urging full civil rights for the Jews.

During the revolutions of 1848, this welter of views among the proponents of national ideas produced a situation in which Jews were sometimes made part of the revolutionary awakening and could even assume positions of leadership, while voices were raised demanding their removal from the "National Guards"; some espoused legal equality for the Jews and others demanded "emancipation *from* the Jews." The failure of the 1848 revolutions was a severe setback for the exponents of the liberal and radical line in the national movements and disappointed many of the Jews who had supported the revolutionary forces. Some of the former now underwent a metamorphosis and turned to monarchist or extreme chauvinist ideas, while a number of Jews who had been active during the period of the revolutions left Europe to seek the fulfilment of their aspiration in the land of liberty, the United States (the *Auf nach Amerika* movement in Central Europe). But European liberalism soon recovered from its crisis; the 1860s witnessed the revival of the liberal and radical camp and heightened pressure for the attainment of national goals, first and foremost to bring about the political unification of Germany and Italy. It is not by chance that during this period the Jews in Central Europe obtained legal emancipation, Jewish emancipation was completed in Britain, and the legal status of East European Jewry improved.

The revolutions of 1848 had a profound influence both on the development of the national movements in Europe and on the Jews' relationship with their environment. They bolstered the national consciousness of many of the smaller national groups that were part of the multinational empires, above all in the Hapsburg Empire. The sense of solidarity among the Slavic peoples intensified as they felt the need for a common stand against German influence, on one side, and the Ottoman Empire, on the other. Not content, for the most part, with cultivating their language, cultural heritage and historical consciousness, they now demanded administrative autonomy. As their aspirations grew to conduct an independent national policy, voices were even heard among them in favor of full autonomy, that is, independence. The imperial government was still able to cater to the nobility and the upper-middle class, but in other strata a growing feeling of deprivation was accompanied by more pronounced demands for appropriate representation in all domains of life.

Following these developments, the status of the Jews in the multinational empires and their attitude towards the national movements underwent a considerable change. If hitherto the Jews residing among these peoples—the vast majority of them predominantly agrarian societies—had fulfilled their traditional role as mediators between estate and village, on the one hand, and the urban centers on the other, now, under the accelerated thrust of the capitalist economy and modern transportation, the sweep of urbanization, and industrialization, a Jewish bourgeoisie sprang up in these areas and competed with the weak local bourgeoisie, not just in the economic realm but in education, culture and the arts as well.

The competition was rendered even more acute because of the Jews' growing integration into the Gentile environment and their adoption of its culture, generally the more potent culture—German or Hungarian in the Slavic environment, and later Russian in the Polish and Ukrainian areas. The result was that the smaller and weaker nations began to look upon the Jews as bolstering the dominant cultural influence at their expense. The Jews were regarded as the bearers of German culture in Czechoslovakia, Hungarian in Slovakia, Polish and German in Galicia, and Russian in Poland.

The majority of Jews were concerned about the disruptive tendencies of the smaller national movements and their effect on the economic and even political unity of the empires. Furthermore, due to the hostility of these national movements toward them, the Jews tended to support the existing state apparatus and adopted a "pro-imperial" posture. The Jews were apprehensive of the possible disintegration of the empires and opposed the establishment of independent nation-states that would sever historically entrenched economic ties. They also feared hostility toward Jews on the part of many leaders of these movements. Even Jews who were disinclined to cooperate with the imperial bureaucracy accepted the stand of those forces that sought to preserve the integrity of the imperial framework, such as the Austro-Marxists or the Bund in its debate with the PPS (the Polish Socialist Party), which demanded that Poland be severed from the Russian Empire. Some tried to extricate themselves from the tangle of contradictory national tendencies by viewing the Jews as a separate national entity, possessing its own goals and interests—that is, by proposing the creation of an independent Jewish national movement.

The completion of the political unification of Germany and Italy, the emergence of Germany as an aggressive imperial force following its victories over Austria and France, the Balkans' attainment of independence—these events signified a new stage in the growth of national sentiments and consciousness throughout Europe, indeed of their incipient transfer beyond the Continent. This same period also denoted a shift in the European nations' attitude toward the "Jewish Question"—the nascent appearance in Europe of antisemitism as an ideology and a political movement.

Concurrently, the "Concert of Europe" era was drawing to a close, and Europe split into rival camps marked by Germany's claims and French-British colonial rivalry, as well as France's ambition to restore the territories lost to Germany. The effect of these developments was to hone the sense of national distinctiveness and the aspirations for national supremacy even in countries where most people had not previously been concerned by national problems. The "national" tendency assumed an extreme form when imperialist, conservative and militaristic circles began to claim that they were its faithful exponents. Liberalism was plunged into a deep crisis. The adherents of universalism, predominantly socialist, also tried to come to terms with the spreading national trends.

As early as the 1860s a change is discernible in the attitude toward the Jews and their place in society. It was probably triggered by the growing number of Jewish entrepreneurs and bankers, most notably the House of Rothschild, and by growing Jewish political activity, especially in the radical camp—Lassalle and Marx being cogent examples. Moreover, the appearance of an organization claiming to represent all of world Jewry—the *Alliance Israélite Universelle*—may also have contributed to the spread of rumors about a Jewish conspiracy to conquer the world and warnings of a "Jewish menace" to the Christian world. Simultaneously, as mentioned above, the legal emancipation of Central European Jewry was nearing completion. The Congress of Berlin in 1878 made recognition of the independence of the Balkan states conditional upon their granting all residents equality before the law, irrespective of origin and creed. Thus equality of rights for the Jews was recognized as a binding international principle. Yet there is no doubt that anti-Jewish tendencies—now coming to be known as antisemitism—took on added momentum in the late 1870s.

Despite disparities in economic and cultural development and differences in political regimes in the Europe of the late 1870s and early 1880s, antisemitism emerged almost simultaneously as an ideology and a political movement in numerous European countries. In Central and Western Europe (France) this fact can be accounted for in terms of the democratization of society and education, the appearance of political parties seeking the mass vote, and the emergence of a popular press. Most scholars agree that antisemitism was the result of economic crises (particularly the crisis in Germany in 1873) and the role that Jews had supposedly played in their genesis, compounded by intense apprehension among all strata of the bourgeoisie about impending economic collapse.

In Eastern Europe, by contrast, antisemitism was in large measure the fruit of deliberate government policy: the desire of government circles to divert public attention from their political and economic shortcomings and impute the responsibility for them to the "foreign, harmful and domineering" element—the Jews, the bearers of the "ruinous ideas" of the West, namely, economic liberalism and a democratic system of government. In addition, public opinion in Eastern Europe was exposed to the impact of Western antisemitic theories, notably from Germany. Intellectuals, including the radical intelligentsia, explained the 1881 anti-Jewish riots in southwestern Russia as a justifiable uprising of the masses against their Jewish exploiters. Antisemitic groups enjoyed considerable parliamentary success in the 1880s in Germany and Austria and were highly influential in France, particularly following the Dreyfus Affair in the last decade of the century.

The growing extremism in the nationalist attitudes of the radical Right undoubtedly afforded the suitable ideological and social backdrop for antisemitic activity. These developments exercised a profound influence on the self-consciousness of many Eastern European Jews, who were prevented by the prevailing political conditions from organizing to repulse antisemitic assaults. There was hardly an influential liberal movement in these countries to serve as an ally for this purpose; even the radical groups took a stance hostile to the Jews. The nature of the regimes and their growing political oppression stifled hopes for legal emancipation as well. There were Jews, particularly among the upper class and the religious leadership, who continued to believe that the situation would improve under the pressure of Western public opinion. Overall, however, there was a marked rise in the number of disappointed Jews who emigrated, turned to revolutionary activity, or nurtured hopes for "a country of our own"—in Palestine or elsewhere—in which the Jews would form the majority and determine their own laws and customs. The intensification of antisemitism in the West toward the end of the nineteenth century spurred Jewish circles there, too, to adopt the Jewish-national approach—whose high point was Theodor Herzl's establishment of the Zionist Organization in 1897.

Manifestly, the appearance of the Jewish national movement and the spread of antisemitism were interrelated. Antisemitism led numerous Jews to abandon hope of achieving full social integration, even in countries where legal equality had been attained, and instead to perceive themselves as outsiders, victims of discrimination, or aliens, to one degree or another. Concomitantly, the definition of the Jews as a people or nation unto themselves on the part of the Jewish national movement, and the positing of political objectives peculiar to that movement, served the enemies of the Jews as convincing proof that Jewish goals and aims conflicted with their own national interests, and that in general they were a harmful alien element. It was not by chance that the most crass document penned by antisemites (written by agents of the Russian police in the years preceding the appearance of Zionism), on a purported Jewish scheme to conquer the world, was named *The Protocols of the Elders of Zion*.

Still, not always were the antisemitic movements successful. In Romania and Russia they wielded considerable influence in broad public sectors, although in the 1880s and 1890s Russian intellectuals underwent a reorientation: not only did they dissociate themselves from antisemitic ideas, they actually began to combat them. They now saw antisemitism as a ploy of the autocratic government designed to gain the sympathy and support of various strata in which Jew-hatred was pervasive. Indeed, circles close to the government were able to ignite outbursts against Jews during the Russo-Japanese War (1904–05), serious anti-Jewish riots in western Russia toward the end of 1905—after the outbreak of the revolution there—and attacks on Jews during the agrarian disturbances in Romania in 1907. However, Russian public opinion split into two antagonistic camps, with the liberal Center and Left vigorously opposing the antisemitic Right.

A similar, if more acute process occurred in France. Despite the major success of antisemitic propaganda in Algeria in the 1890s, the struggle between the Dreyfusards and the anti-Dreyfusards split French society, while the attitude toward the Jews played an important role. At bottom, this was a struggle of the French nation over its future direction and character; it was a contest between the radical-republican camp and the clerical-monarchist camp, the military identifying with the latter. The defeat of the anti-Dreyfusards and the separation of Church and State pushed the antisemitic groups onto the sidelines of French public life until the 1930s, when the Nazis' assumption of power in Germany strengthened them to the point of a formidable political force.

In Germany, on the other hand, antisemitism penetrated society in many spheres, abetted by court circles, the nobility and the senior bureaucracy. Liberal groups who opposed this trend were dubbed "Jew-defenders." Antisemitic slogans were absorbed into the platforms of centrist and right-wing parties and cropped up in publications of numerous public organizations. The antisemitic approach became the hallmark of German patriotism. The absorption of antisemitism by the larger parties may account for the failure of the specifically antisemitic parties and organizations and the decline in their parliamentary representation at the start of the new century. As for the Social-Democratic Party, which opposed antisemitism, its struggle against the phenomenon was not energetic and consistent—indeed, the party itself had still not gained full public legitimacy, not even after the lifting of the ban on its activity in 1890.

Generally speaking, it can be said that in the years leading up to World War I, the influence exercised by antisemitic parties and groups on society and public opinion waned in most European countries. Their ideological impact was confined to the fringes of the political map, within the circles of the radical Right.

The outbreak of World War I brought with it a surge of national sentiment. Even the great majority of socialists enlisted "in the defense of the homeland," evincing a distinctly patriotic spirit. The suffering engendered by the War heightened feelings of hostility toward the enemy and intensified suspiciousness and hatred for foreigners; it is thus no wonder that the enmity toward the Jews resurfaced. In Russia, the authorities blamed the Jews for military failures and the economic difficulties caused by the War. Polish Rightists took advantage of opportunities to brand the Jews as traitors to both the Russian and Austrian governments. German military commanders accused the Jews of stirring up the ferment that gripped workers and soldiers because of the suffering brought on by the War. After their defeat, they advanced the slogan that Germany had not been overpowered but had faltered because the Jews and socialists (and perhaps the Catholics, too) had "stabbed it in the back." (Disregarded was the fact that it was precisely the Rathenau plan—by a statesman of Jewish origin—to put the economy on a total war footing that had enabled Germany to hold out for so long under the conditions of economic siege.) The deposition of the Kaiser, the rise of the Left to power and the Communist revolutions in Bavaria and Hungary were all cited as examples of the Jewish conspiracy against Germany.

The international recognition of every nation's right to self-deter-mination—that is, an independent political existence—which took root in public opinion following World War I due to the collapse of the multinational empires, could be considered a triumph for the idea of nationalism. In the political arena, however, it generated many difficulties. It was the Communists, usually in favor of inter-nationalism and universalism, who adopted the slogan of self-deter-mination and utilized it to stir up national groups in Europe and Asia against the colonial powers. The victorious Allies, who under the pressure of US President Wilson adopted this principle, delin-eated in rather arbitrary fashion the borders of the old and new nation-states and tried to impose Western-type democratic regimes on them. Since a multitude of diverse considerations were brought to bear in determining their boundaries, some of the new states (e.g. Poland and Romania) harbored large national minorities (members of national groups that were not part of the ruling power in these territories) or formed federal states in which one nation was more influential and dominant than the others (e.g. Czechoslovakia, Yugoslavia).

The Allies, taken aback by the strength of nationalist tendencies in the new or expanded states, tried to foist on them international treaties protecting their minorities that were both far from effi-cacious and prompted adverse reactions in these countries as an infringement on their sovereignty. Claims of historical rights over certain areas, always based on the glorious past, aggravated the tensions between the national states, in some cases even sparking wars between them. National feelings mounted in them all, while the considerable political and economic dependence of most of these states on the Great Powers wounded their national pride.

In this atmosphere the Jewish minority, which was dispersed

throughout all the national states, was particularly vulnerable. The large numbers of Jews in the Communist parties, regarded as the subverters of all the "capitalist" states, magnified the historic enmity toward Jews, irrespective of their social standing or views. Pogroms were perpetrated in some countries. In areas where wars raged between different political formations, such as in the Ukraine and White Russia, tens of thousands of Jews were murdered and hundreds of thousands injured. Not even the stabilization of the borders and the consolidation of the various regimes brought a decline in anti-Jewish feeling. The attempts of public bodies in the West to protect the Jews and ensure their rights in accordance with the treaties for the protection of minorities only exacerbated the attacks on the Jews, who were portrayed as an alien element, enemies of the state, and agents of Communist Russia or of Western plutocrats.

Beyond all this, the relations between the Jewish minority and the majority was a complex affair. In the agrarian societies of these new national states, the Jews (and the Germans) fulfilled many functions of an urban middle class—not only in the economy but in the press, cultural life, and the sciences. The attainment of independence was accompanied by the self-evident assumption that in addition to their positions in the state bureaucracy, the members of the majority should be preeminent in these domains as well. Many clung to the belief that state institutions should assist the so-called indigenous population to control every aspect of the economy, of society and culture (e.g. the "Latvia for the Latvians" slogan) and gradually oust the Jews from their positions in these realms. This approach to the national state had the effect of giving an official imprimatur to the already deeply rooted antagonism toward the Jews. Jewish dissent from this policy—whether taking the form of opposition or revolutionary activity, Jewish organization and cooperation with other minorities, or soliciting the aid and protection of Western Jewry—was perceived by large parts of the public in the national states as hostile activity undermining the state's authority and impinging on national sovereignty. The notion that the Jews were traitors and enemies of the state took root in many quarters.

These developments played into the hands of traditional antisemites and enabled them to portray their anti-Jewish activity as being grounded in true patriotism. The antisemites' activity ranged from perpetrating anti-Jewish riots and organizing against the Jews to boycotting them and lobbying for the passage of discriminatory legislation. They were bolstered by the spread of tales concerning the Jewish conspiracy to seize control of the world (*The Protocols of the Elders of Zion*) and by propaganda on the part of the Catholic Church and highly influential Western circles against the ruinous impact of Communism—propaganda that was laced with antisemitism. The attempt by masses of Jews in the early 1920s to emigrate from Central and Eastern Europe to Western Europe and the US met with opposition from both the authorities in the countries of immigration and large sections of the population, including the trade unions, which feared unemployment as a result of competition by immigrants willing to work more for less pay.

National feelings also heightened the hostility toward Jews in Germany and the Soviet Union. In the former, the radical-conservative Right (the National-Socialists) were successful in raising to the level of paranoia the bourgeoisie's fear of the Communist menace, allegedly spread by Jews (Jews were in fact conspicuous in the Communist Party and its leadership). Notwithstanding the close cooperation of German Army commanders with Soviet leaders, right-wing propagandists continued to posit Russia and its "Jewish rulers" as the paramount threat to Germany's very existence. All the difficulties and failures of the Weimar Republic were held to stem from the weakness of the ruling Social Democracy and the debilitating influence of the Jews on it. Antisemitism became a powerful factor in Weimar Germany and helped pave the way for the Nazis' assumption of power.

In the Soviet Union, social tensions were the primary cause of the deteriorating attitude toward the Jews (the Jewish image of the new bourgeoisie that arose for a brief period as a result of the New Economic Policy [N.E.P.]; the accelerated migration of a large number of Jews from the "Pale of Settlement" in western Russia into the interior, where few Jews had lived before the Revolution; the high number of Jews in the Soviet government apparatus, the universities, and in culture and the arts). But national tensions also played a preponderant role—for example, the government plan to transfer Jews to agricultural settlements in White Russia, the Ukraine and the Crimea encountered resistance from the local population, which believed the Jews were receiving preferential treatment in the form of "the best lands"; or attempts to encourage the national culture of the smaller peoples ("Ukrainization," "Belorussification," and the like) while the Jews in these areas were perceived as the conveyors of the dominant Russian culture.

Despite the fact that the Soviet government had conducted a fairly protracted propaganda campaign against antisemitism in the late 1920s, even suppressing antisemitic manifestations, Stalin's appeal to cultivate Russian nationalism and to glorify the Russian national past encouraged the antisemitic elements deeply embedded in the Russian historical tradition. True, the suppression of all expressions of opinion during the years of the Stalin terror precluded the voicing of antisemitic ideas, too. But the population's attitude toward the Jews during the Nazi occupation, and the official postwar anti-Jewish policy, which gained widespread support, provide faithful testimony that the roots of enmity towards the Jews were never eradicated from the minds of many peoples in the Soviet Union—not even from the intelligentsia, who, it will be recalled, for the most part dissociated themselves from antisemitism in the pre-Soviet period.

In the West, too, there was a gradual change for the worse in the attitude toward the Jews. When the Jewish refugee problem arose, following the Nazis' assumption of power in Germany and the strengthening of antisemitic parties and tendencies in the national states of Eastern and Central Europe, the countries of Western Europe reacted by closing their gates to the refugees. They were unwilling to change this policy even after the anti-Jewish measures were exacerbated and the situation of the Jews in many countries became insufferable. Economic crises and political tensions produced growing animosity toward aliens in general and Jewish outsiders in particular.

Following the parliamentary success scored in several countries by anti-Fascist fronts composed in the main of Communists and Socialists, the political Right and large parts of the Center organized for an all-out war against the Left, which was perceived to be acting on behalf of the Jews. Circles that wished to placate Hitler and reach a compromise with him expressed the view that the Jews were the primary obstacle to the attainment of a peaceful settlement and were essentially pushing Europe into war. In Britain this posture gained the support of those who feared that the Arabs would join the Axis; to forestall such a move, they were prepared to ignore the Zionists' claims and the needs of the Jewish refugees for a haven in Palestine. Propagandists in many countries harped on the supposed disparity between Jewish interests and aspirations and those of the European nations. The overall result was a steep deterioration in the attitude toward Jews in both Europe and America, while Nazi

Germany made anti-Jewish discrimination and persecution a central issue in its relations with other countries.

Toward the end of the 1930s, when legal discrimination against Jews, and antisemitic propaganda had become accepted norms, the leaders of England and France, on the one hand, and of the Soviet Union, on the other, courted Hitler. Each side wanted to reach understanding and a *modus vivendi* with him, in the hope of deriving the maximum political benefit. The possibility of resistance to Fascist aggression was not seriously considered. Indeed, it was not at all surprising that once Hitler attacked Poland and launched his military campaigns, Europe, frightened and disunited, fell into his hands like a ripe fruit. Finding that he had achieved the total isolation of the Jews and that the antisemitic front was gaining many adherents, he began to carry out his plan to annihilate the Jews.

The events of this period showed that those with pretensions of being the standard-bearers of national aspirations and the purported guardians of national honor were the most eager to subjugate their country's policy to the objectives of Nazi Germany and comport with its demands. This is all the more true of the leaders of such nations as the Ukrainians and Lithuanians, which did not achieve or were unable to preserve independent political status: they became pawns in Hitler's hands and took an active part in effecting the extermination of the Jews. In their radically aggressive forms, national pride and loyalty went a long way toward harming other peoples but failed to ensure the true interests of the nation exhibiting them.

This book clearly demonstrates the process by which national ideology in Europe was radicalized during the nineteenth and the first half of the twentieth centuries, as well as its intimate bond with active Jew-hatred and antisemitism. The annotated documents substantiate and reinforce the author's analyses and conclusions. He has revealed one of the key elements of antisemitic ideology, activity and its role in preparing the hearts and minds of Europeans for the extermination of the Jews.

Introduction:
Early Beginnings

The writings on Jew-hatred and antisemitism often refer to extreme nationalism or chauvinism as the cause of discrimination and persecution of Jews. Studies on European Jewry before the Holocaust and during World War II abound with descriptions of the rabid nationalism in various countries that affected the fate of the Jews. So deep are the roots of both nationalism and antisemitism that it is no easy task to trace the point of origin of either. Moreover, each has branched out widely in the modern era.

The concept of "nationalism" is something of a catch-all phrase for various movements which evolved in numerous places over a lengthy period of time. In contrast to the movements which stressed universal human qualities, nationalism tended to emphasize the *unique*, i.e. the divisive elements between peoples. A disparity therefore exists between the generalization inherent in the notion of "nationalism" and its substantive content in any given case. A further difficulty in grasping the essence of nationalism derives from a certain vagueness in distinguishing between the terms "people," "nation," and "nationality," or between "nationalism" and "chauvinism," and so forth. The Latin *natio* took on different and at times contradictory meanings in different European languages (Akzin, pp. 8–10). These terms are also emotionally charged, as they entail the self-identity of groups of people. (One should consider, for instance, the emotional resonance evoked by the dichotomy of "Greeks" and "barbarians," or between "Jews" and "Gentiles.")

Similarly, the study of antisemitism must also cope with linguistic ambiguity. The term "antisemitism" itself is relatively new, its coinage is usually attributed to Wilhelm Marr (1819–1904), who sought

1

a word to express the modern enmity *vis-à-vis* the Jews, in contrast to traditional Christian hostility toward Judaism. Jew-haters in the nineteenth century sometimes wished to dissociate themselves from Christian tradition and posit other factors—economic, social, cultural, and even racial—that aroused their opposition to the Jews (Berger, pp. 9–11). Moreover, Jew-hatred in its traditional form was still extant and continued to wield its own influence, both directly and indirectly, in this period.

Nationalism and antisemitism played highly significant historical roles in modern Europe, and the two phenomena are interrelated. Extreme nationalism—or chauvinism—tends to evince hostility towards outsiders, and may be instrumental in generating enmity toward the Jew as the classical alien. Yet it bears noting that nationalism is merely one among many elements which has nurtured modern antisemitism, and that not every manifestation of nationalism is necessarily also antisemitic. Since these elements also undergo occasional changes within a particular national movement, they must be seen in historical perspective and be examined within their particular context. Furthermore, European nationalism is best viewed as an evolving phenomenon and not as a fixed construct. The process of Jewish integration into European society was concurrent with the consolidation of national consciousness and with the organization of society on a national basis. The old model of Christendom, with its typical class divisions, gave way to the new ideal of national identity, which in theory encompassed all social strata; its implicit thrust was toward democratization and the sharing of the masses in state affairs. Concomitantly, the differences between the various nations also took on sharper edges, and as a result the Jews, if they wished to become part of society, were obligated to identify with the people among which they lived, to the point of merging seamlessly into the nation. Beginning in Western Europe, this process subsequently spread to Central and Eastern Europe, but its unfolding was gradual, multifaceted and protracted, and its various incarnations bear some scrutiny.

I shall begin by dwelling on the convergence of emergent nationalism and Jew-hatred at several historical junctures that essentially preceded the emancipation of the Jews. Salo Baron analyzed the expulsions of Jews from England, France, Spain and Portugal in the later Middle Ages, referring in this context to "national unification movements," "national sentiments," and "growth into a national state" as the common factors underlying these expulsions (Baron, 1967, pp. 200, 209, 216, 226, 236, 249).

This explanation points to the innovative element of *general expulsions* of Jews, as distinct from the partial expulsions which had occurred frequently in the past. The expulsion of Jews from an entire state was feasible only under the aegis of a powerful central government. In the Middle Ages the centralized administration in the kingdoms of England and France was more developed than in other realms, and indeed the expulsions of the Jews occurred when feudal monarchy was at its height. Still, these were medieval kingdoms, where the underlying relations were feudal and the mentality was markedly Catholic. In this world, "national unity" was not yet a commonly felt aspiration; furthermore, the expulsions in question had a socioeconomic rationale, so that there was no need to resort to "national" explanations (Na'aman, pp. 436–437, Braudel, p. 820).

The expulsion from Spain, which occurred toward the end of the Middle Ages, must be seen against the background of the collapse of the Muslim foothold in the Iberian Peninsula. By this time the realm of the "Catholic Monarchs," Ferdinand and Isabella, bore some of the trappings of a nation-state. On the other hand, no popular movement and no developed national consciousness, such as appear in modern nationalism, were as yet discernible (Kohn, p. 154).

The link between the various expulsions of Jews in the thirteenth to fifteenth centuries and the rise of nationalism seems a far-reaching conclusion: on the one hand, there was the growing power of the feudal monarchy and the rise of early absolutism, while on the other, the unprecedented countrywide expulsion of Jews. Yet can these elements be considered nationalism? Certain traits, such as patriotism and xenophobia, are of ancient lineage, but they do not account for the new elements within nationalism. Modern nationalism is typified by the rising power of the masses in society and the spread of a national ideology. The expulsion of Jews for religious reasons differs from modern antisemitism, which divests itself of theological justifications for its Jew-hatred. In other words, while the expulsion from Spain does testify to the strengthening of the state as an institution and to the manifestation of organized Jew-hatred, it does not fall into the category of the national antisemitism that emerged in the nineteenth century.

Another phenomenon which appeared in Spain and Portugal following the expulsion of the Jews also bears noting. After Jews and

Muslims had accepted Christianity *en masse*, the majority society sought to distance itself from the "New Christians." The Christians adopted this attitude toward the converts—fostering pride of origin and purity of blood (*limpieza de sangre*)—notwithstanding that in theory, at least, Christianity preaches the dissemination of the faith irrespective of class or origin (Galatians 3:28). Scholars disagree on whether this phenomenon constitutes an early form of the racism which would become rampant in the nineteenth and twentieth centuries (Yerushalmi, pp. 19–21).

Although the desire for purity of blood in Christian Spain may resemble modern racism, a clear distinction must be drawn between the two phenomena. Every society—and particularly a conservative society such as that in Spain, which stresses *lineage*—is reluctant to accept a large-scale absorption of new elements. Although racial discrimination was rife in the Iberian Peninsula, it was not an act of faith, as in Nazi Germany. The fact is that in the course of time the New Christians were assimilated into the Christian society on the Iberian Peninsula as differences of origin faded into insignificance.

Generally speaking, the transition from one era to the next and from one way of life to another is a gradual process. Thus although a sharp line seems to divide the Middle Ages from the Modern Era, the actual boundaries between these epochs are less distinct. The triumph of the old over the new may be merely superficial, with vestiges of the traditional modes persisting at deeper levels. Thus Salo Baron referred to the insularity which appeared "in the national state of the Middle Ages" and was maintained, despite the emancipation of the Jews, until it resurfaced in modern antisemitism.

Prevalent in the Middle Ages was the ideal of a single political framework throughout Christendom. The idea that each state had the right to its own sovereign status was slow to take hold. The decline of the universal ideal entailed the crystallization of political frameworks which are usually characterized as "national," even when they still lacked the distinguishing features of modern nationalism. Starting with the premise that a "nation-state" would by definition resist any alien element, Baron concluded that the readmission of the Jews into England and France in the modern period was contingent upon their ability to assimilate into a non-Jewish society. He also pointed out that the emerging national consciousness would not grant the Jews the right to be different and regarded this intolerance as a regression to the spirit of the Middle Ages (Baron, 1929a, pp. 503–515; 1929b, pp. 148–158). The historian was contending here with the phenomenon of a modern society which is ostensibly moving in reverse and adopting a system that recalls periods long gone. Among other points, this phenomenon raises the question of the *continuity* of Jew-hatred. We thus encounter a basic question in the study of antisemitism: Is there a connection between the various manifestations of Jew-hatred in different periods and different countries; and if so, what is the nature of this connection?

Noting the durability of the negative Jewish stereotype in the European consciousness, Shmuel Ettinger concluded that continuity did exist. He located this stereotype at the junction between traditional Jew-hatred and modern antisemitism and showed how the forces of the past operated under present conditions. Thus, for example, the new antisemitism absorbed certain elements from antiquity, particularly from the struggle of the Church against Judaism. These two elements—*continuity* and *change*—tend to intertwine and interweave through history and the same can be said of Jew-hatred (Ettinger, 1988, pp. 1–12).

1

Romantic Nationalism

Both nationalism and antisemitism were influenced by romanticism. A rather loose term, romanticism is difficult to delineate. Thus, it is perhaps worthwhile to look it up. According to the *Encyclopaedia Britannica* (1973, p. 560), "romanticism is a term loosely used in both a historical and an aesthetic sense to designate the numerous changes in literature and the arts . . . in reaction against neo-classicism." It is also seen as "a quickening of nationalism, marked by a return to local origins." Referring to romantics, *The Dictionary of the History of Ideas* tells us (1973, p. 206): "Since all forms of liberalism, as well as the industrial civilization . . . were hostile to them, they opposed the free play of business transactions." Another authority on the subject describes some pertinent features of romanticism as follows: "Utopian dreams for the future side by side with nostalgia for the past; a marked nihilistic mood accompanied by a fervent yearning for a faith" (Schenk, p. xxii).

The inherent difficulty in applying the concept of "romanticism" becomes more apparent as one moves beyond the purely aesthetic sphere in search of an overall definition of the term. The late historian Jacob Talmon, after describing the resistance to the classical outlook shared by the pioneers of romanticism in various parts of Europe, goes on to write: "In a sense every variety of romanticism was a protest, even the various conservative versions. For surely the reactionary tendencies of German romanticism in the later years of the French Revolution and under Napoleon were an expression of resistance to a conquering and dominant force as well as support for the established order" (Talmon, pp. 135, 157). As a result of revolutionary events, then, the romantic feeling was powerfully entrenched in the social and political realm and became the driving force for a certain type of nationalism. From romanticism, this nationalism borrowed the notion of the individually unique, while pitting emotion and passion against the sterile rationalism of the eighteenth century. All these elements were then grafted onto the *folk*, which became the host of authentic romanticism by virtue of its deep-rooted singularity. Far from being a political and social movement only, nationalism aimed at a cultural and historical revival and aspired to self-realization based on the contours of the past. The nation was not perceived as a contractual relationship between individuals but as a social organism functioning according to its own disposition, like a natural being.

A credible contemporary description of romantic nationalism has come down to us in what is admittedly a polemical essay by Saul Ascher (1767–1822), a Berlin bookseller and scholar who is known in Jewish history as a precursor of religious reform. In 1815, while the Congress of Vienna was in session, Ascher published a work entitled *Germanomanie* ("The German Illness" or "The Illness of Germanism") in which he described the nature of the reaction which had arisen in Germany following the defeat of Napoleon. Writing in an ironic vein, he addressed himself to the fusion between romanticism and nationalism:

> Germany, it is said, has since time immemorial been bequeathed to a people that is distinct from all others in character, mode of thinking, language and customs. It is the duty of every true German to restore this individuality, undermined by the passage of time and the course of events. Thus, the primary condition thereof is to remove from German soil all things alien, brought in from the outside, and to declare Germany at the same time a closed state. (Ascher, pp. 19–20)

Though Ascher was fulminating against the philosopher Johann Gottlieb Fichte (1762–1814) (Low, pp. 143–154; Mendes-Flohr & Reinharz, 257–258), the main target of his polemic was the Berlin historian Christian Friedrich Rühs (1781–1820), an outspoken critic of the emancipation of the Jews who denied their ability to integrate into a Christian state. Ascher retorted that the barrier to emancipation was not Christianity but its abuse by romantic nationalism. He held that the Catholic revival among the adherents of this German nationalism was part of a trend wishing to check progress and impose a medieval imprint on society. The Jews, by contrast, could restrain the dogmatic tendencies and participate in the quest for freedom and progress. Ascher's opponents burned this essay in public during a nationalist rally held in 1817.

The debate over emancipation was then at its height. During the Restoration, the rights accorded the Jews in Germany during the Napoleonic conquest were reduced and effectively revoked. The fact that those rights had accrued to the Jews through the agency of the French conqueror had marked the imposed emancipation with a stigma. Even more extreme than Rühs was the Heidelberg philosopher Jakob Friedrich Fries (1773–1843). In his essay *On the Danger to the Well-Being and Character of the Germans Presented by the Jews* (1816), Fries justified the hatred of the masses for the Jews and intimated that the acts of violence against them might be resumed. Only the extirpation of Judaism—a vestige of the barbarous past, as he saw it—could improve the Jews.

The difference between these two essays reveals something of the duality which typified the attitude of romantic nationalism toward Christianity. Indeed, in the view of Jacob Katz, Fries's rabid extremism against the Jews derived from his negative attitude toward Christianity (Katz, pp. 21–84). Actually, in the subsequent development of the antisemitic movement, its Christian elements were sometimes relatively restrained, compared with the rampages of the radical nationalists.

Yet these theoretical disputes were but faint echoes of a broad and stormy public debate marked by violent outbursts. In 1819 German towns and villages were swept by a wave of rioting which spread beyond German lands and has gone down in history as the "Hep, Hep" movement. (Some believed this to be a Latin acronym for "Jerusalem is destroyed"—*Hierosolyma est perdita*; however, it was probably an utterance used on goats and sheep that was adopted for Jew-baiting.) The disturbances, which were prompted by the debate over the rights of Jews, quickly became a pretext for restricting those rights even further. They had been preceded by anti-Jewish propaganda; among other things, the antisemitic fulminations of Fries were read aloud in the beerhouses and the anti-Jewish extremism of Rühs was vigorously supported by the nationalistic *Burschenschaft* (*Encyclopedia Judaica*, p. 330).

The noteworthy development in this context is the reciprocal interaction between thinkers, propagandists and the popular masses. The impact of these ideas was particularly pronounced on the younger generation, which had grown up in an atmosphere of liberation from the foreign yoke. Educators, writers and preachers instilled the Germans with pride for the German nation and were hostile to everything that was not German. This was the backdrop to the rise of the anti-Western strain in German nationalism and to the nascent vision of the resurrection of a greater Germany. German nationalism longed to embrace all speakers of German dialects, irrespective of existing political borders, and to build itself on the foundations of the glorious past without external, alien influences. In the highly charged atmosphere that took hold following Napoleon's defeat, newly formed organizations of young people were even bent on reintroducing medieval codes of chivalry as an expression of vaunted German uniqueness.

The rise of extreme nationalism with its concomitant hatred of the alien was also reflected in society's attitude toward the Jews. Hugo Valentin has provided striking testimony on the intensification of hostility towards the Jews in Germany by comparing the reactions to two theater productions. In 1788, when Shakespeare's *The Merchant of Venice* was staged in Berlin, the producers felt compelled to issue an apology and assure the public that no anti-Jewish sentiment was intended. However, by 1820 it was necessary to justify to the public what appeared to be an inordinate fondness for the Jews in the dramatization of Lord Byron's *Hebrew Melodies* — so greatly had the attitude toward the Jews changed in just one generation (Valentin, p. 52).

On the eve of the French Revolution it seemed that Jew-hatred in Europe would gradually give way to tolerance. However, the situation was aggravated following Napoleon's defeat, due in part to the rise of aggressive nationalism. At the same time, antisemitism also fed on social and economic tensions stemming from a growth in the Jewish population in the towns and the commercial competition waged against it by the non-Jewish middle class (Greive, p. 22). Yet it should not be concluded that enmity for the Jews was expressed by all the strata of society; certain circles, notably the enlightened ones, objected to the Jew-baiting, and during the wave of rioting some of them actively aligned themselves on the side of the Jews. Similarly, the authorities acted to quell the rioters, and occasional instances of Jewish self-defense are known as well.

It bears noting that the 1819 disturbances erupted against a backdrop of general social unrest and were also marked by violence against non-Jewish adversaries. Nationalism at this time was congruent with political radicalism, and some professed to read the anti-Jewish riots as reflecting a revolutionary spirit. The authorities viewed the growing ferment with alarm, fearful that the violence against the Jews would trigger an attack on the regime itself (Rürup, p. 51). Certainly the social turmoil and the emergent national consciousness helped foment the disturbances, but the developments were rather multifarious, and at all events the anti-Jewish riots bore no revolutionary character.

Although romantic nationalism was born in Germany and found its first vigorous expression there, it was by no means a purely local phenomenon. To the contrary, its spirit swept across the continent, particularly to the east, where it found fertile ground among peoples and ethnic groups with a nascent national consciousness. Romantic nationalism had its greatest impact on the peoples residing in the mixed regions of the multinational empires. There it lent tremendous impetus to the emergence of a local culture and language, the formation of historical awareness, and the crystallization of a national identity. Gradually, romantic nationalism also trickled into the consciousness of long-established nations, wielding a potent influence on the Russians, the French, and the English too.

Far from functioning merely as an imported commodity, romantic nationalism acted as a stimulus which generated indigenous developments in each setting. It possessed the capacity to transform nationalism into a unifying element which could override class distinctions and other internal differences. It blended diverse social elements into a single cohesive system bearing a shared identity. As the pace of change became increasingly rapid, this type of nationalism seemed able to offer a stable, deeply-rooted alternative to a type of social organization that was no longer viable.

Almost inevitably, the emphasis on each nation's uniqueness had the effect of sharpening differences between peoples, and very soon neighboring ·ethnic groups found themselves becoming rival national movements. In time, this model would tend to typify nationalism in general, leaving little room for open-mindedness. Moreover, this trend had the effect of intensifying internal fanaticism and fanning intolerance toward minorities and outsiders. Ultimately, even the moderates among the nationalists were compelled to fall in line with a burgeoning extremism which was driving the national movements into mutual strife. This left its mark not only on the national movements themselves but also on the relations between states and had a circular effect on the general atmosphere, particularly during periods of crisis.

Thus the stage has been set for the dramas that will play themselves out in the coming chapters, as the thrust of growing fanaticism and national rivalry is directed time and again at the Jews and Judaism.

Against Romantic Nationalism

The following is taken from a contemporary source. The author discusses the "Jewish Question" in the context of internal conflicts between opposing trends in German society, such as the ideas of the Enlightenment and the romantic school of German nationalism.

Mr. Rühs, having become a citizen of the world again,[1] after being liberated from his *Germanomania*,[2] should make milder demands of the French and English and consequently also of the Jews— milder demands especially of the latter—than those he mentions, namely: that in the event of a presumptive organization of the German Constitution[3]—
—The relation between Jews and Germans be exactly determined;[4]

[1] The movement of the European Enlightenment evinced a markedly cosmopolitan approach, and its spokesmen considered themselves "citizens of the world," bound up with all mankind and especially with the cultured human beings. The German Enlightenment shared this approach. Since the time of Johann Gottfried von Herder (1744–1803), a disciple of Jean Jacques Rousseau (1712–1778), the idea had gained currency in Germany that a unique "folk spirit" existed within each nation—which was therefore called upon to cultivate that spirit. This outlook, which was to have far-reaching implications for German society, culture, and thought, left its mark on romanticism, nationalism, and spurred the flowering of historical thinking. It was also reflected in "historicism" as a method.

[2] Germanomania (also known as Teutomania, after the Teutons, an ancient German tribe), Gallomania, Anglomania—the end of the eighteenth century saw growing opposition in Germany to the phenomenon of Gallomania self-effacement vis-á-vis French culture—which had prevailed during the Enlightenment. In France itself the English style of life—Anglomania—was increasingly emulated, and paradoxically this fashion also found its way into Germany and the other countries of Europe. Germanomania was held as counteracting all foreign influences.

[3] The German Reich ("the Holy Roman Empire of the German Nation") came to an end in the Napoleonic era and was not restored after the French Emperor's defeat. The Congress of Vienna (1815) established a federation of the German states, and a constitution was drawn up. While Saul Ascher was writing his booklet, various German states discussed and approved their respective constitutions. These developments did not entail the renewal of the German Reich, as Romantics such as Rühs had hoped.

[4] The proposal to incorporate into the constitution an article defining the relations between Jews and other citizens would be tantamount to relegating the Jews to a special status. Such a position would have been appropriate in a period when the legal standing of the Jews was unique, but when differentiations also existed

—Their increase in numbers be prevented;[5]

—Their conversion to Christianity be facilitated, this being the primary and indispensable condition of transforming them into Germans.

Who would not recognize here Herr Rühs, the *Germanomaniac*? Every step taken for and against Jews in Germany should, according to Mr. Rühs and his friends, be looked at through the spectacles of *Germanomania*. Everything should depend upon *Germanomania*. To determine the relations of the Jew towards the German! As if these relations should be any different from the relation of the Jew to any other nation, or as if the German may not take any other nation as an example. Moreover, the increase in the number of Jews through immigration should be prevented! As if it had not been done already. And finally, to promote the conversion of Jews to Christianity, so that they be transformed into Germans! As if Christianity were an indispensable condition of Germanhood! Which reminds me, that the Germans as Tacitus describes them . . . were quite brave Germans, without being Christians.[6]

Mr. Rühs knows the right answer, as befits a true *Germanomaniac*. He demands, out of "higher" considerations, to exclude the German Jews from the obligation to defend the *Vaterland*.[7]

between other classes in the society, both in theory and in practice. A proposal of this kind was inconsistent with a state based on the equality of all citizens before the law. It did conform, however, to a point of view which wished to reintroduce medieval customs.

[5] As Ascher goes on to point out, Jewish immigration to Germany was restricted. There were at the time numerous differences between one state and another, one town and another, and this affected the Jews as well. Some locales even reintroduced the restrictions barring young Jews from raising a family in their hometown. In particular, the Jews' right to engage in various professions was restricted.

[6] The first-century Roman historian Cornelius Tacitus was the author of a work known as *Germania*, which describes that land and its peoples. Tacitus emphasizes the heroism and healthy simplicity of the ancient Germans, contrasting them with the refined and decadent Roman civilization. He also takes note of the Germans' violent religious rites, including human sacrifice. Romantic nationalism, wishing to revive ancient German myths, had recourse to the writings of Tacitus as supporting evidence. Thus Ascher, for his part, also cited Tacitus in order to refute the contention that Germandom was anchored precisely in the "Christian state."

[7] The legislation of 1812 in favor of the Jews in Prussia (where the two disputants, Saul Ascher and Professor Rühs lived) granted the Jews civil rights. Henceforth the Jews were also eligible for military service. The opponents of emancipation argued that the Jews' religion prohibited them from serving in the army; hence they were not like all the other citizens and were not even entitled to citizenship. To this some of the proponents of emancipation retorted: To the contrary, to have the honor of serving in the army, Jews would be only too glad to violate their religious precepts! Ascher takes issue with his adversary's denunciation of Jews who have forsaken

In any case, when one looks at Mr. Rühs' ideas, opinions and utterances (of which I have presented to the reader only a small part) and puts them together, one recognizes the image of a true *Germanomaniac*. And I may now put the question to the impartial reader:

Whether this way of thinking, built on principles which are opposed to the spirit of the time[8] and to the progress[9] of human education,[10] whether this way of thinking is not bizarre at this time—and, like any distinct phenomenon in the world of the spirits,[11] should not only be described according to its origin, development and image, but be preserved by a name of its own in the annals of history.

I tried to present the reader with a mere sketch. Maybe some day in the future a more skillful and more clever hand will paint a more perfect picture of it. Then, in the gallery of German errors, next to *Gallomania* and *Anglomania*, *Germanomania* will take its proper place. (Ascher, pp. 64–70)

Summary: Romantic Nationalism and the Jews

Romantic nationalism developed in Germany in the wake of the resistance to Napoleon and to the influence of the French Revolution. In striking contrast to the message of universal liberation pro-

their religion; he argued that non-Jews were also drifting away from religion (and at all events he supported a reform of the Jewish religion).

[8] The term *Zeitgeist* was used by Herder (who has already been mentioned) and by Johann Wolfgang von Goethe (1749–1832), Germany's greatest poet, in a neutral sense as the "spirit of the times." The philosopher Friedrich Hegel (1770–1831) uses the term in the singular and in a sense close to the modern meaning, that is, something *appropriate* to its time. This is also what the author is driving at: Rühs is expressing views which are long out of date!

[9] The idea of progress, in the sense of man's dominance over nature and the increasing rule of reason, was regarded as a basic element of the Enlightenment. The enemies of progress included conservatism and backwardness, which were characterized by resistance to changes in society, religious fanaticism, class narrow-mindedness, mystical or romantic obscurantism, and the like.

[10] By using the term "human education" the author seems to reveal his general outlook. Education, or *Bildung*, was considered the principal avenue to the betterment of man and society. Saul Ascher, the Jew, was suggesting that Rühs had removed himself from the main thrust of German culture.

[11] The "world of the spirit" refers both to the French ideal of lucid thought and to the somewhat deep-probing German approach. By contrast, Ascher employs the ironical expression "world of the spirits," meant to evoke ghosts, devils, and so forth. With one stroke, then, he downgrades "Germanomania" from an exalted place in the realm of the spirit to something base, no more than a superstition.

claimed by the French conquerors, a movement emerged which cultivated unique and authentic German roots. Romanticism generally disparaged intellectual abstraction, seeking instead to cling to real life, vent emotion, adore the countryside, and give free rein to creativity. This was tantamount to a rebellion by the individual against the conventions of society and, on a different plane, constituted a revolt by the young against the outmoded ideas and ossified traditions of their parents. However, in the atmosphere which reigned in Germany in the Napoleonic period, romanticism was actually an adjunct to the nascent nationalism. Not satisfied with individual emotion, romantic nationalism wished to give expression to the emotions of the people, take root in the landscape of the homeland, and seek a genuine German creativeness.

The marriage with romanticism lent momentum to the national awakening, while also furnishing it with ideological content. Romantic nationalism railed against Western influences, seeing in them sterile rationalism, superficial universalism, and a materialist civilization. The resistance to these ideas was often accompanied by a critique of the forms of government and social customs of the West. The advocates of romantic nationalism tended to prefer authoritarian government to a representative system, to dwell on the heritage of the past, and to be suspicious of change and innovation. Romantic nationalism viewed as *alien* a whole series of phenomena and ideas which would become increasingly important in the course of the nineteenth century, such as capitalism, liberalism, democracy, and socialism.

The model of romantic nationalism did not remain confined to Germany alone. It spread eastward and southward and influenced other emerging national movements. The national movements that adopted this model did not feel obligated to acknowledge their debt to Germany. Far from it, the relations between Slavs and Germans followed the pattern set when German nationalism had responded to the challenge of Napoleon's army. Similarly, the national movements of the Slavic peoples that had absorbed German nationalism viewed Germany as a source of Western—hence alien and harmful—influence. Moreover, the model of romantic nationalism, which was ostensibly grounded in the unique and the inimitable and in professed resistance to alien influences, soon affected the long-established nation-states as well. There occurred a bizarre and unexpected turn of events: the Jacobin nationalism of the French Revolution and of the "Peoples' Spring" had inscribed on its banner 'liberation for all peoples,' but the national movements essentially displayed mutual enmity and spurned the message of universality. It was expressly romantic nationalism which spread, notwithstanding its own resistance to alien influences. Each national movement took refuge behind its own walls to play out its particular variation of the same tune.

The encounter of the Jews with romantic nationalism also entailed a paradox. On the face of it, Germans simply objected to the equality of rights accorded the Jews by a foreign conqueror. This much is self-evident, and with Germany's liberation from the Napoleonic yoke steps were indeed taken to restore the *status quo ante* where the Jews were concerned. Nor should it come as a surprise that the equality of rights granted the Jews under French auspices had the effect of stigmatizing the Jews as an anti-national group. In other words, to the already oppressive burden of the religious clash between *Christians* and Jews was now added a national clash between *Germans* and Jews. The emancipation of the Jews, which German society had viewed with scepticism from the outset, was now branded as treason and forced to backtrack.

All this would seem fairly understandable, however unsatisfactory it may have been to Jews who had already considered themselves full-fledged Germans and were now once more deprived of their rights (for to lose rights which one had already possessed can be even more frustrating than not having them in the first place). What is more puzzling is the turnabout which occurred in this period and later typified the attitude of other national movements toward the Jews. For generations the paramount allegation against the Jews, and one that consistently recurred in various forms, was that they were "a people that dwells alone, that has not made itself one with the nations" (Numbers 23:9)—in other words, a closed, peculiar group, alien to universalism to the point of abhorring mankind. Suddenly a radical shift occurred and the quality which had been disparagingly attributed to the Jews became a hallmark for all peoples, as the aspiration to universalism gave way to a longing for national uniqueness. Language, history, custom, folklore, faith, ritual, even landscape—each of these domains was a treasure house of the nation's spirit, to be cultivated under the aegis of nationalism and brandished in the face of other national groups. The result is that once more the Jews were excluded from the family of nations because they were supposedly incapable of identifying with the national genius. In the past they had been tainted by particularism; now they became the very archetype of universalism.

Antisemites had even maintained that for appearance's sake the Jew was advocating universalism, but in reality he behaved like a fervent nationalist. Long before the Jews' national movement arose, their enemies were saying that they were a nation within a nation, a state within a state, a kind of anti-national nationality, outwardly espousing a universalist approach but in fact owing loyalty only to their own kind. The extraordinary fusion of a particular history and a universal message, as embodied in Judaism, vexed mankind for many generations. This coupling held fast in the era of nationalism, yet new elements were added to it.

2

Revolutions and Counterrevolutions

The Polish Uprising of 1830

In the previous chapter we took note of the "Hep, Hep" riots, which occurred during the era of the Restoration, after Napoleon's downfall. The so-called "Holy Alliance" had lasted for fifteen years when the older line of the Bourbons in France was ousted in July 1830. The French example sparked similar attempts elsewhere. In Brussels a revolt broke out, leading to Belgium's secession from the Kingdom of the Netherlands, as created by the Congress of Vienna. A national war of independence comported well with the challenge to the *Ancien Régime* which had been reinforced by the powers of the Holy Alliance. The forces which fought for national liberation were part of the struggle for democratization and parliamentary representation. Similarly, the leaders of the great powers in Europe were often resistant to social change and national movements alike.

As part of the revolutionary tide of 1830, a revolt against Russian rule broke out in Poland. It forced the Czarist army out of Warsaw, while the mobs took advantage of the chaos to attack Jewish homes and pillage Jewish property. After order had been restored, differences of outlook emerged between the Polish rebels and Jews who wished to join the national militia. Among the Jews were ardent supporters of the revolution, but they encountered rejection from the Polish leaders. Special units set up for Jewish volunteers were underwritten by the Jewish population and engaged in police and patrolling duties only. When Jews were permitted to serve in regular units, many Poles were incensed, fearing that as a result Jews would gain civil rights. Something of the atmosphere can be gleaned from the fact that Poles were opposed to bearded Jews serving as Polish

17

Army personnel. Furthermore, in a typical paradox, the abolition of Russian censorship during the revolt enabled the publication of anti-Jewish pamphlets, which had been prohibited by Czarist regulations.

The Polish public also suspected that the Jews were sympathetic to the Russians and were spying for them. Yet the denunciation of the Jews as enemies of the revolt stood in striking contrast to the favorable attitude toward the uprising manifested by the educated and younger Jews. Expressions of support for the revolution even came from some Jewish communal institutions and rabbis. Jews suspected of spying were executed without trial, while others were killed secretly. The events brought in their wake an abuse of Jews; even old people and children were not spared.

However, the Polish revolt was viewed positively by Jews abroad, and expressions of sympathy and support began streaming into Poland. This was reported by the Polish press, as were instances of identification and sacrifice for the revolution by the local Jewish population. The democratic circles in the Polish national movement were favorably disposed to such Jewish participation and were inclined to grant the Jews civil rights. In contrast, some leaders of the revolt took an overtly hostile attitude toward the Jews, arrogantly dismissing their contribution to the success of the uprising in both body and spirit. The ultimate failure of the revolt triggered a controversy both at the time and in the subsequent historiography: contemporaries tended to the view that the young rebels had acted rashly and had erred in refusing to heed the council of their wiser elders (Shatzky, p. 534). In our own century a conspiracy theory was adduced, alleging that Jews and Freemasons had plotted to thrust Poland into a hopeless revolt to further the prospects of revolution in France and Belgium (Levin, p. 34, n.2; Davies, pp. 322–325)

The Polish revolt had certain features which often recurred in the relations between the Jews and the national movements:
— Doubt in the Jews' ability to integrate into the nation.
— An ambivalent attitude toward the Jews as partners in the national struggle.
— The unleashing of Jew-hating popular forces.
— The overthrow of the "old regime" as a catalyst for the disruption of public order.
These indicators would reappear with greater intensity in the "Peoples' Spring" in 1848.

The Polish Insurrection of 1830–31

The following passages are taken from a Hebrew-language memoir written by a Plonsk Jew, Ya'akov Halevi Levin, ten years after the events described here. His recollections focus on the fate of a distinguished Jewish family whom the Poles accused of abetting the Russians. As the narrator proceeds, the underlying outlooks of both sides emerge, reflecting the attitude of the Jews toward the revolt, and the image of the Jews in the eyes of the Poles.

A Statement by the Accused Jew

Your brother am I, son of your mother, soil of Poland. From my youth my father and my mother raised me among youths, your sons as am I. With them I played in the sand. And from that time friendship pulled me to you, took root in my heart and caused me to be as one body and one soul with you; and were it not for the law of religion that separates us, I would give my daughters to your sons and take your daughters for my sons, for ever have I been ravished by your love. My flesh feels your pain and my innermost feelings reach out to you. Your troubles are my troubles and your happiness is my happiness. Therefore, how shall I do evil to my soul and betray my brothers by abetting another nation—a nation which my brethren stand against, a nation whose tongue I do not know, and which has itself not known Israel, yet seeks only its evil and will never wish it good?[1]

Testimony in Favor of the Accused by a Non-Jew

When soldiers from our Polish brothers, Lithuanians,[2] some six hundred strong, came to his house, he willingly gave them food and drink, meat and good spirits. Not so when Russian soldiers came to him: unwillingly did he give them meager helpings and bad spirits, you could smell their stench from afar. And I heard him say to his wife, his sons and his whole household: I do not like to give these food and drink, but what can I do? Can I fight against them, with the ruler's scepter and sword in their hands? And if I refuse to give bread, then I shall have to give meat and

---

[1] The argument is based on the deep inner feeling of the Jews for Poland and its people—with the only reservation relating to religious differences—and points up the common interest shared by Jews and Poles where their attitude toward the Russian authorities is concerned.

[2] The Lithuanian fighters in the rebel ranks were greeted warmly and hosted generously by the Jew because of his sympathy for the Polish uprising. The revolt was marked by the renewal of the historic union between Poland and Lithuania.

wine too, so that they can eat and drink, besides what they will plunder from me.[3]

The Statements against the Accused

This is our land of Poland, with its precious sons grown from seedlings in the paradise of our land, this Poland! Little foxes that destroy our vineyards—are these not the perverse Hebrews who dwell among us? Even though these Jews may be small compared with our own great and esteemed nation, yet with their tongues and their sharp teeth they can chop down a tree and eat it, branches, leaves and all. —These are the kinds of bad deeds these Hebrews inherited from their forefather—"a plain man, dwelling in tents" [Genesis 25:27], who in his naïveté duped his brother, our father, Esau, by taking his birthright and giving nothing in return . . .[4] Their cruel heart spared not even their brother and they sold him to the Ishmaelites, and this has been their way since time immemorial! When they came to dwell in another land, they fabricated all manner of pretexts against the inhabitants thereof, until they provoked them to war, for heroes they were and they expelled [the inhabitants] and dwelt there in their stead.[5] Peruse the Book of Records and you will find many evils even greater than these, which they have done in the world. Wherever they come, there is no truth and no peace. Even today their evil heart wished to push us out so they could dwell here in our stead . . .

These Hebrews came from a far land because they were expelled from there, and we, because of the love of the stranger which has always resided in us, took pity on them and said: Let them also dwell in our land, let them take from the best fruit of the land and be sated.—And shall they also drink our blood and be drunk? And with their tongues lick everything around us? . . . For as long as they are here, on our soil, the Kingdom of Poland shall not be firmly in our hands—we shall be in bondage to a kingdom of aliens . . . These perverse Hebrews who dwell among us will tell him all that we hold secret, hidden in our treasures.[6]

---

[3] The Russian Army, dispatched to put down the uprising, forced itself on the Jewish host who, because of his support for the rebels, dished out poor-quality food and drink.

[4] The ironically naive Jacob is posited as the symbol of Jewish cunning, while the Pole is here identified with the honest Esau. This is not the typical Christian image but stems from the influence of Deism and eighteenth century rationalism.

[5] The story of the selling of Joseph and the conquest of the Land of Canaan are motifs testifying to the negative character of the Jews throughout history.

[6] The early settlement of the Jews in Poland remained in the historical conscious-ness of the Poles as an act of hospitality toward the Jews, whereas now the Jews

The Author's Argument to the Authorities

We knew, we too knew, that we are Polish-born. Amongst you we have always dwelt secure, and we hope to find shelter thus in your shadow forever, and how shall we then betray you and lend a hand to the strangers in the land? What do we have in common with them, that we would know them and estrange ourselves from you? . . . Master of all our lands! The truth is the very opposite— each and every one of us would give his very flesh for his Polish comrade, would spill his blood, give his very life only to save you, our brothers the sons of this country, for our souls are bound up with your souls in a powerful bond, with iron links, and shall never be separated. And please do not be bewildered, sir, that we did not offer you our sons to fight against the enemy: it is not for hatred of the inhabitants and love of the foreigners that our sons are held back, but so that we do not melt your hearts as ours are melted. For ever since we fell from our position, faintheartedness has been implanted in us from our fathers and our fathers' fathers, so that no spirit rises up in any of us at the sound of the rifle barrel . . . The Jew is a worm, not a man of war . . . We shall not spare our money . . . Ask please, sir, how generous we have been since your day of battle![7] (Levin, pp. 57, 64, 75, 80, 102, 106, 113–114)

The "Peoples' Spring"

In the middle of the nineteenth century the winds of revolution began to blow in many countries of Europe. February of 1848 saw a renewed uprising in Paris, and the unrest soon spread to the rest of France. In Alsace these events were accompanied by acts of hostility against representatives of the authorities and against the Jews. It was alleged that the Jews were lending money to farmers at usurious rates—but anti-Jewish acts were perpetrated in the towns there as well (Delpech, p. 319). Because the authorities were sometimes slow to intervene the Jews were compelled to come to their own defense. The economic and religious tensions which marked the Alsace region had made it a persistent trouble spot during the French Revolution, in the Napoleonic era, and again in 1830. The local inhabitants spoke a German dialect, and their attachment to

---

were repaying kindness with evil, as it were, by spying on behalf of the Czar. The Jews are presented as an obstacle to Polish independence.

[7] The author apologizes that the Jews are unfit to serve in the army because of their traditional cowardice and are thereby liable to affect the fighters' morale. Instead, the Jews atone through money for what they do not provide in body but are completely loyal to the uprising.

France was rather precarious. Thus, it seems likely that one cause of the hostility toward the Jews was the latter's outspoken support for France; French law had granted them equal rights, and they were ardent French patriots (Harris & Sédouy, p. 14). At all events, the local inhabitants strongly disapproved of the Jews' equality of rights. Nothing was easier for the French than to attribute the antisemitism in Alsace to the "German blood" flowing in the veins of the inhabitants, and this was also the view of many Jews (Szajkowski, 1970, pp. xxix–xxx; Szajkowski, 1955, pp. 98–99). When Alsace-Lorraine was annexed by Germany in 1871, many of the local Jews moved to France, which for them was the cradle of liberty and emancipation, and they adhered to the French nationality and its prestigious culture. In time, the Jews of Alsace would constitute an appreciable portion of French Jewry.

Manifestations of hostility tinged with nationalism also appeared in territories annexed by Prussia as part of the partition of Poland. The Jews of Posen and Upper Silesia were inevitably swept up in the clashes between Poles and Germans and consequently found themselves involved in the local national struggles. While the majority of the Jews professed neutrality, some identified with the Germans against the Poles. This development may have been the pretext for the riots perpetrated by a Polish mob against Jews in several Posen villages (Jersch-Wentzel, p. 121). Hundreds of Jews signed a petition calling for the German character of the region to be guaranteed, and some Jews volunteered for the civil militia against the Polish rebels (Toury, p. 52). Posen had been a part of Poland until 1793, when it was annexed by Prussia. The Prussian authorities had tried to eradicate the area's Polish character but were relatively well disposed toward the Jews. During the uprising many Jews from the rural districts fled to the towns, never to return to their former places of residence. The Polish population launched an economic boycott against non-Poles, thus perhaps initiating the tradition of economic struggle against minorities, and especially against Jews, in Poland. In the course of time, however, the Jews of Posen became an integral part of German Jewry, entering industry, the services and free professions; quite a few of them moved westward, settling elsewhere in Germany (Bartyś, p. 191). As they had in Alsace, the Jews of Posen also preferred to leave the outlying district and move closer to the metropolitan areas—to a modern economy and high culture.

Undoubtedly it was the Hapsburg Empire which faced the most

complex national problem. According to a conservative estimate, no fewer than twelve different nationalities resided in the Austrian Empire. Some of the national movements were active in the revolutions of 1848, and in some instances they fought against one another: in Italy there was an uprising against the Austrian garrison force: elsewhere, Czechs and Croats pressed for autonomy while Hungary declared its independence and took no notice of the demands of the country's Walachs, Croats, Serbs and Slovenes. The Jews, who were scattered throughout the Empire, were indirect victims of the clashes that broke out between their many neighbors. Bloody riots against the Jews themselves erupted in Slovakia and Bohemia-Moravia—areas which would later be incorporated into Czechoslovakia—and in Hungary. Galicia, the region of Poland which had been annexed by Austria, had still not recovered from the revolts there two years earlier.

The situation in Hungary enables us to gain a better understanding of the "Jewish Question" throughout the Hapsburg Empire. Hungary was a multinational country within the Empire, and the Jews were well represented in its mixed districts. Although the majority of the Jews did not yet obtain a secular education, by 1848 certain radical groups among them were ardent supporters of the patriotism espoused by the Magyar majority. On the one hand, the Jews were integrated into the Magyar culture, while at the same time Jewish immigrants streamed into the country from the outside. The local population viewed the Jewish newcomers with considerable antipathy, and the net effect of the wave of immigration was to underscore the evident imcompatibility between the Jews and the society around them. Nevertheless, the liberal circles led by Lajos Kossuth (1802–1894) allied themselves with the Jews in the national struggle. In the long run, the Magyar national movement divested itself of its reservations concerning the Jews' economic function and their clannishness, coming increasingly to regard them as Hungarians of the Mosaic faith (Barany, p. 56).

The Jews of Bohemia-Moravia adopted the German culture and professed allegiance to the Emperor, who had bettered their lowly status. The German-speaking city-dwellers did not look kindly on the Jews' improved status, while the Czech inhabitants accused the Jews of abetting the Austrian regime in its efforts to impose German culture. Yet the 1840s also saw attempts at a dialogue between Czechs and Jews. One of the leaders of the Czech national movement, Karel Havlíček (1821–1856), took exception to this development, arguing that the Jews were a national group of Semitic origin and loyal to the Jewish people, whereas "anyone who wants to be a Czech must cease to be a Jew." However, Havlíček was more inclined to change his attitude toward the Jews after having despaired of pan-Slavic cooperation (Goldstücker, pp. 67–71).

Something of the underlying complex relations between the Jews of Bohemia-Moravia and their multinational surroundings surfaced at this time. As Jews were among the entrepreneurs of the local industry, an economic and cultural gap separated them from the Czech proletariat, who were of rural origin. Jews were also the bearers of German culture (notwithstanding the enmity shown them by the non-Jewish German population); they turned to the indigenous Czech culture late and only half-heartedly. In consequence, the dichotomy between the Jews and their neighbors assumed class and national-cultural dimensions, alongside the original religious distinction (which had become increasingly less significant in the eyes of the Jews themselves). These conflicts brought about an identity crisis among the Jews and even undermined the sense of all-Jewish solidarity. Jewish Prague, torn between divergent loyalties—a certain affinity to Judaism, the cultivation of German culture, and a Czech-national orientation—exemplified the tragic aspect of emancipation coupled with nationalism (Haumann, p. 230). Only later would Czech Jews find a solution to their personal identity crisis in Jewish nationalism.

It bears stressing that during the "Peoples' Spring" radical ideas still prevailed and were reflected in the readiness of the national movements to recognize the rights of other national groups, among them the Jews. The revolution was followed by a counterrevolution which brought a turnabout in the political situation and the dominant frame of mind. Once the "old regime" seemed restored, the national movements changed their tune, becoming less liberal and less democratic and tending more towards conservatism and insularity. The political map, which in the first half of the nineteenth century was split between conservatives and innovators, between multinational empires and movements of national liberation—front against front—was now atomized into a highly complex mosaic of forces, movements and interests competing within diverse frameworks.

The failure of the 1848 revolution was also a watershed for many among the intelligentsia, drawing them toward conservatism. Additionally, the collapse of the revolution generated a shift from a radicalism of the Left to a radicalism of the Right—a development which is particularly notable in the lives of some of the period's leading antisemites: Wilhelm Marr (1819–1904), who is considered to have coined the term "antisemitism"; the composer Richard Wagner (1813–1883), author of *Judaism in Music* (1850); and the writer Fyodor Dostoyevsky (1821–1881), a Slavophile nationalist and antisemite.

Disappointed in the revolution and its goals, these figures now espoused a nationalism which ostensibly gave expression to the people's soul—and which placed the Jews beyond the pale. The notion of the *alien* formed the linchpin of the various antisemitic attributes; a number of negative character traits were imputed to the Jews:

— Tribal loyalty and hostility toward others.
— Parasitism and greed.
— Shallow intellectualism.
— Subversiveness and arrogance.

By contrast, other peoples were depicted as innocent and generous, marked by their depth of feeling and dreaminess. Given this picture, nothing could be simpler than for the Jews to take advantage of the people's naivete and even gain its sympathy out of compassion. The Jews were alleged to be exploiting the weakness of the people in order to utilize it for their own ends. This was the juncture at which criticism of the Jews merged with the romantic frame of mind, rejecting as it were the rule of Mammon, anxious to prevent the disintegration of society and its values, and fearful lest the existing order be subverted. The following quotations may serve to illustrate this approach:

Wilhelm Marr, *The Victory of Judaism Over Germandom*:
The historical fact, that Israel became the leading social-political great power in the nineteenth century, lies before us. It is already notorious to what extent we lack the physical and intellectual strength to dejudaize ourselves.[8]

Richard Wagner, *Judaism in Music*:
How naive does their desire for emancipation therefore appear, for it is *we* who find ourselves in a state which obligates us to fight for emancipation from the Jews. The situation in the world shows that the Jew has gone well beyond emancipation. He *rules* and

[8] Marr, "The Victory of Judaism over Germandom." In Mendes-Flohr & Reinharz (eds.), *The Jew in the Modern World*, p. 272.

will continue to rule as long as money means power.[9] [Emphases in the original.]

Fyodor Dostoyevsky, *The Diary of a Writer*:
Step out of the family of nations, and from your own entity and thou shalt know that henceforth thou art the only one before God; exterminate the rest, or make slaves of them, or exploit them. Have faith in the conquest of the whole world; adhere to the belief that everything will submit to thee.[10]

The point of departure is national-romantic with a strong emphasis on the ordinary people and their polar opposite in the form of the Jews, who symbolize capitalism, liberalism and a rootless intelligentsia. In the eyes of these authors, the Jews evinced flagrantly anti-popular and anti-national tendencies. To account for their spurning of their revolutionary past, these antisemitic writers maintained that they were merely being disabused of illusions, including the illusion that the Jewish problem would be resolved through emancipation. The exposure of the Jews' true nature was indicative to them of the entire flawed social system.

It is noteworthy that the antisemitic literature tended to generalize about "the Jew," "the Russian" or "the German" as creatures with immutable characteristics. The terms of generalization—"Judaism," "Germanism," and the like—were also much resorted to, showing that these entities were simultaneously a social organism and an abstract essence. In other words, a Jew was not merely an individual but a representative of immutable Jewry, which by its nature differed from all the rest of mankind.

The concept that each people was supposed to be unique did not prevent antisemitic nationalists from evoking virtually identical notions, when they depicted "the Jew" or "Judaism" as the polar opposite of "the soul of the Russian people," "the genius of the German nation," and so forth. Even as the national movements grew increasingly hostile toward one another after the "Peoples' Spring," they continued to share a common feature, namely, enmity towards Jews—which now began to be incorporated into their ideologies. The future would also see some abortive attempts at international collaboration among antisemites from various countries. Despite their usual chauvinism, antisemities tend to rely on the experience of their counterparts in other countries, thus presumably signifying

[9] Wagner, *Judaism in Music*, pp. 5–6.
[10] Dostoyevsky, *The Diary of a Writer*, p. 646.

that all Jews are the same. In any event, a striking similarity under-
lies the allegations and stereotypes propounded by antisemites
from different nations: identical traits are usually attributed to the
Jews, despite the seemingly divergent conditions in each movement
and country.

A Letter from Leopold Zunz to a Friend[11]

The following is taken from a private correspondence between two
German Jews, following the events in the Prussian capital during
the 1848 revolution, which are accompanied by antisemitic outbursts.

Berlin, April 7, 1848

Your dear letter from Shushan Purim reached us on the day of
the Great Funeral,[12] and since then, king, government and parliament sanctioned the principle that civil rights are not dependent
on any religious beliefs whatsoever.[13] Notwithstanding all kinds
of harassment of and against Jews, which I personally do not
think worthwhile bothering with, there is no doubt that our cause
has won a decisive victory in civilized Europe, and with this conviction let us celebrate redemption next Passover.[14]

... Jews here have taken part in the fighting, and about eight
of them were killed or died of their wounds.[15] A father, from out of
town, lost two sons. At the funeral on March 26, I, and later

[11] Leopold Zunz (1794–1886), one of the founders of the *Wissenschaft des Juden-
tums* ("Science of Judaism"), laid the foundations of Jewish Studies as a systematic
discipline. He espoused a liberal outlook and advocated—particularly during the
period of the "Peoples' Spring"—a solution of the "Jewish Question" in conjunction
with the advancement of society as a whole. The events of the time and the hopes
Zunz pinned on them resonate in this letter (which reads like a personal document
and indeed was not intended for publication). It is typical of the period that Zunz
dismisses manifestations of Jew-hatred as the vestige of a phenomenon already long
defunct.

[12] The funeral processions of the fallen were transformed into victory demonstrations. Rabbis and clergymen called for cooperation between the different
religions.

[13] Equality between religious denominations was in practice annulled in Prussia
in 1850, when an amendment to the constitution designated Christianity as the
state religion.

[14] "Redemption" is used here in a double sense, as a remembrance of the Exodus
from Egypt and as the Festival of Liberation at this time.

[15] There were apparently 21 Jews among the 183 persons who fell in March 1848.

Sachs,[16] delivered the orations. After that three salvos were fired. (Glatzer, p. 139)

The Polish Revolt, 1863

This chapter began with the Polish insurrection of 1830 and will conclude with the Polish insurrection of 1863.

The Czarist authorities tried to forestall a rebellion by neutralizing various population groups; thus agrarian reform was introduced for the peasants and a degree of emancipation was assured for the Jews. Nevertheless, Jews still evinced sympathy for the Poles and even took an active part in the revolt.

After the failure of the revolts led by the aristocracy and gentry, a new trend arose among the Poles led by the bourgeoisie and aimed at the formation of an infrastructure for the consolidation of the Polish nation. The new current directed national energies toward "organic work"—development of resources and the promotion of industry, commerce and the sciences. Thus prospects also opened for the Jews to take part in economic development and assist in the national effort (Leslie, p. 47; Shatzky, pp. 617ff). At the outset, Polish positivism had seen in the Jews a desirable element and a faithful partner in the building of the Polish nation. The new development effected a sweeping change in the country and in the standing of the Jews in Polish society. However, those inclined toward romantic nationalism maintained that the Jews had bought off the leaders of the new mode as part of a scheme to lull and thwart Poland's national aspirations. At a later stage, "positivists" too began to draw a distinction between beneficial economic activity, such as that engaged in by the Poles themselves, and unproductive commerce, namely that of the Jews (Garntsarska-Kadary, 1975, pp. 52–53; Garntsarska-Kadary, 1985, pp. 282–284). The swift headway made by the Jewish bourgeoisie and intelligentsia threatened to stamp the modernization process in Poland with an imprint too manifestly "Jewish" for Polish tastes. The diligence and initiative of the Jews, favorably received and held to their credit at first, would later be seen as a drawback (whether due to competition and envy, or to rooted antisemitic feelings).

On a different plane, Jewish fealty to Polish nationalism was also called into question because of the economic ties which some Jewish

[16] Dr. Michael Sachs (1808–1864), a religious preacher and scholar of Jewish studies, was also numbered among the founders of the "Science of Judaism."

circles maintained with Czarist Russia (cf. Billington, p. 448). Furthermore, since 1868 Jews had enjoyed the right to move between the Polish region and other areas in the Pale of Settlement, and Jewish immigration began from outlying districts into Congress Poland. In addition to being outsiders, the so-called "Litvaks" were suspected by the Poles of serving as agents of Russification (Davies, p. 251). The phenomenon already noted in connection with Magyar nationalism recurred in the Polish case: the majority peoples claimed that the arrival of Jews from outside prevented the integration of the local Jews into the polity. This migration also intensified the demographic problem of Polish Jewry: according to data from the end of the century, Jews constituted fourteen percent of the population of Congress Poland, had a high birth rate, and were particularly concentrated in the cities and small towns.

From the Memoirs of Marcus Jastrow, 1860–1862

Passages from an essay published in 1870 by Dr. Mordechai Marcus Jastrow (1829–1903)—who at one time served as the preacher of the "enlightened" Temple in Warsaw—on the awakening of the national movement and on Polish-Jewish fraternity on the eve of the Polish insurrection of 1863.

> In these demonstrations there was manifested a call for unification with the brothers of the Mosaic faith.[17] The people wished to acquire as an ally this element which was important numerically and spiritually. Obviously, everything depended on the reaction of the Jews and especially of their leaders, the rabbis and the preachers, and in particular their paramount representative, Rabbi Meisels.[18] The Jews had the choice of forgetting about the persecutions and humiliations of the past and extending a brotherly hand to the inhabitants of the country, who called for reconciliation and fraternity, or rejecting this hand—in which case the mob would be incited to persecute the Jews and Jewish

[17] In February 1861 a parade was held in Warsaw which ended in a demonstration against the Russian authorities. The army fired into the crowd, killing and wounding Poles and Jews who had taken part in the demonstration. One of those killed was a Catholic priest who had been carrying a cross. When he was cut down by the bullets of the troops, a Jew who had been marching in the demonstration took up the cross, until he, too, was shot and killed.

[18] Dov-Ber Meisels (1798–1870), the Chief Rabbi of Warsaw during the insurrection, had been a supporter of Polish nationalism as early as the 1830 revolt. In 1861 he was arrested for his support of the rebels and was temporarily expelled from the city.

blood would be spilled in the streets of Warsaw, and even more in the smaller towns, a development which would have been convenient for the government.[19] To all appearances, [the government] would be defending the Jews against the Polish rebels, would be assuming a mantle of liberalism, and would suppress the liberal national movement and thereby intensify the Jew-hatred of the Poles.

Would Rabbi Meisels sign the Czar's memorandum when summoned to the greatest of the magnates, Count Zamoyski?[20] Would he identify himself and all of Polish Jewry with the interests of the country? Meisels did not hesitate much. On February 28, in the Count's reception room, he took pen in hand and signed his name alongside that of Archbishop Fijalkowski.[21]

... The fraternity of religions, even if it stems not a little from empty demonstrativeness, implanted in the Polish people the idea of the Jews' equal rights and in the course of time will eradicate the Poles' enmity toward the Jews, an enmity which is more national than religious in nature.[22] The blood of Jewish youth was spilled on the battlefields for Polish liberty. Jewish families suffered greatly because of death, expulsion and the flight of their family heads and sons. The Jews contributed immense sums of money to the national cause, Jewish writers devoted their work to the Polish cause in the country and abroad. All this is cement binding all the strata of the people. (Jastrow, pp. 210, 222)

[19] The authorities could only benefit by emphasizing the differences between the various population groups, and could have used the pretext of defending the Jews in order to suppress disloyal elements among the Poles.

[20] Count Andrzej Zamoyski (1800–1874) headed a committee which organized the insurrection, together with the Jewish industrialist and banker Leopold Kronenburg (1812-1878). Also active at the same time was a more radical group, which sought social changes in conjunction with national liberation. At this stage the idea was mooted to dispatch a petition to the Czar, with the support of all sections of the population, requesting autonomy for Poland.

[21] Archbishop Fijalkowski died that year, and his funeral in Warsaw became a major national event. The funeral ended with repressive measures being taken by the authorities, particularly against Catholic clerics. Both Rabbi Meisels and the author of the memoir himself were likewise arrested at this time.

[22] Notwithstanding his optimism regarding the fraternal relations between Poles and Jews, the author did not disregard the residue of enmity and scorn for the Jews or the situation in which the leaders of the Jewish population found themselves: caught between the rebels and the masses, on the one hand, and the Czarist regime, on the other. The author stressed that the Poles' hostility toward the Jews was more national than religious in character and thus subject to improvement as more and more Jews integrated into the Polish nation.

Summary: The Jews between Revolutions

The "Peoples' Spring" was something of a watershed between two historical epochs. Before the revolutions of 1848, nationalism saw itself as being locked in combat against the "Holy Alliance" (in the broad sense of that concept) side by side with other forces which were struggling against the old regime: liberals, democrats, and radicals of various stripes. This stage saw the formation of a kind of united front between the different national movements and the other opposition forces. Since national indentity had not yet reached a stage of cohesion in which a sharp distinction was drawn between one nation and another, cooperation among the national movements seemed feasible. The events of 1848 left in their wake rifts, disappointments and rivalries between various national movements. The revolution put to the test the slogan of international solidarity—and it was found wanting. In addition, the alliance which had to some extent been forged between the national movements and the opposition elements in the society was breached. The developments which had marked the rise of romantic nationalism in post-Napoleonic Germany were to be played out again and again in the second half of the nineteenth century. National clannishness intensified internally and aggressiveness manifested itself externally.

The Jewish interest was in large part bound up with the victory of the liberal elements. Until the "Peoples' Spring" there had been no conflict between these elements and the integration of the Jews into national life in various countries. Jews possessing sufficient awareness pinned their hopes on this trend. However, in the second half of the century the lines were redrawn and the Jews were caught in a withering crossfire of conflicting national and social interests: national identification was no longer reconcilable with the previous political orientation, and readiness to absorb Jews into society was being assailed by counter-reactions. In the multinational states the Jews found themselves entangled in the contradictory situation caused by the need to profess allegiance to only one of the various nationalities. Against this backdrop, antisemitism no longer seemed to be a vestige of the past, but a definite by-product of modern nationalism.

At the same time, it was clear that the Jews did not yet occupy a prominent place in the life of the nations, that their integration into society was proceeding quite slowly, and that large Jewish groups still lay outside the principal course of events. The national and social struggles affected chiefly the upper strata and did not yet involve the popular strata in the society. Just as the national movements were borne by rather narrow elites, so it was only the exceptions among the Jews who were directly involved in events. Yet the Jews did occupy a place in the public consciousness, due to an historical residue and the web of relations woven over many generations, as well as the role Jews were currently playing as pioneers of modernization. The Jews were a saliently urban element, and due to their past socioeconomic performance, their skills and their connections, as well as the agility which characterizes a discriminated minority, some of them had attained prominent positions, initially in the economic sector and thereafter in the cultural realm and even in politics.

Paradoxically, the appearance of individual Jews as citizens involved in the nation's life served to underscore precisely their historical and contemporary affinity with the Jewish groups that had been left behind. The assimilated or converted Jew could make crude attempts to become part of the surrounding society, but his efforts at integration could not conceal his Jewish origins or his ties with other Jews. Hovering specter-like behind the Jew who became a Frenchman, a German, or a Hungarian, seemed to be large reserves of Jews of the old type—and this perception caused apprehension among non-Jews. Even Jews who had resided in a country for generations continued to be regarded as not really belonging, as foreigners threatening to flood the country with more of their kind, subvert its essence, and obscure its unique character. This is a recurring motif in modern antisemitism, particularly under the influence of nationalism.

3

The Rise of
Political Antisemitism

The 1870s saw the onset of a cycle of economic crises which continued
intermittently for about twenty-five years. Antisemitism came to a
head in this period. Although its root was not always economic,
times of crisis usually generate social and political tensions. It is
generally believed that antisemitism in Germany and Austria arose
in reaction to the emancipation of the Jews. The general public was
under the impression that the success enjoyed by many Jews had
come at the expense of the non-Jews. Both Germany and Austria
had experienced rapid growth and prosperity followed by periods
of economic crisis. The deteriorating situation played havoc with
political and economic liberalism, with which the Jews were in large
measure identified. In place of free trade, a hallmark of liberalism,
the captains of industry and agriculture now urged protective tar-
iffs. An insular approach toward national economies developed, and
concomitantly, growing state intervention was manifested in many
areas of life. Gradually the nation-state fulfilled a central role in
society and was often admired as the embodiment of the national
soul.

France, so often jolted by upheavals in the past, was affected by
the economic crisis rather late. The eventual collapse of the economy
in France was attributed, as previously in Central Europe, to ques-
tionable Jewish business ethics. Several countries saw the rise of
social-Christian movements which competed with socialism by
forming worker's organizations imbued with a Christian-national
spirit. These movements espoused social justice without revolution,
"productive" as opposed to "exploitive" capital, and opposition to the
"mercantile spirit" of the Jew. The more extreme elements started

antisemitic movements whose declared aim was to combat the excessive influence of the Jews—and this was the genesis of political antisemitism. As a minority group excluded from the old establishment, the Jews had become entrepreneurs *par excellence* and demonstrated a sense of innovation which seemed to portend menacing unrest. Outspoken antisemites accused the Jews of harboring malicious intentions, said to originate in their own nationalism which was, supposedly, inimical to the majority peoples.

German antisemitism entered the political arena in 1879, when Chancellor Otto von Bismarck (1815–1898) abandoned the liberal coalition in favor of a conservative policy. This move heralded a far-reaching change in both the German polity and the Jewish condition. The depression brought on by the crisis of 1873 hardened the opposition to economic liberalism and weakened the National Liberal Party. Concurrently, a conservative alliance was formed of the *haute bourgeoisie* and the aristocracy with the Catholic Center, resulting among other things in legislation banning the Socialist Party. The National Liberals went into decline and began to recant their traditional principles. The new line was interpreted as a reaction against the Jews, who were identified with the liberal tendencies in the economy and in politics. Blame for the failure of liberalism was placed upon the Jews, who had been among its chief exponents.

The new political course likewise had many ideological ramifications, which were delineated most notably by the historian Heinrich von Treitschke (1834-1896). He rekindled the romantic nationalism of the early part of the century, now tailored to fit a great power which was unmistakably on the rise but felt it had not yet been accorded its due place in the world. Treitschke was also at the center of a polemic on antisemitism, which broke out among the intelligentsia following the creation of the Social Christian Party of the court-preacher Adolf Stöcker (1835–1909). Treitschke, while seemingly dissociating himself from the crude manifestations of antisemitism in its vulgar form, nevertheless welcomed the masses' instinctive eruption against the Jews. His article, published in November 1879, triggered a wave of responses from both Jews and non-Jews. When Treitschke replied to the criticisms, the polemic assumed the dimensions of a full-scale debate on the Jews' standing in German society.

Originally Treitschke had intended to deal not specifically with the Jews but with Germany's future. His sharpest critique was directed at phenomena such as liberalism and socialism, nihilism and materialism. In his own eyes his critique of the Jews did not seem harsh. Although he coined the classic phrase "The Jews are our misfortune," he did not seek to alter the status of the Jews, merely to reduce their influence. According to him, the Jews were impeding Germany's cohesion at a time when the country was struggling to preserve its distinct character against foreign influences. Treitschke differentiated between the Jews of Germany and those in England and France who, he maintained, had integrated smoothly into the social fabric in both countries. In contrast, he argued, Germany suffered from a mass immigration of "assiduous pants-selling youths . . ., whose children and grandchildren are to be the future rulers of Germany's exchanges and Germany's press." In other words, the Jewish problem had arisen in the course of the mass migrations from the East. Treitschke did not forget to dole out compliments to a few German Jews who had made an effort to integrate themselves into the life of the German nation.

Among those who took issue with him, Treitschke was particularly disparaging of Heinrich Graetz (1817–1891), whose influence as a historian he considered tantamount to incitement to Jewish fanaticism. "There is no place on German soil for dual nationality," he pronounced and called on the proponents of Jewish nationalism to emigrate from Germany and found their own state elsewhere. A nationalistic intolerance of nonconformists was quite prevalent in broad circles of German society. The antisemitic trend celebrated its victory at the Tivoli Conference of the Conservative Party in 1892, whose platform called for restraining "the ruinous Jewish influence." This resolution closed the circle of the mass antisemitism of the 1880s. The "professional" antisemites, who preached an unabashed Jew-hatred, were fading from the public stage, but in exchange antisemitism became a legitimate component of the ruling ideology (Boehlich, 1965, pp. 11, 12, 44; Sheehan, pp. 272–283).

In the last quarter of the nineteenth century, German antisemitism not only ran broad and deep but was highly diversified. It encompassed traditional Jew-hatred—both Catholic and Protestant—and economic and social antisemitism with incipient racist antisemitism on the fringes. But it was the nationalist component that was shared by many of the antisemites during this period. After Germany achieved its much coveted unity, becoming a great-power on the international stage, German nationalism assumed a more aggressive form externally and a less tolerant attitude internally. Its considerable achievements notwithstanding, Germany perceived itself as lagging behind England and France—a self-image which accounts for many of the phenomena that marked its subsequent history, including its attitude toward the Jews. When Treitschke spoke of the Jews' "dual nationality" he was giving expression to a broad consensus. The Jews tried to do their part in forging a standardized German identity, but from time to time they nevertheless found themselves standing out due to their dissimilarity. The Jews, in concert with the circles that favored their integration into the society, insisted that this difference was confined to religion alone—that is, the Jews were "Germans of the Mosaic faith" just as other Germans were Lutherans or Catholics. However, the enemies of the Jews contended that the totality of the differences between them and the country's other inhabitants exceeded the bounds of religion. Moreover, even the religious difference pointed to a dissociation from the German entity in a society which was suspicious of minority or deviant groups (Strauss, p. 433).

Heinrich von Treitschke: "What We Can Expect" [1]

The following document reflects the attitude toward the Jews of a prominent spokesman of German nationalism at the end of the nineteenth century. The Jews' insularity and their negative influence are assailed.

What we have to demand from our Jewish fellow-citizens is simple: that they become Germans, regard themselves, simply and justly as Germans, without prejudice to their faith and their old sacred past which all of us hold in reverence; for we do not want an era of German-Jewish mixed culture to follow after thousands of years of German civilization. It would be a sin to forget that a great number of Jews, baptized and unbaptized, Felix Mendelssohn,[2] Veit,[3] Riesser[4] and others, not to mention the ones now living, were Germans in the best sense of the word, men in whom we revere the noble and fine traits of the German spirit. At the same time it cannot be denied that there are numerous and power-

[1] In this essay, published in 1879 by Heinrich von Treitschke in the "Prussian Yearbooks" which he edited, Graetz is attacked for his alleged Jewish fanaticism.

[2] The composer Felix Mendelssohn-Bartholdy (1809–1847) was a grandson of Moses Mendelssohn and a convert to Christianity.

[3] Philip Veit (1790–1854), an artist, was also a grandson of Mendelssohn's and a convert to Christianity.

[4] Gabriel Riesser (1806–1863), deputy chairman of the National Assembly in Frankfurt during the revolution of 1848, was Jewish and a leading liberal and fighter for emancipation.

ful groups among our Jews who definitely do not have the good will to become simply Germans. It is painful enough to talk about these things. Even conciliatory words are easily misunderstood here. I think, however, some of my Jewish friends will admit, with deep regret, that recently a dangerous spirit of arrogance has arisen in Jewish circles and that the influence of Jewry upon our national life, which in former times was often beneficial, has recently often been harmful. (Mendes-Flohr & Reinharz, p. 281)

The Austro-Hungarian Empire

The 1870s and 1880s saw an intensification of antisemitism in the Hapsburg Empire as well. The special status granted to Hungary in 1867 aroused bitterness among other nationalities and heightened the frustration of the German-speaking population in particular. The Germans feared that they were about to lose their predominant position in the Empire. The rising influence of Hungary, on the one hand, and the mounting pressure exerted by the various Slavic peoples, on the other, compelled the authorities to pursue a balanced and cautious policy. It was against this background that the advocates of Greater Germany began to make themselves heard, their demand being for union with the redoubtable neighboring German Reich. This aspiration, if consummated, was bound to bring about the dissolution of the Austro-Hungarian Empire. Considering these sentiments, Vienna's tactic was to tread carefully between the contradictory national and social trends. Following the compromise with the Magyars in Hungary, a measure of autonomy was also granted to the Poles in Galicia. The central government relied to a considerable degree on the cooperation of statesmen of different ethnic backgrounds in running the country. Nevertheless, a steady erosion was discernible in public support for the central government throughout the Empire.

In this multinational situation, the Jews were generally among the groups that actively supported the empire's continued existence. True, Hungarian Jewry identified with Magyar nationalism, and even among Galician Jews the Polish orientation was gaining in strength, but in theory these trends did not conflict with the traditional loyalty to the Emperor. The Jews also served the government as a buffer against the isolationist interests of certain aristocratic cliques. As in Germany, the Jews in Austria were among the chief exponents of liberalism. The liberal orientation suited the Jews—

a dynamic group in the economy—and was consonant with their aspiration to integrate into the country's political and social life, since the liberals espoused equality of rights and combated clerical influences.

The crisis of 1873 undermined the resilience of liberalism as an economic policy; nor did liberalism as a political system escape unscathed, with the result that the national conflicts became more acute. The groups that were hardest hit by the crisis imputed the responsibility for their condition to the rule of capital, and particularly of the Jews, whom they regarded as the symbol of bourgeois liberalism. The ongoing democratization and the extension of the franchise lent support to a political structure with a markedly antisemitic slant. Soon Vienna was seething with varied antisemitic activity: radical pan-German, conservative-Catholic, petit-bourgeois. Concurrently, antisemitism flourished in other regions, interacting with the local national conflicts:

— Czech antisemitism propelled by anti-German sentiment;
— Slovak antisemitism in protest against Magyarization;
— Polish antisemitism which was anti-Russian, anti-German and
    anti-Ukrainian in character; and
— Magyar antisemitism in protest against the integration of the
    Jews in Hungary. (Rosensaft, pp. 57–86; Wistrich, pp. 187–188)

This was the atmosphere in which the famous blood libel was perpetrated at Tisza-Eszlar, in Hungary, in 1882–1883. A village girl disappeared just before Passover, and a rumor spread among the local farmers that she had been murdered by the Jews. After the suspicions found their way into the press, at the initiative of a local priest, antisemitic representatives in the Budapest parliament demanded an investigation to determine whether ritual murder was involved. The government tried to calm the situation, but the opposition, which sought to detach Hungary from Austria, used the event to excoriate the government. Legal proceedings were instituted against Jewish suspects, and the surging antisemitic incitement soon produced riots. Ultimately the suspects were exonerated after the case had gone through several hearings, but in the meantime violent outbursts against the Jews erupted in various locales in Hungary and a state of emergency was proclaimed. One version has it that the riots were planned with the aid of German antisemites and that the rioters were recruited from nationally and socially deprived groups (Katzburg, 1985, p. 4). The affair foreshadowed other blood libels, such as that in Xanten, in the Rhine District, in 1891, marking the exploitation of deeply ingrained religious prejudices for modern political purposes. (This will be elaborated upon in the next chapter.)

Austrian Jews or Jewish Austrians

The following are the divergent views of two Jewish leaders concerning antisemitism and the national orientation of the Jews: Rabbi Dr. Samuel Josef Bloch,[5] who favored supporting the Empire as such and was against Jewish involvement in various national struggles (1885); and Prof. Alois Zucker,[6] who espoused a Czech orientation, in the course of a speech against antisemitism in the House of Representatives (1890).

Neither the Germans nor the Czechs regard us as belonging to their respective nations [*Stammesgenossen*][7] and we need not covet such honor either.[8] We are neither Germans nor Slavs[9] but *Austrian Jews or Jewish Austrians.*[10] We can neither act as "Deutsch-national" nor as "Czech-national" without making fools of ourselves. For our fellow Jews in Bohemia there is no other way but to surrender to facts, as well as to political sense and the duty of self-preservation, and to place ourselves *outside of these two national groups.* . . . As Jews we cannot but support the rights

[5] Galician born Joseph S. Bloch (1850–1923) was a rabbi in a Vienna suburb and campaigned against antisemitism. He gained fame in his polemic against August Rohling (1839–1931), who had vilified the Talmud. Bloch published a militant Jewish weekly and represented a Galician constituency in the Austrian Diet.

[6] Zucker, a Jew, served in the Diet as a member of the "Czech club." He claimed to have been elected unanimously to serve as rector of the University of Bohemia (yet had turned it down), as proof of the friendly relations that obtained between Czechs and Jews.

[7] The author uses the term *Stammesgenossen*, which connotes ethnic partnership between members of the same people, as distinct from the usual national criterion in Austria, namely, language.

[8] A sarcastic barb directed against Jews who try to curry favor with a specific national group. These Jews supposedly enjoy the honor that befalls them whenever spokesmen of the nationality in question make a friendly gesture toward them.

[9] The prevailing distinction made by the public between the rival national movements already extended beyond ethnic differences and was sliding toward racial terminology—"Slavs," for example, superseding "Czechs," and "Poles."

[10] Bloch did not determine his choice between two diametrically opposed concepts: on the one hand, Jews who were inhabitants of Austria (just as there were also Jews in Germany, Russia, or France); and Austrians who were also Jews (as Austrians might be Catholic, Protestant or Orthodox). However, his general outlook is based on the notion that the Jews in Austria are the linchpin of the entire Empire.

of all national groups in the state, equal rights for all citizens. [Emphases in the original.] (Bloch, pp. 40, 42)

The national battles which are being fought in Austria constitute a mere phase in the political development. These fights must turn into competition between nations,[11] and I believe that in this competition of nations the Jews may have an advantageous position. As Jews have no language and other things in common, one cannot speak about a *Jewish nation*.[12] Thus it is only natural that Jews living in mixed-language areas should join one nation or another; and this is how the problem might be solved. When I join a certain nation, when I am active and contribute to the development of the people, no sincere nationalist can reject me, since there exists competition between nations.[13] . . . I wish to express the hope that antisemitism may not blossom in Bohemia, or will be nipped in the bud.[14] [Emphasis in the original.] (Zucker, *Reden gegen den Antisemitusmus*.)

Russia and Romania

The largest Jewish community on earth—forty-five percent of world Jewry—resided in Greater Russia. The majority was forced to live in the "Pale of Settlement," which was limited mainly to Poland, White Russia and the Ukraine, and was prohibited from moving to other areas of the Empire. The policy toward the Jews was an outgrowth of the absolute rule which prevailed in the country and bore the stamp of the Russian Orthodox Church. Discrimination against the Jews persisted in Russia even after most of the civilized world had granted equality of rights to all inhabitants, at least on paper.

As new trends took root in the 1870s, the situation of Russian Jewry took a turn for the worse. These trends followed the publication in 1869 of *The Book of the Kagal* by Jacob Brafman

[11] The author distinguishes between unrestrained national struggles and fair competition based on fixed rules. Competition of this kind could, perhaps, divert existing aggression into positive channels and thus prove beneficial to all concerned.

[12] When these words were spoken in Parliament, incipient signs of a Jewish national movement had already appeared in Austria; however, the Jews were not yet considered a nation.

[13] Zucker thought that no national movement could afford to forgo the political and financial help of the Jews while it was fighting for its place in the multinational Empire.

[14] The speaker admitted that hostile feelings toward the Jews existed among the people but hoped that these would subside in the course of the Jews' cooperation with the national movement.

(1825–1879), a converted Jew who purported to expose the Jews according to authentic sources. The book, which was based on distortions of material taken from the minutes of the Minsk Jewish community in White Russia, was meant to show the alleged danger the Jews posed to Russia.

The Russian establishment was divided between assimilators and extremists who did not believe in changing the Jews and wished to be rid of them. The debate on the "Jewish Question" broke out against a backdrop of fanatic nationalism triggered by the Polish Revolt in 1863 and steeped in a belief in the need to save Russia's purity from Western influences. Just as the Poles had accused the "Litvak" Jews of abetting the Russian influence in their country, so the Jews in Russia were perceived as the allies of Polish nationalism. At the same time the Jews had also become a symbol of dangerous innovations—capitalist initiative and Western influences—that impinged on the spirit of "Holy Russia." Resistance to the encroachment of the West characterized Church circles and most of the establishment but was also marked among those revolutionaries who drew their inspiration from popular Slavophile traditions (Gleason, pp. 35–37).

Following the assassination of Czar Alexander II by a revolutionary in 1881, a wave of anti-Jewish riots swept through southern Russia. These protracted and bloody events, known in Jewish annals as the "whirlwinds in the south" (Isaiah 21:1), also spread to other parts of the country and left a trail of death and devastation. Quite possibly the riots were organized by extremist agitators close to the ruling circles. The authorities failed to quell the disturbances, and sometimes evinced sympathy for the rioters. The unchecked course of the riots showed the Jews of Russia how isolated they were, and demonstrated that virtually all sections of the society—the revolutionaries included—were tainted with enmity toward them and remained indifferent to their fate.

The riots were a turning point in terms of the future status of the Jews in Russia, for the hostile atmosphere led to new measures against them. The authorities initiated a public inquiry into the damage allegedly caused by the Jews to the majority population, and regulations were promulgated restricting Jewish economic activity. Although these restrictions were announced as temporary measures, they remained effective for thirty-five years. The restrictions on the Jews were of social and political significance, and their message was clear for all to see: the riots were taken as the peoples' just revenge against the Jews who had dispossessed them. The victims of the riots and of the decrees—the Jews—were portrayed as themselves responsible for the fate that had befallen them. As a result, the Jew was branded as the enemy of the people and was turned into a political scapegoat. Incitement against the Jews was utilized to divert public opinion from the challenge posed by modernization and the growth of national consciousness in the Pale of Settlement, among Poles, Lithuanians, Ukrainians and White Russians (Ettinger, 1976, pp. 881–885).

An interesting question arises in any discussion of antisemitism as a means to divert public opinion: Does the antisemite himself believe his fabrications about the Jews, or does he merely exploit them for propaganda purposes? On the face of it, an antisemitic agitator might bear no personal animosity toward the Jews and still be capable of arousing enmity according to need and circumstances. One is reminded here of Vienna's mayor Karl Lueger (1844–1910), for one, who though friendly with Jews on a personal level used antisemitism as a political tool. Antisemitism thus asssumes a dimension of abstraction or externalization—a phenomenon which brings to mind the spread of antisemitism in places where there are no Jews at all, without a patent connection to reality. This is a particularly complex issue when applied to Nazi antisemitism and Hitler's role in the Holocaust.

I now turn to Romania, a country well known for its antisemitic tradition. After attaining independence, Romania sought to expand its borders, giving rise to both an aggressive nationalism and anti-semitism. The Romanians used the old argument that the Jews were foreigners and hence had no claim on Romanian citizenship. They held that only a few Jews had lived in Romania at the beginning of the century, the rest being immigrants who had exploited and abused the local inhabitants. Influential Jewish groups throughout the world, headed by the Paris-based *Alliance Israélite Universelle*, pressured the Bucharest government to grant the Jews civil rights. In 1878 the Congress of Berlin required Romania to recognize the rights of all the country's inhabitants, irrespective of ethnic origin or religion, as a condition for recognition of its independence. However the Romanian authorities did not honor their commitments. Indeed, their response was to issue expulsion orders against Jews who constituted a "menace to the state" and to harass the Jewish population by means of administrative measures. Even under international pressure the Romanians refused to alter their position and continued to deny the Jews (with certain privileged exceptions, such as veteran soldiers) their promised rights.

Antisemitism in Romania fit in with the struggle against foreigners and efforts to weld the Romanian national identity. As the middle class, particularly in Moldavia, was largely Jewish, antisemitism went hand-in-hand with the emergence of the Romanian bourgeoisie, which competed with the Jews but retained a feudal outlook, invested its capital in land and was dismayed by the prospect of modernization. The struggle against the Jews was perceived as an extension of the struggle against the excessive privileges granted foreigners during the period of Ottoman rule. Hence the constant emphasis on the contention that the Jews were no more than aliens. Jew-hatred in Romania was also intertwined with the tradition of the Orthodox national church and was further nourished by Russian influences. The anti-Jewish policy rested on an antisemitic lobby in both major parties, economic pressure groups, and not least on the support of the religious establishment. Underlying the policy was an antisemitic ideology tinged with a conservative-nationalist bias and a populist slant. Both trends cultivated the romaticism of a peasantry deeply rooted in the land and opposed both capitalism and industry, which were identified with the Jews. It bears stressing that in Romania, as in Czarist Russia, discrimination against the Jews was official state policy (Weber, pp. 501–507).

Memorandum to the Czar

The following document was written by the future Russian Minister of the Interior, Nikolai Pavlovich Ignatyev (1832–1908), upon the accession to the throne of Alexander III in 1882.

In Petersburg there exists a powerful group of Poles and Yids[15] which holds in its hands direct control of banks, the stock exchange, the bar, a great part of the press, and other areas of public life. Through many legal and illegal ways it exerts an enormous influence over the bureaucracy[16] and the general course of affairs. Parts of this group are implicated in the growing plunder

[15] Even though the wording seems to indicate that these were Polish Jews, the remainder of the document makes it clear that the reference was to both Jews and Poles.

[16] The conservatives suspected the bureaucracy of adopting an overly independent stand.

of the exchequer and in seditious activity. . . . Preaching the blind imitation of Europe[17] . . . these people . . . recommend the granting of the most extensive rights to Poles and Jews, and representative institutions[18] after the Western model. Every honest voice . . . is silenced by the shouts of Jews and Poles who insist that one must listen only to the "intelligent" class and that Russian demands must be rejected as backward and unenlightened.[19] (Rogger, 1983, p. 201)

France

Since the French Revolution, France had seemed to be the epitome of liberty, equality, and fraternity. True, Jew-hatred stemming from Christian sources persisted, but it was perceived as merely a vestige of the old prejudices that would soon die out. The Jews were granted equal rights in 1791 and Napoleon accorded Judaism the status of a recognized religion, like Catholicism or Protestantism. Clearly, these developments helped integrate the Jews into French life as citizens with equal rights and obligations—ostensibly no different from anyone else. Enmity toward the Jews now seemed to be harbored only by arch-conservative Catholics.

Yet antisemitism was also present within the French Left, which identified the Jews with exploitive capitalism. Jew-hatred in France in the nineteenth century was often linked with a certain ill-feeling toward capitalism and modernization. Those who followed with alarm the unravelling of the French social fabric under the twin pressures of industrialization and urbanization or those who fought against exploitive capital tended to cite the Jews as the progenitors of capitalism. Rothschild became the very essence of capitalism in France; when the socialist circles railed against the injustices of the bourgeois society, they pointed at *him*. Gradually other types of antisemitism—nationalist and racist—also evolved together with a fusion of nationalism, racism and national socialism containing antisemitic ingredients (Sternhell, pp. 339–342).

[17] The characteristic recoil from Western influences is reflected here.

[18] That is, an elected house of representatives such as the parliament of the constitutional monarchy in England.

[19] The dichotomy is between the Enlightenment and the authentic Russian tradition, considered primitive by exponents of the West. It was not by accident that the advocates of modernization were alleged to be Poles and Jews—the point being that this trend was alien to Russia. The combination of "Poles and Jews" after the Polish insurrection signifies cooperation between different elements that fuse into a dangerous and alien power.

And there was more: French national feeling rose after France was defeated in the war against Prussia (1870–71), the German emperor was crowned at Versailles, and Alsace as well as parts of Lorraine were annexed by the German Reich. The hostility toward Germany and the revanchist spirit now became the focus of French national ambitions. Generations of Frenchmen were educated in a spirit of anti-German patriotism. The liberation of Alsace-Lorraine remained a permanent item on the French national agenda, preoccupying politicians and men of letters alike as a traumatic national experience.

Testimony to the extent of antisemitism in France is provided by the fact that *La France juive* by Edouard Drumont (1844-1917) became a great bestseller. Over 100,000 copies were sold within a year of its publication in 1886, and eventually it went through over 200 editions. The book is a mixture of social and economic criticism, nostalgia for France's days of glory, racist and Catholic sentiments, and anxiety in the face of change. Drumont claimed to have exposed the so-called Jewish "secret conspiracy." He owed his success in part to his broad appeal to different sectors of society and his ability to aim at, and hit, a variety of targets simultaneously. Antisemitism in the France of the 1880s was a subject of broad public interest and served to explain the country's lengthy economic crisis. But the full-fledged nationalist element was not wholly manifest until the eruption of the Dreyfus Affair (Poliakov, pp. 39–42).

The Affair began in October 1894 when Drumont's paper reported that Captain Alfred Dreyfus (1859–1935), who served on the general staff, had secretly been arrested on a charge of treason. Rumors abounded that Dreyfus had sold military secrets to a foreign power (at first thought to be Italy and later Germany) and that he had confessed. It was also being said that his downfall was the result of debts incurred because of women, gambling, and the like. Soon it became apparent that the Affair was damaging Franco-German relations and adversely affecting the prestige of the French high command. The press covering the trial created great excitement and the public was divided, for and against Dreyfus. When he was court-martialled in closed session in December 1894, the tension was palpable. Dreyfus was convicted, his appeal was rejected—and only then was it reported that he believed he was being persecuted because he was a Jew. In early 1895 a public ceremony took place in which Dreyfus was stripped of his rank; he was then exiled to Devil's Island in the Atlantic Ocean. A few public figures, among them Émile Zola (1840–1902)—who was convicted of libel—maintained that officers of the general staff had conspired against Dreyfus in order to save their own skins.

The Affair split the public into two hostile camps: on the one side were the Republican loyalists, who believed in Dreyfus's innocence; on the other were the backers of the Army, who applauded the verdict against the "Jewish traitor." In 1898 demonstrations were staged against Dreyfus's supporters in various places in France and anti-Jewish riots broke out in Algiers. The real traitor confessed in 1899, but although a retrial was held Dreyfus was not exonerated. He later received only a pardon, and it was not until 1906 that Dreyfus was fully acquitted (see Chapman, 1972; Halasz, 1955).

The Dreyfus Affair was a landmark in French history, not only in terms of the attitude toward Jews but because it forged two ideological and political camps that were to prove highly durable. In time, the struggle over Dreyfus's innocence became the focal point of a general confrontation between two sections of the French public: the secular-republican camp, which proclaimed its allegiance to the heritage of the French Revolution; and the conservative-clerical camp, which was prepared to sacrifice an innocent person so as to preserve what was purported to be the honor of the French Army. The reliance on Dreyfus's Jewishness as overwhelming proof of his treason derived from deep-rooted prejudices. There were nevertheless some people with antisemitic leanings who backed Dreyfus, since they were able to distinguish between specific personal guilt and a negative disposition toward the Jews as a group. On the other hand, some anti-Dreyfusards maintained that Dreyfus deserved to be punished even if he were *not* guilty of the crime attributed to him; in this view, the struggle did not involve the loyalty of one person but the supposed disloyalty of the Jews to France. For such people the Affair became a symbolic contest between *the spirit of France* and the "anti-French" Jewish spirit (Duroselle, p. 68).

The ingredients of a nationally motivated antisemitism were clearly visible in the Dreyfus Affair. Nationalism became the criterion which determined human behavior in general: the nation was perceived as a unique entity confronting other nations in a war of all against all while simultaneously combating the enemy within. At the head of the hostile forces stood the Jew, the epitome of the foreigner. He lived in France but his ramified reach embraced the world; since he was not flesh of the nation's flesh and bone of its bone, he was always ready to betray the country. These arguments were occasionally joined by others, but overall the Jews were seen not as a diversified group of live human beings but as a fully formed stereotype. To the ancient myths of "the eternal Jew" and of Judas Iscariot who betrayed Christ was now added the image of the Jew as the enemy of the nation.

The waning of the Dreyfus Affair brought with it a decline in the impact of antisemitism in France. Unlike Germany, where anti-semitism was incorporated into the conservative platform, in France it remained the purview of extreme fringe groups. These groups exercised a certain influence in conservative circles, among intellec-tuals and, during a crisis, even on the streets of Paris, but for the time being antisemitism seemed to have gone out of fashion. In French society as a whole, the Affair served as a catalyst for political deployment marking the closing of one chapter in the historical interaction between the two halves of France (Ettinger, 1975, pp. 12–13).

Antisemitism Justified

In 1893, about a year before the Dreyfus Affair erupted, a book attacking antisemitism by a liberal Catholic historian, Anatole Leroy-Beaulieu (1842–1912), was published in France. In the author's view antisemitism was a negative phenomenon but con-tained an element of truth.

> It would be well to give the preference to the natives, to the French Frenchmen. It must be admitted, however, that precisely the opposite practice has prevailed in France under the Third Repub-lic. The important part that strangers play in our affairs, has been one of the features and one of the faults of the system that has obtained during the past fifteen years.[20]

> In this respect, the complaints of *la France Juive*[21] and of the Antisemites have not been altogether groundless; and this fact, in itself, fosters the Antisemitic agitation. It should not be con-sidered an advantage in France to have been born in Hamburg or

[20] The author decries the Third Republic, especially since the advent of the con-servative Republicans, also known as "Opportunists," who conducted an anti-cleri-cal policy.

[21] *La France juive* ("Jewish France") is the name of the famous book by the anti-semite Drumont, who in this period led the attack against Jewish influence in France. Drumont's newspaper was the first to write about the scandal that would burgeon into the famous Dreyfus Affair which was to split France for years to come.

in Frankfurt, nor should it be a recommendation in the eyes of the government to have brothers or cousins in Berlin or Vienna, or even in London and New York.[22] It is not right that adopted sons should be preferred to the children of the house, nor, that at the public board the immigrants or their sons should have the choicest morsels and the promptest attendance. Let us have no inverted privileges. In our assemblies and in our newspapers we have too often seen newcomers from beyond the Rhine or elsewhere, many of whom had never drawn lots with us for military service,[23] laying down the law to our native-born citizens, giving lessons in patriotism and in French at the same time, revealing to our children the meaning of the Revolution and the mission of the French spirit.[24]

For us, fatherland means something else and something deeper.[25] We have no more chosen it than we have chosen our mothers, and it seems almost impossible to change it as it would be to change our mothers. That Israelite is mistaken;[26] we do feel ourselves rooted in French soil, as firmly as a tree that clings to the earth with all its roots and living fibres. Our fatherland was here before us; it has borne and nourished us; we belong to it; we are bound to it with indissoluble ties. . . .

For the Jews, emigration is not the same thing as for our countrymen.[27] Most of the Jews who are streaming towards the northern

[22] The author maintains that France needs the immigrants because of the country's low natural birth rate. Although he notes that his criticism is directed equally at the behavior of Christian immigrants, his principal target is unmistakably Jewish. He also accepts Drumont's claim that the influential French statesman Léon Michel Gambetta (1838–1882) was Jewish or of Jewish extraction.

[23] The point is apparently that they did not serve in the army (according to the recruiting procedure by lot).

[24] This is, of course, a sarcastic jibe against the arrogance of Jews prominent in French cultural and social life, who were eager to represent the sacrosanct values of the national tradition: patriotism, language, the Revolution, and the French spirit.

[25] The author contests the view that national identity is a function of personal choice and argues that national affiliation is an existential experience of the group, deriving from the interrelation of man and nature.

[26] His adversary in this debate was apparently Michael Aharon Weil (1814–1889), the first Chief Rabbi of Algeria. A similar stance was voiced in 1882 by the renowned French scholar Ernest Renan (1823–1892) in his famous lecture "What Is a Nation?" (his reply: "a daily plebiscite!").

[27] It bears recalling that the purpose of the essay was to justify the absorption of Jews into French society and repudiate the antisemitic position. Yet at times, the author emphasizes the foreignness of the Jews—and this is even more striking against the writer's fundamentally sympathetic attitude toward them. In the author's view, the Jews *can* be absorbed by the nation; nevertheless, French Jews are perceived as lacking the natural sense of belonging that other Frenchmen possess.

or the southern seas, are not changing their country; they are in search of a country. And they are grateful to those who will grant them one.[28] (Leroy-Beaulieu, 1904, pp. 338–343 *passim*)

Summary: In Times of Upheaval

Passing through a series of economic crises, Europe in the last quarter of the nineteenth century entered a stage of extended political consciousness. Industrialization, urbanization, secularization, the greater impact of the urban masses, the growth in the circulation of the popular press, and the extension of the franchise all left their mark. The old order may not have been collapsing at a uniform pace, but it did so with growing palpability. The need was felt for a new guarantor of social cohesion, particularly in view of the rise of the workers' movement and the spread of the socialist idea. The socialist movement espoused the international unity of the working class, rejected in theory national solidarity, and took a hostile attitude toward the bourgeois state. This outlook was perceived as a threat not only to property and to the interests of the bourgeoisie or to the remaining privileges of the aristocracy but to the very existence of the social order.

The development of capitalism and the processes of democratization which found their way into many European countries exposed large sections of the public to the influence of socialism while at the same time helping to convey the message of nationalism. Nationalism penetrated various social strata and exercised an influence on the workers indirectly and cumulatively, to the point where it became a new focal point for societal organization. In the nation-states the *state* was perceived as the embodiment of the national entity and frequently became the object of loyalty and adoration. The political conflicts in the multinational states increasingly reflected the struggle between rival national movements. At the end of the nineteenth century nationalism was broadly perceived as a struggle between different national organisms. Nationalism purported to speak in the name of all strata, to mold the nation into a

[28] Here we find the practical argument regarding the Jews' ability to assimilate: since they are strangers everywhere, they are ready to make the effort to be accepted and to adopt a national identity. In comparison, other immigrants have a natural homeland, and find it difficult to adopt a new national identity elsewhere—but this is not the case with Jews. Moreover, the very speed with which the Jews integrate sometimes arouses opposition; the author shares this feeling, but does not oppose their integration altogether.

single body and to represent the spirit of the people. The reserved or even hostile attitude of international socialism toward nationalism was accepted by parts of the working class; this in turn transformed nationalism into a dividing line between those who were supposedly loyal to the people and an internal enemy who, in alliance with foreign elements, was causing the disintegration of the national entity, in the name of harmful ideals.

The economic crises and their attendant social turmoil played havoc with the liberal system that had predominated in the countries of Central and Western Europe. Liberalism went into decline both as an economic doctrine and as a political force. The liberal parties either lost their power or changed their posture. Against this backdrop antisemitism emerged as a political movement and a mobilizing ideology. After the enlightened countries of Europe had granted emancipation to the Jews, voices were heard calling for a re-examination of the Jews' status with the aim of curtailing or abolishing those rights altogether. The Jews, for centuries the archetype of the alien in European society, were once again publicly excoriated as an element foreign to the body-politic. Internal needs within mass society made the Jews an object easily maneuvered to secure certain political goals. Here was the link between nationalism and political antisemitism, which manifested itself in particular parties and organizations or permeated the rhetoric of the political establishment. The Jews were readily made into scapegoats for economic depressions, and they were often denounced as traitors to the nation. Hence the notion that antisemitism was merely a political tool serving reactionary forces but had no innate significance—in other words that major political change, or even an amelioration of the economic situation, would deprive antisemitism of its sustenance. This hypothesis might constitute a response to the problem in its narrow, immediate sense, but it does not answer the trenchant questions relating to antisemitism in its entirety.

4

The Turn
of the Century

Background to Jewish Nationalism

The end of the nineteenth century in Europe was marked by an economic upsurge and an abating of social tensions. Contemporaries dubbed the first years of the twentieth century *la belle époque*. Although tensions seethed below the surface, externally, at least, optimism reigned. Economic well-being and the comfort introduced into day-to-day life by a spate of technical inventions were more tangible than sporadic portents of doom. The Jews, too, welcomed the new century in the expectation of better things to come.

It was likewise during this period that the Jewish national idea took shape and political Zionism entered the limelight of public opinion. Yet this development added a new focal point in the confrontation between the Jews and their adversaries, as it seemed to manifest Jewish isolation once again. True, the dissemination of the antisemitic claim that Jews were foreigners created an atmosphere conducive to the propagation of the national idea among them, but the emergence of Zionism also furnished the antisemites with evidence for the suspicions they harbored about the Jews. Not that the antisemites had ever lacked for reasons to disparage the Jews: to demonstrate that the Jews were aliens in the nation in which they sought integration, they would cite the *Alliance Israélite Universelle*, whose very name testified to its being a supra-national organization. The enemies of the Jews frequently cast aspersions on the *Alliance* as the ostensible spearhead of a secret conspiracy of world Jewry against the nations. Zionism, in contrast to the *Alliance*, openly affirmed the existence of a separate Jewish nation and thereby blatantly confirmed what Western Jews had always been at pains to deny.

On the face of it, Zionism and antisemitism shared a common platform, and in fact some antisemites had supported Zionist aspirations. Herzl, for his part, evinced a certain understanding for the basic premise of antisemitism, and even tried to persuade the antisemitic Russian Minister of the Interior Plehve to take a stand in favor of Zionism (Herzl, pp. 1523–1528, 1534–1540). Indeed, Zionism occasionally found an attentive ear in statesmen who wanted to rid their country of Jews or who feared a possible aggravation of the "Jewish Question." In time, however, hardened antisemites realized that they could not give Zionism their unequivocal support, since implicit in the movement was the renewal of Jewish life. In the last analysis, antisemitism tended to reject Jewish nationalism, which was beginning to have an impact as a stimulating and revitalizing force among European Jews. On the other hand, Jewish nationalism provoked an adverse reaction in other national movements, which advocated the assimiliation of the Jews and looked on Zionism as a competitor (Davies, p. 68; Heller, pp. 42–45).

At all events, undue importance should not be attached to the clash between antisemitism and Jewish nationalism, since *assimilation* was the preferred target for the barbs of the antisemites. Yet an internal contradiction would seem to be present here: did not the antisemites vilify the Jews as an alien body which could not be absorbed by the nation? Nationally inspired antisemitism was disappointed by the Jews' refusal to disappear as a distinct group. Despite the efforts of emancipated Jews to seek integration into society and blend with the local peoples, Jewish traits stubbornly persisted. Notwithstanding the conversions and the mixed marriages, and despite the slackening of communal and religious affinities, organized Jewish life endured and the waves of Jewish immigration inhibited the process of total assimilation.

On the other hand, the influence of Jews was felt in the economy and in cultural life, as well as in politics and public life. The entry of the Jews into new walks of life was perceived by their adversaries as tantamount to a Jewish takeover of society. The Jew who acted as an ordinary citizen possessing equal rights and obligations, without reference to his Jewishness, was perceived by his neighbors first and foremost as a Jew. Whereas the Jewish individual tended to attach full value to his formal status and expected to be judged according to his own merits, those around him were inclined to see him as a typical representative of the Jewish minority. It was here that the flagrant disparity came out between the Jew's self-image as an individual, or even of the Jews' self-perception as a group, and their image in the eyes of society (especially the antisemitic stereotypes) (Weltsch, p. xxi).

For the antisemites, the "Jew" was simultaneously a greedy capitalist and a subversive revolutionary, a rootless individualist and a loyal member of the Israelite tribe. If his assimilation into the dominant society was successful, he might be accused of affectation, or at any rate of indulging in spineless imitation. Not even by converting to Christianity could the Jew escape the burden of his origin. The new Jew-hatred tended to give religion a wide berth and even harbored anti-Christian tenets. For modern antisemites, conversion was no solution; to the contrary, they rejected Christianity because of its Jewish origin. Such trends were not entirely new, but now they received a new impetus and penetrated groups previously immune to them. This was a reaction not only to the Jews' integration into society, but also to the rapid changes that characterized the period.

Take for instance the Second Industrial Revolution which is said to have occurred at the end of the nineteenth century—a revolution of electricity and steel that superseded the coal and iron of the First Industrial Revolution. The processes of modernization were greatly accelerated, bringing about sweeping transformations in Europe and affecting the international scene. The world saw global competition among the Great Powers; any achievement of one power was perceived as a setback for its rival and as boding ill for the nation's well-being. Nor were the inter-power rivalries and concomitant spread of colonialism confined to the level of foreign affairs and the elite circle of professional diplomats; increasingly they were the affair of the "man in the street." Imperialist policy was boosted by the spread of a low-priced popular press and enjoyed broad public support in the countries that practiced it. The public at large drew no distinction between self-defense and aggression, or between reasons of state and the people's interest; it tended to identify completely with the dominant line—all in the name of nationalism. The imposition of one's rule over backward areas was viewed as an exalted national mission.

Whether due to the unfolding political events or to the ideas then in fashion, the intellectual climate was charged with aggression. To counter the rise of international socialism, the Right in various countries hoisted the banner of aggressive nationalism. This was a nationalism laced with xenophobia and at times with antisemitism too. From here the road was short to the emergence of proto-fascist thought and superimposing a racial interpretation upon antisemitism. For the sake of accuracy, I wish to point out that fascism is not necessarily identical with either racism or antisemitism (fascist Italy was neither racist nor antisemitic before 1936), nor, for that matter, is racism inevitably congruent with antisemitism. Yet under the circumstances these divergent elements coalesced in various forms. Initially this was only discernible on a theoretical level within small circles and ideological writings; only at a later stage did this indoctrination filter down to the general public. The extremism of the Right was sometimes paralleled on the Left: the trade unions in the industrialized countries benefited from economic prosperity, and the working class elites did not really oppose the nationalist politics of their respective governments. Thus the left-wing opposition became all the more outspoken in its combat against imperialism. As mentioned, an established tradition had identified the Jews with capitalism; now an antisemitic tone found its way into anti-imperial-ist rhetoric as well (see, e.g. Holmes, pp. 67–70).

Although one cannot be two contradictory things at the same time (bourgeois and revolutionary, cosmopolite and nationalist, and so forth), the "Jew" was portrayed by the antisemites as a multi-faceted figure. Antisemitic propaganda reconciled these contradictions by pointing to the supposedly demonic nature of the Jew or by reference to a secret conspiracy of the Jews against society. According to the antisemitic line, Jews pretend that each of them acts on his own, whereas in reality they have secretly assumed different roles—one is a bourgeois, another is a revolutionary—while there is no substantive difference between them. Their alleged objective is to lead the non-Jews astray and destroy the social fabric with the ultimate aim of seizing control of the world. To this, racial thinkers add that the Jew is what he is not by his own will but by biological necessity, a primeval fate of blood and race that is ineluctable. The Jew, then, seeks to subvert the foundations of society, for this is his innate calling. One must bear in mind, though, that it took time for all these threads to gather into a single skein. At this juncture, however, our discussion revolves around what may be termed the age of national-ism—which left its imprint on antisemitism, too. Still, as time goes on, various new shades and nuances would be woven into the anti-semitic loom.

Herzl's Interview with the Russian Minister of the Interior

The following are passages from Herzl's diary notes following two meetings with Vyacheslav von Plehve[1] (1846–1904) in St. Petersburg, capital of Czarist Russia, in 1903.

Plehve: The Russian state is bound to desire homogeneity of its population. We realize, of course, that we cannot obliterate all differences of creed or language.[2]

For instance, we must concede that the older Scandinavian culture has maintained itself in Finland as something that has become organic.[3] But what we must demand of all the peoples in our Empire, and therefore also of the Jews, is that they take a patriotic view of the Russian state as an actuality.[4] We want to assimilate them, and to this end we have two methods: higher education and economic betterment. Anyone who has fulfilled certain conditions in both these respects and whose education or prosperity, we therefore have reason to believe, has made him loyal to the existing order is given full civil rights. However, this assimilation which we desire is a very slow process.[5]

. . . To be sure, we can confer the benefits of a higher education upon only a limited number of Jews, because otherwise we should

[1] Plehve had been in charge of the police during the anti-Jewish riots of 1881, and was suspected of fomenting them. Herzl's visit thus angered many Russian Jews, including Zionists. Plehve's later position as Minister of the Interior was of immense political importance. Herzl wanted him to use his influence with the Ottoman government in favor of Zionism in Palestine, out of a common interest to abet Jewish emigration from Russia. Plehve was shot and killed by an assassin a year later.

[2] Plehve admitted that if possible, he would have forced everyone in the Czarist Empire to convert to Russian Orthodoxy and speak only Russian, thereby fulfilling his desire for homogeneity, as he put it.

[3] Russia conquered Finland from Sweden at the beginning of the nineteenth century and accorded it a semi-autonomous status. The final decade of the century witnessed vigorous Russification in Finland, and in the year of the interview (1903) Finnish autonomy was revoked and Russian imposed as the official language.

[4] The Russian Minister of the Interior is here expressing his obdurate opposition to national rights for the peoples of the Empire. He equates patriotism with loyalty to the state as is, implying that innovation is tantamount to poor citizenship. In Czarist Russia, opinions like these emanating from a highly-placed government personality carried a good deal of weight.

[5] The reforms of Czar Alexander II allowed "useful" Jews, such as wealthy merchants, to reside outside the Pale of Settlement and also encouraged high school graduates. After young Jews began flocking to Russian schools, the Jewish quota for high schools and universities was drastically reduced. In theory, then, the authorities espoused the gradual integration of the Jews, but conducted in practice an anti-liberal policy, which became still more stringent after the assassination of Alexander II.

soon run out of posts to give the Christians.[6] Also, I am not blind to the fact that the economic situation of the Jews in the Pale of Settlement is bad.[7] I also admit that they live in what amounts to a ghetto; but it *is* a large area—13 *gouvernements* [government districts]. Lately the situation has grown even worse because the Jews have been joining the revolutionary parties.[8] We used to be sympathetic to your Zionist movement, as long as it worked toward emigration. . . . But ever since the Minsk conference we have noticed *un changement des gros bonnets* [a change of big-wigs].[9] There is less talk now of Palestinian Zionism than there is about culture, organization and Jewish nationalism.[10] This doesn't suit us. (Herzl, pp. 1523, 1525)

The Kishinev Pogrom as an Omen

An event that shook the Jews occurred in 1903: Kishinev, the capital of Bessarabia, had been under the Czar's rule for some ninety years but had been untouched by the anti-Jewish riots of 1880–81. The pogrom of 1903 followed a campaign of incitement conducted by a right-wing politician named P. A. Krushevan, with the aid of his antisemitic newspaper *Bessarabetz*, accusing the Jews of committing ritual murder in the town of Dubossary in the Kherson District. The government apparently used antisemitism as a means to release the pressure that had built up among the Moldavians; it may also have reacted to the involvement of Jews in the revolutionary movements. Be that as it may, the authorities stood by as the mob perpetrated a brutal massacre which left about fifty Jews dead and several hundred injured.

[6] Notwithstanding Plehve's liberal gesture in his talk with Herzl (which duly impressed his interlocutor), he made no secret of his opinion that the idea of Jews being given rights equal to Christians was untenable.

[7] The population density in the Pale of Settlement, together with socio-cultural changes that intensified toward the end of the nineteenth century, aggravated the situation of the Jews and triggered mass emigration from Russia, much of it to the United States.

[8] Here Plehve comes to the real point: it was not the Jews' situation that bothered him but their revolutionary activity. Young Jews were motivated to join revolutionary parties, among other reasons, as a reaction to government policy, which offered no hope of improvement except by revolutionary means.

[9] In 1902 the Second Congress of Russian Zionists convened at Minsk, the only time with the authorities' permission.

[10] Plehve was kept well-informed about the Zionist operations and was, indeed, disappointed in the local Zionist activities, which strengthened Jewish nationalism within Russia, whereas Plehve wanted the Jews out (even though emigration from Russia was legally restricted).

The Kishinev pogrom raised the alarm that stirred Jews everywhere out of their complacency. In the wake of the slaughter, the great Hebrew poet Chaim Nachman Bialik (1873–1934) wrote a monumental work which had a powerful impact on Jewish national consciousness and on Jewish self-defense. The world press reported the events at length, and protest rallies were organized in many countries, with Jewish and non-Jewish personalities taking part; even the Russian intelligentsia condemned the massacre publicly (Greenberg, pp. 50–52; Ettinger, 1976, p. 886). The subsequent investigation failed to reach unequivocal conclusions about the causes of the riots—neither about the degree of responsibility borne by the central authorities nor about the social character of the perpetrators—or about the depth of the popular enmity toward the Jews. It is possible that in this as in other cases, a number of different factors—national, social, religious and political—were at work, so that when the local authorities loosened the reins, pent-up emotions erupted violently in the most convenient direction: against the Jews.

The Kishinev events prefaced a new wave of riots throughout Russia. They broke out as early as 1904, in the midst of the Russo-Japanese War, on the pretext that the Jews were disloyal to the country and were evading the draft, and they reached their peak during the revolution of 1905. With the reins of government grown rather slack following the Russian drubbing at the hands of Japan, the struggle between the supporters of the regime and their adversaries began to take a violent turn. Heading the antisemitic camp was a right-wing organization which also fought against the liberal intelligentsia and against the national aspirations of the Finns, the Poles, and others. The proponents of this radical Right enjoyed support from circles close to the Czar and from the Church. In contrast to the 1880s, anti-Jewish disturbances were no longer a singular phenomenon but became an integral part of the rising current of ferment and violence in the country. *Thousands* of Jews died in the 1905 riots, but by then organized Jewish resistance often struck back at the rioters. During the period of reaction following the 1905 revolution, army and police personnel were sometimes directly involved in the pogroms, and Jews apprehended while offering armed resistance were sent to prison for breaking the law.

At the height of the revolution, the Czar yielded to the demand to convene a legislative assembly and signed a declaration granting political rights (the "October Manifesto"). This was greeted by demonstrations of support by the majority of the public, while conservative groups agitated against it. The charged atmosphere undermined the discipline in the ranks of the Army, and the security forces were frequently unable to control the situation. It was against this backdrop that the October riots struck out at the Jews. In consequence, Jews threw their support behind the regime's opponents, in the hope that the "Jewish Question" would eventually be resolved by means of a radical change of regime. In fact, the Jews suffered more than most, but it was widely believed that their plight was only an interim stage on the way to their full integration into Russian society. In contrast to 1881, the revolutionary forces no longer tended to interpret the riots as a release for the ostensibly justified fury of the masses. Now the rioters could be identified with the Czar's loyalists and the Jews seen as victims of the government's despotism. These altered perceptions seemed to place the Jews in the same front with all the forces combating absolutism—the revolutionaries, the liberal bourgeoisie and the movements for national liberation—hence the widespread notion that the pogroms had been instigated by reactionary elements exploiting the primitive instincts of the backward strata in Russia in order to combat the forces of progress.

Nevertheless, it bears stressing that the Jews were among the principal victims of the counterrevolution (Harcave, pp. 198–205). True, enlightened public opinion was not indifferent to the suffering of the Jews in the revolution of 1905—as it had been in 1881—but it tended to view the anti-Jewish riots merely as an outburst of the anti-revolutionary forces. The singularly antisemitic character of these riots was overlooked in the liberal and revolutionary responses. The disparity between a liberal stance which blurs the unique nature of the attacks on Jews and the position of the rioters and their dispatchers recurs frequently in the annals of antisemitism: whereas one side accords the Jews an unwarranted status as the most prominent enemy of the nation and its values, the other side sees the Jews as a rather marginal factor. For the liberals, any other assessment of the actors and events is liable to attribute an undue role to Jews, which in turn would ostensibly support the antisemitic argument. But less generous explanations have also been adduced for the liberals' disregard of the special Jewish aspect, such as their reluctance to stand out as the defenders of the Jews or the influence of Jewish assimilationists, who shy away from Jewish solidarity (Slutsky, 1976, pp. 21–22).

The divergent assessments of the role played by the "Jewish Question" in the heat of the events remain unresolvable. Historians are frequently divided over the impact of the Jewish factor in public consciousness and on the minds of decision-makers. While some Jewish historians seek out every iota of evidence for Jewish involvement, non-Jews tend to ignore the Jewish ingredient in history generally (see, e.g. Marrus, 1980, p. 88). This obliviousness is akin to the national-liberal tradition which seeks the integration of the Jews into society whereas a historian who pays attention to the specifically Jewish elements might even be suspected of harboring antisemitic tendencies.

Some see proto-fascist features in the organizing of the Right in the 1905 revolution. There is no question about the interaction of several characteristic elements on the Russian Right: nationalism and antisemitism, combined with radical populism and support for the Czarist regime. As in similar movements elsewhere, antisemitism served as the cement for binding several elements which generally do not cohabit—above all, radicalism and conservatism. The new Right actively evoked antisemitism in its appeal to the lower strata and in its effort to drum up broader public support for the government. In this the radical Right had an advantage over the old conservative Right in a period which saw the growth of political consciousness among the lower classes (Rogger, 1986, pp. 189–211; Laqueur, pp. 79–87).

The Kishinev Pogrom

The following selection describes the atmosphere that prevailed before the Kishinev pogrom, notably the systematic and protracted incitement against the Jews.

Then, in 1902, we saw unmistakable signs of reaction, which became more intense and more arrogant, among the members of the monarchist gang.[11] Not a day went by without new judicial restrictions on the Jews, with the antisemitic press—headed by

[11] The Kishinev riots were perpetrated during the Greek Orthodox Easter (April 6–8, 1903; April 19–21 according to the Gregorian calendar). As is well known, blood libels usually appeared about that time of the year, sparked by the legend that Jews needed Christian blood to bake their unleavened bread for Passover. The author testifies that the incitement preceded the blood libel at Dubossary. He associates the organizers of the riots with the radical Right, which strove to mobilize broad popular support for the Czar.

the Kishinevite Krushevan[12]—using every means at its disposal to play up extreme antisemitic politics and prepare the ground for "St. Bartholomew's Eve."[13] The provocateur and fabricator of libels, deputy district officer Ostrogov, Krushevan's assistant on the paper (who also serves as censor), blesses the swords and directs the action through his slogans.[14] It was in the period of Nikolai's psychosis, in the time of the Czar's aggressive antisemitism,[15] under the aegis of the said Ostrogov, that Krushevan's dementia reached new heights. He invites from Jassy the "infamous" Professor Cuza,[16] sets up a big meeting at the edge of town, in the place known as the "vale of enchantments," and declares that "St. Bartholomew's Eve" will be held at Passover 1903.

. . . Different groups of Jews prepare themselves for the pogrom: the rabbi and his assistants betake themselves to the head of the church, and there the well-known story is played out once more: the pontiff asks in puzzlement whether we Jews are truly certain that there is no sect among us that uses the blood of Christian infants to make matzo, as there are Christian sects that murder children and extract fat from their bodies to make candles.[17]

[12] Krushevan, who was of Moldavian origin, had adopted Russian culture. From 1897 he edited an antisemitic newspaper in Kishinev. In 1902 he began publishing an antisemitic paper in the capital, St. Petersburg, enjoying government funds thanks to Minister of the Interior Plehve.

[13] St. Bartholomew's Eve: on the night between August 23 and 24, 1572, and in the following days, thousands of Huguenots were massacred in Paris and elsewhere in France by their Catholic enemies. The slaughter became the symbol for religious-inspired massacre and persecution. The term is also used here by one of the speakers at a rally, even though it originates in Western Christianity.

[14] The investigation carried out after the riots on behalf of the Czar found no proof that Ostrogov was implicated in organizing the disturbances: he was nevertheless transferred to Tiflis, Georgia. The author relates that not long after Ostrogov's arrival there, a massacre was perpetrated against the Armenians.

[15] Czar Nikolai II (r. 1894–1917) on several occasions expressed his negative attitude toward the Jews. Considered to be of weak character, he was strongly influenced by conservative and antisemitic advisers. In 1902–1903 peasant revolts and massive workers strikes erupted in Russia, leading the authorities to take violent repressive measures. The author held progressive views and saw a common source for the government's antisemitic policy and the suppression of other groups.

[16] Alexandru Cuza (1857–1946) was an economics professor at Jassy University and a delegate to the Romanian Parliament. In 1910 he was among the founders of the National-Democratic Party, which favored restrictions against the Jews. Here he was invited as a guest lecturer from across the border to preach his antisemitic doctrine in Czarist Bessarabia. In the 1930s he was sympathetic to Nazi Germany and was a member of the short-lived Romanian government that preceded the dictatorship of King Carol in 1938.

[17] The reference may be to heretical sects to be found throughout Russia, some of which performed deviant Gnostic rites. These sects were generally persecuted by both church and state, and rumors about their secret rituals were difficult to confirm. The claim that human sacrifice, while not part of normative Judaism, may have

And why should we not confess frankly, like Christians? Finally he promises to try to persuade the district officer to prevent the pogrom, though he cannot vouch for it.

The youth react differently: they are angry, obtain arms from under the ground, and organize the butchers in the slaughter-house, in the markets, to sharpen knives and hatchets for self-defense. (Bernstein-Cohen & Koren, p. 127)

The Revolution of 1905

The following are passages from a Russian-language proclamation issued at the end of 1905 in the Crimea by the Jewish social-democratic workers party *Poalei Zion*[18]. The document calls for solidarity with the forces struggling against the regime but emphasizes the special Jewish fate.

By now the role played by the Czar's officials in the riots must be clear to all. Everyone knows already that the pogroms were perpetuated everywhere, at the order of the higher authorities, by the "Black Hundreds"[19] and their leaders, the Czar's faithful servants. In the final hour, when the despotic regime signed its own death-sentence through the October 17 Manifesto,[20] all those who are suppressing the Russian population, those who are plundering the state coffers, decided to extinguish with our blood the spreading flames of the Russian Revolution.

Why is it that we serve as a lightning rod for the dying Czarist regime? Why should we have to pay for its crimes? Why is it that we are almost the only ones against whom it manages to direct the wrath of the oppressed, ignorant masses?[21]

been practised by deviant Jewish sects was quite common in Russia. This claim was later made in the Beiliss Affair as well.

[18] This leaflet was issued by a Zionist-Socialist group in the Crimea, influenced by young Ber Borochov (1881–1917). Borochov, while espousing the building of a Jewish Palestine, also advocated a class war and a struggle against the regime in Russia.

[19] The "Black Hundreds" was the name given to extreme right-wing terrorist groups that aided the regime by combating revolutionary cells and perpetrating pogroms against Jews. They opposed the national aspirations of non-Russians, and unofficially enjoyed the assistance of the police and even of church circles. They sometimes drew to their ranks habitual criminals and all sorts of adventurous types.

[20] In the October Manifesto, issued on October 17, 1905 (October 30 according to the Gregorian calendar) the Czar proclaimed a series of civil rights: freedom of conscience, speech and association; enhanced parliamentary representation; and the Duma's involvement in legislation and supervision of the administration. The proclamation was issued under revolutionary pressure and sharply deviated from the traditional absolutist stands—indeed, the reforms did not last very long.

[21] The authors of the leaflet, far from despairing of the Russian people, saw the

The reason is our abnormal state in the diaspora.

For twenty centuries we have been dispersed far and wide, and everywhere we are an isolated group, socially and nationally. The ruling classes have always exploited the situation of the wandering nation, the people without a territory. Forced to give up their rule in favor of the people that rebelled, they aroused the dark animal instincts against the eternal scapegoat, against the eternal Jew,[22] in order to divert the people's attention from the true enemies that are suppressing them, from themselves.[23]

. . . Our abnormal social structure will disappear when we stand on an equal footing with the other nations, when we constitute a majority in our own territory, in the Land of Israel.

Our abnormal lack of political rights, which is translated into riots and similar manifestations, will disappear when we constitute a cohesive and armed force, when we defend with our own breast our right to life and liberty.[24] (Peterseil, pp. 16–17)

Modern Blood Libels

What differentiates the blood accusation, as it recurred in Christendom for centuries, from the renewed blood libel on the threshold of the twentieth century?

As will become apparent, the new blood accusation contains all the ingredients that characterized its predecessors in generations past, that is, a residue of hatred and prejudice in the society surrounding the Jews, a projection of beliefs rooted in Christian mysticism relating to the ritual meaning of blood, the use of the Jews as

riots as resulting from government manipulation. They interpreted Jew-hatred as reflecting the ignorance of the masses. Their tacit assumption was that once the masses would be released from their present condition, they would cease to heed antisemitic incitement. The riots, then, served the regime and did not reflect the true wishes of the people.

[22] The Eternal Jew is a legendary medieval figure based on a verse from the New Testament (Matthew 16:28) in which Jews are presumably condemned to endless wandering. From Western Europe the legend reached the Slavic countries, where it took on local coloring.

[23] The writers allude to the impact of superstitious belief on simple folk as a diversion from their real problems through attacks on Jews.

[24] The authors see the long-term solution in emigration to Palestine, but in the meantime they call for active self-defense against the rioters as part of the common front of all the peoples of Russia in their struggle against the regime. The assumption that the rioters are just an enflamed mob resolves the apparent contradiction between the Jews' armed struggle and the commitment to international solidarity. The Zionist-Socialists proclaim to see no contradiction between the national goals and class consciousness, or between the present struggle and the future in Palestine. The document attempts to explain antisemitism as a phenomenon of political reaction, while Jewish nationalism is viewed as part of the struggle for social progress.

an outlet for the release of aggressions, and so forth. Although past centuries also saw the purposeful exploitation of Jew-hatred to further the aims of political and religious establishments, it is the advent of the twentieth century that precipitates the use of anti-semitism as an instrument for political purposes. The rise of the masses, their concentration in the cities, the expansion of elementary education, the circulation of the popular press and the challenge of modernization all hastened the disintegration of the traditions which had formerly served to cement society. Nationalism became a counterbalance to these currents and reinforced socialization, while antisemitism enhanced the individual's sense of belonging to the majority group by ostracizing the deviant Jew.

The old vessel of traditional Jew-hatred could easily be blended with national or racial hostility. The blood accusation which Christians raised against Jews in the context of the conflict between Judaism and Christianity acquired an additional significance: it sought to prove that in essence the Jew had not changed, his modern appearance notwithstanding, and that he was fated to remain an alien who evoked dread. Paradoxically, the blood accusation presented the Jew in a light which was the reverse of the prevalent antisemitic allegations. In this period, as is known, the Jews were accused of being dangerous innovators whose influence eroded the foundation of society, but the blood accusation added to this a primordial, irrational dimension. When a Jew was accused of ritual murder he was supposedly acting on behalf of the Jews, or at least of some Jewish sect, thus revealing the dark side of Judaism. Hence, those who pretended to be modern people wishing their neighbors well were actually the enemies of humanity whose loathing for other peoples drove them to commit every imaginable atrocity. The blood accusation, then, nourishes the contention that the Jew has no local roots and cannot take part in the life of the nation.

In the modern era rumors about the disappearance of people (very often children) spread far and wide rapidly. The rule of law and modern techniques enabled the authorities either to deal with it effectively or to allow rumors to run rampant until the imaginary culprit was found—for instance, a Jew suspected of committing murder for ritual needs. At this stage the police and the judicial apparatus became involved, while the press and public opinion were drawn along. When the suspect was apprehended and an official investigation began, the prosecution then submitted an indictment to secure his conviction, and the prestige of the judicial system, an official institution, was mobilized against the accused. Such confrontation was extremely potent in authoritarian regimes, especially when the population identified itself with the national state. It is not surprising, then, that the blood accusation served the goals of the antisemites even after the influence of religion had waned.

In the period when religious tolerance was supposedly at its height, two blood accusations that were to receive much publicity occurred in Europe: in 1899 in the Austro-Hungarian Empire and in 1911 in Czarist Russia. Two murders committed in backwater districts inhabited by ordinary country folk quickly became major judicial affairs, engaged various branches of government in the capitals, and aroused public opinion on an international scale (like the Tisza-Eszlar Affair in Hungary in the 1880s mentioned in Chapter Three).

In 1899 a country girl was found with her throat slit in a wood near the Czech village of Polna. Leopold Hilsner, a local Jewish cobbler's apprentice, was accused of the murder by the ultra-nationalist press in Prague. Both the Czech nationalists in Prague and the German antisemites in Vienna held that a ritual murder was involved, and political spokesmen of various shades were soon involved in the case. At a trial held in an atmosphere of mass hysteria, the jury condemned Hilsner to death. Anti-Jewish riots broke out in the provinces and in Prague itself. The future president of Czechoslovakia, Thomas Masaryk (1850–1937) proved that the trial had been a travesty of justice and demanded that the legal proceedings be reopened. A second instance again found Hilsner guilty but dismissed the intimations of a ritual murder. In the absence of decisive evidence, the Emperor commuted the sentence to life imprisonment, and many years later the prisoner was granted clemency.

The stand taken by Masaryk, then a professor at the University of Prague, triggered a vitriolic debate, particularly among Czech students. Some of them protested vociferously against his position, others took his side. To restore order, the university authorities decided to suspend Masaryk temporarily, a step that assumed symbolic significance in the struggle between the different wings of the Czech national movement (Červinka, pp. 145–153; Haumann, pp. 223–225). What transformed a local murder into a *cause célèbre* was the fusion of popular Jew-hatred and political interests stemming from the national conflicts in the Austro-Hungarian Empire. Nor did the differences between the Czech national movement and the

German ultra-nationalists in Vienna prevent both sides from exploiting the affair for their own ends.

The advent of the twentieth century saw several further attempts to accuse the Jews of blood libels. Among others, there were cases in 1900 in Vilna and in the West-Prussian town of Kunitz, and in 1903 in Dubossary, in the Kherson District, which was the pretext for the Kishinev pogrom mentioned above. But the case that shook the world began in 1911 in a suburb of Kiev, in the Ukraine. The body of a twelve-year-old boy was found in a cave in a local wood, not far from a brick factory where Mendel Beiliss was employed and lived with his family. At the funeral, leaflets were circulated calling for vengeance against the Jews, who had allegedly caused the boy's death in order to draw off his blood. The investigation of the crime was accompanied by incitement and intrigues, and the Czar himself followed the developments. Beiliss was arrested on a ritual murder charge. The trial exposed the corruption of the governmental apparatus, which had raised a collective accusation against the Jews at the instigation of the extreme Right (the so-called "Black Hundred" organization) (see Samuel, 1966; and Greenberg, pp. 88–94).

The malicious scheme against an innocent man outraged enlightened public opinion, and even some hardened antisemites expressed their reservations. The blood libel was termed a second Dreyfus Affair. After two years of investigation, arrest and trial, Mendel Beiliss was exonerated and set free. Yet the jury, while finding Beiliss to be innocent, left room for doubt concerning the motive for the murder. Liberal opinion interpreted the verdict as a victory for its stand, but the Black Hundred and its supporters stressed that the Jews *as a group* had not been freed of suspicion.

Following the revolution and the opening of the archives in Russia, proof was found for the hypothesis propounded at the time of the trial: the boy was actually murdered by a gang of criminals who feared that he would inform on them to the police. Evidence was uncovered that even the judicial authorities had known the truth. The Beiliss Affair served its organizers to buttress popular support for the absolutist system of government. The architects of the plot believed that Beiliss' conviction would mobilize national feelings to help prop up the crumbling regime. With the exception of a handful of fanatics, who apparently believed the blood accusation literally, policy-makers and senior officials acted cold-bloodedly "to strike at the Jews and save Russia" (in the words of a popular Russian adage) (Rogger, 1986, pp. 40–45).

The Beiliss Trial

The following is the text of the leaflet which was circulated at the funeral of the boy whose body was found near Kiev. The funeral was held shortly before Easter, hence the implications for the ritual murder imputed to the Jews.

ORTHODOX CHRISTIANS![25]
The Yids have tortured Andryusha Yuschinsky to death![26] Every year, before their Passover, they torture to death several dozens of Christian children in order to get their blood to mix with their *matzos*. They do this in commemoration of our Saviour, whom they tortured to death on the cross.[27] The official doctors found that before the Yids tortured Yushchinsky they stripped him naked and tied him up, stabbing him in the principal veins so as to get as much blood as possible.[28] Russians![29] If your children are dear to you beat up the Yids! Beat them up until there is not a single Yid left in Russia. Have pity on your children! Avenge the unhappy martyr![30] It is time! It is time! (Quoted in Samuel, 1966, p. 17)

A New Kind of Nationalism

Looking back, the period preceding the First World War appears as a lull between the surging antisemitism of the 1870s and 1880s and the riots and upheavals that attended the War and its aftermath. Yet this period, too, saw an abundance of antisemitic activity: anti-Jewish riots occurred not only in Eastern Europe but in places as

[25] Kiev is today the capital of the Ukrainian Republic in the Soviet Union. When the event occurred, a Ukrainian national movement was already in existence. The leaflet appeals to the adherents of the Greek Orthodox Church, i.e. both Russians and Ukrainians.

[26] A week after the boy's disappearance his body was found, almost completely drained of blood. The body was covered with stab wounds.

[27] The tortures preceding the murder are part of the blood libel which was already widespread in the Middle Ages. The deicide attributed to the Jews signifies that they consciously repudiate Christ and symbolically re-enact the Crucifixion on the date that Jesus himself died on the cross.

[28] The loss of blood served the prosecution as a major argument in trying to prove the intention of the culprit: the victim's blood was said to be used to bake unleavened bread for Passover and attributed to the customs of a Jewish sect.

[29] The leaflet no longer addresses Orthodox Christians but "Russians." Its authors did not draw any distinction between the two terms, as they presumably disregarded Ukrainian nationalism.

[30] Several of the children whose names were cited in blood libels in the Middle Ages were regarded as saints.

far apart as Saloniki, in the midst of the Balkan wars; Morocco, in the wake of the international crises there; and even Wales, during a miners' strike. Still, what stood out in the period was the difference between the large Jewish communities in Eastern Europe and the Jews in the West. The majority of the former had no civil rights and often lived in poor conditions; these years were the peak of Jewish migration westward and particularly overseas.

In contrast, the Jews in Western and Central Europe seemed increasingly destined to integrate into their countries of residence as citizens possessing equal rights and equal obligations. Antisemitism, while continuing to be a source of concern to the Jews in these countries, was not official or semi-official policy as it was in Russia and Romania. Nevertheless, the antisemitic manifestations that occasionally surfaced in Central and even Western Europe, together with instances of social and economic discrimination, whether overt or covert, demonstrated how fragile was the formal emancipation. Zionists and doom-sayers pointed to these phenomena as testimony to the Jews' tenuous position. But such warnings were unable to dislodge the Jewish orientation toward full integration (while preserving certain religious particularities or assisting fellow Jews in Eastern Europe). Beyond a natural feeling of solidarity, the Jews in the West were moved by an essential need to enlist in the aid of their brethren in the East; the existence of anti-Jewish discrimination in Czarist Russia was concrete proof that the Jews were not the same as other people. Furthermore, there was a lingering fear that the "Eastern Jews" who were immigrating to the West would disrupt the process of integration into society and arouse heightened antisemitism.

This period also saw the appearance of other phenomena whose ramifications may not have been fully comprehended. For one thing, the commonplace term "nationalism" gradually took on a new meaning. Here a rather paradoxical process was at work, standing the original sense of the word on its head and radically altering its meaning. How did this come about? On the face of it, the national idea was firmly vested in the established nation-states, besides which more national movements were cropping up in the multinational empires. Apparently nationalism was a deeply rooted and durable phenomenon and could be expected to grow and expand. But there was also a reverse current, which saw in nationalism a regression in the development of humanity. For some, nationalism reflected a parochial insularity which would block the free flow of people, ideas and goods. The emphasis could be placed either on free trade or on human liberty, but liberal doctrine saw an internal affinity between the various types of freedom.

The socialists were also generally suspicious of nationalism, and the radicals among them inveighed against nationalism as an attempt to obfuscate the class war and undermine the international solidarity of the working class. The moderates, recognizing a need to show consideration for the national feelings of the masses, sought a way to confine nationalism within a controlled framework (such as the plan for cultural autonomy in the Austro-Hungarian Empire). In 1900 the permanent office of the Socialist International was established in Brussels (until then the International had functioned through conferences convened every few years). Those so inclined could view this development as signifying the spread of the cosmo-politan trend and hence as a danger to nationalism.

Countering the international and anti-national orientation of the radical movements, a new "national" approach manifested itself in right-wing circles. For various groups on the Right, patriotism, which was fundamentally directed at the entire nation, irrespective of class and viewpoint, became an asset reserved for patriots of a very specific type. Organizations dedicated to the defense of nationalism sprouted up in numerous countries, and the terms "nationalists" or "patriots" were seen as the exclusive prerogative of the Right, be they old-time conservatives or right-wing radicals. These organizations generally drew their members from the middle class, with a spicing of activists from the nobility and the intelligent-sia. Prominent among them were officers, society ladies, and stu-dents (Shafer, pp. 218–219, 446; Smith, pp. 62–65). Externally, these organizations took an apolitical line, but very often they played a part in helping to entrench the conservative regime. At all events, when the political establishment was disinclined to accept their "national" ideology, these groups quickly revealed their funda-mentally rebellious character.

The "patriotic" Right saw its mission as the defense of the national values which were being menaced by the rise of anti-national forces. The danger could emanate from the outside, but just as often from internal adversaries: from the revolutionary Left and the Free-masons, from the Jesuits in Protestant countries and from the Prot-estants in Catholic countries; but above all from the Jews, whether as part of the "anti-national" camp or as Jews *per se*. It is noteworthy that the groups targeted by the "national" camp varied from place to place and from time to time, and that different outlooks existed among these groups. But it is difficult to find a nationalist group that did not take recourse to antisemitism in one form or another. Of course, this was no coincidence; the Jews were a minority in every country of Europe, and while there were many other minority groups in many of these countries, only the Jews were a universal minority. One could almost say that they were also a perpetual minority. The historical residue of the Jews' foreignness and the enmity toward them combined with the contemporary situation to produce the stereotype of the Jew as the classical enemy of nationalism.

A certain ambiguity hovers over the years preceding the First World War. On the one hand it was a period of respite, an attempt to hold on to the old world charm as portrayed by moderate conservatives—stability and order, rule by a privileged caste, a society built on the premise that one should know one's place, respect for religion and tradition, slow progress of the underprivileged provided they merited it, benevolent rulers who benefited their subjects but knew how to deal with recalcitrants. At the same time, however, insoluble conflicts developed: galloping modernization raised the political consciousness of new strata in society, economic and social disparities thrust up radical forces on the Left and the Right, street voices reached the international arena, and foreign policy intertwined with domestic policy. Despite the aristocratic style still predominant on the surface, democratization matured in the depths.

The pervasive ambiguity was also felt in the attitude toward the Jews and their place in society. Official antisemitism existed in Russia, but the enlightened circles now dissociated themselves from it. In Central and Western Europe the antisemitic wave receded in the early years of the new century. Nevertheless, antisemitism exercised considerable influence at both the social and the political levels. Thus the reaction against new immigrants in England at the beginning of the century gave rise to several organizations whose activity was tinged with antisemitism. Various ultra-nationalist groups in Germany espoused antisemitic goals alongside their diversified political and economic activity. In France the royalist and antisemitic movement *Action française* founded in 1899 left its imprint on a whole generation. Four out of every seven German delegates in the Vienna Diet represented a platform containing antisemitic planks. In all these cases nationalism had diverse aims but shared an underlying antisemitic motif (Holmes, pp. 89–94; Greive, p. 84; Wilson, pp. 379–383; Pulzer, pp. 205–206). Following the failure of parties founded on a specific antisemitic platform, anti-semitism became an integral part of the activity of different organizations and factions within the "national" camp. Thus, merely saying "nationalism" now usually connoted antisemitism.

"The Four Confederated Estates"

The following is taken from an article deploring France's takeover by foreigners which the royalist and antisemitic leader and thinker Charles Maurras (1868–1952) published in 1912 in his movement's Paris-based paper.[31]

. . . From above, from below, the Frenchman is trapped. He does not waste his time complaining any more, for as high a level as his protest might reach, it would be submitted, prior to consider-ation, to several representatives of the four confederated estates—Jewish, Protestant, Masonic, and *Métèque*—with whom necessarily lies the real power.[32]

Well, well! What one sees around today was perceived twenty years ago in literature. More than career concerns, or ideas, or good taste, it is the French spirit that has been compromised. Indubitably, the foreigner knew how to starve out our compat-riot—all the doors were carefully guarded, watched by lackeys of the barbarians and *métèques*.[33] Editors and publishers who con-

[31] The movement and its journal were both called *l'Action française*. The leader, Charles Maurras—writer and journalist—inaugurated his political activity by laud-ing the officer involved in the forgery leading to Dreyfus's conviction. His political writing was greatly inspired by his aesthetic criticism. He rejected the French Revo-lution and parliamentary democracy, aspiring to reestablish the monarchy in order to buttress nationalism. Maurras sought to utilize the Catholic Church as a barrier against anti-nationalist influences, but his writings were condemned by the Vatican as heresy.

[32] Maurras maintained that Protestantism and Judaism were interrelated. He regarded France as the successor of ancient classicism while attributing to the Ger-manic peoples the acceptance of the Reformation, imbued with the spirit of Jewish individualism. The Freemasons had for generations been looked upon as a subvers-ive sect, and their alleged ties with the Jews constituted a major theme in Catholic antisemitic literature. The term *métèque*, or half-caste, was a favorite of Maurras' and became part of the antisemitic lexicon in France (see n. 33 below). His reference to the *real power* paradoxically recalls the distinction between the merely formally recognized Third Republic—*le pays légal*—and the real France, *le pays réel*.

[33] Just as Maurras cherished the classical world, so he regarded his adversaries as inimical to that cultural model. Hence the term "barbarians," which originated in ancient Greece and meant foreigners and even enemies of culture. The term was com-monly employed to describe the hordes that invaded Rome, while it is applied here to an invasion of France by outsiders. The term *métèque* is taken from the Greek—*metoikos*—where it referred to a foreigner resident in Athens who did not enjoy politi-cal rights.

PLATE 1. "Return of a Jewish Volunteer", an oil painting by Moritz Oppenheimer, portrays the return of a German Jewish volunteer from the war of liberation fought against Napoleon. (Oscar Gruss Collection, New York)

PLATE 2. An engraving depicting riots in Durmenach, Alsace. The caption reads: "Revolt against the Jews. February 23, 1848."

PLATE 3.   Caricature of Jews serving in the local militia during the Polish insurrection. (Isaac Einhorn Collection, Tel Aviv)

PLATE 4.   "The Wandering Jew". An 1852 woodcut by Gustav Doré.

PLATE 5.   Caricature from a Russian antisemitic periodical, 1906. (Eduard Fuchs, *Die Juden in der Karikatur*, Munich, 1921)

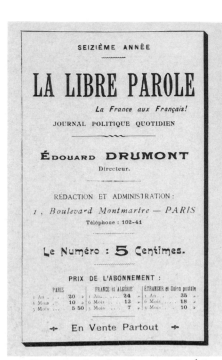

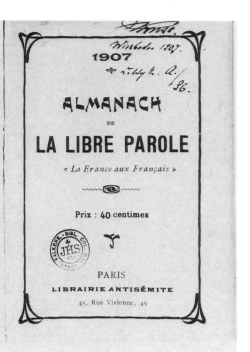

PLATE 6. An advertisement for Édouard Drumont's antisemitic journal *La Libre Parole* and the title page from its 1907 almanac.

PLATE 7. Caricature of Baron de Rothschild's ancestors.

PLATE 8. Édouard Drumont addressing an antisemitic rally in Neuilly, Paris.

PLATE 9.   A picture from the *London Illustrated News* of 12 January 1895. The
caption reads: "The degradation of Captain Dreyfus in Paris on his way to the
prison van."

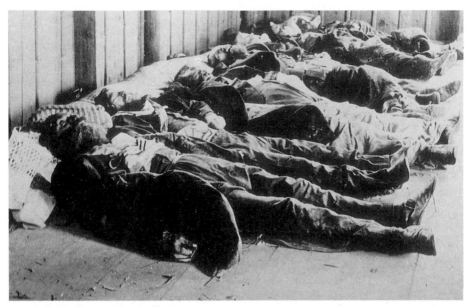

PLATE 10. Victims of the Kishinev pogrom, 1903. (Jewish National and University Library, Jerusalem)

PLATE 11. Pogrom victims in Yekaterinoslav, 1905. (Jewish National and University Library, Jerusalem)

PLATE 12.   An artist's rendition of the pogrom in Bialystok, 1906. (Moissaye J. Olgin, *The Soul of the Russian Revolution*, New York, 1917)

אל היהודים בפולין.

מהרגע הזבֶֹּא מצַרֵיךְדֹבֹּחֵבֶוָזֹ אֹסו לֹשֶבֶֹנֵֹזָ בֹרֵיֹם אֹלֵיוֹם תֹזֹלֵיֹסֹטֹ, מֹסֹנֹדֹה וֹאֹטֹסֹדֹרֹיֹה אֹוֹנֹגֹרֹיֹם,
כֵֹאַֹר בֹֹגֹבֵֹרֵֹ סֹילֵן.

הֹקֹרֹיֹצֹיֹח הֹרֹיֹסֹח מֹהֹרֹה לֵֹיֹם לֹחֹסֹלֹם כֹל נֹשֹבֹה שֹבֹנֵֹי הֹשֹחֹתֹרֹוֹם חֹיֹלֵוֹחֹיֹנֹ, אֹחֵֹר עֹדֹם לֹא
יֹחֹיֹבֹ יֹסֹיֹרֹהֹם.

דֹמֹיֹר נֹשֹא מֹ עֹלֹיֹם מֹסֹבֹב וֹהֹוֹס | סֹיֹרֹדֹיֹח־אֹיֹח נֹגֹיֹד, חֹלֹס הֹרֹה וֹהֹטֹשֹרֹאֹ, חֹיֹרֹה
וֹדֹוֹד כֹל יֹצֹיֹא וֹשֹבֹֹוֹרֹח בֹֹכֹל מֹנֹצֹעֹח הֹבֹֹלֵֹגֹח וֹהֹחֹבֹֹרֹח, בֹֹרֹיֹחֹיֹם.
הֹרֵֹא יֹחֹר סֹדֹר נֹאֹתֹקֹם חֹתֹח מֹבֹֹלֹח צֹו הֹבֹֹרֵֹל סֹל פֹיֹסֹקֹדֹה, הֹנֹה אֹ נֹאֹס אֹיֹכֹם
כֵֹיֹרֵֹיֹדֹ וֹשֹבֹֹרֹה מֹסֹבֹֹם הֹרֵֹיֹם הֹאֹיֹרֵֹיֹח, הֹקֹיֹרֹה חֹתֹח חֹזֹרֹח לֵֹחֹוֹלֵֹיֹ, בֹֹכֹל שֹחֹר מֹיֹם סֹבֹֹבֹ,
וֹהֹיֹיֹר לֵֹצֹבֹֹא לֹוֹצֹֹרֹח כֹל יֹסֹבֵֹי הֹאֹרֹץ, סֹוֹרֵֹיֹצֹיֹח הֹיֹהֹוֹדֹיֹם עֹיֹמֹד לֹהֹוֹסֹד כֹל יֹהֹוֹדֹיֹח חֹזֹקֹם.
אֹל תֹמֹנֹ לֵֹהֹבֵֹלֵֹח אֹח וֹשֹבֹֹם כֹל יֹהֹי הֹבֹֹנֹחֹוֹח וֹטֹיֹדֹח, בֹֹאֹסֹד קֹרֵֹנֵֹם זֹה סֹבֹֹטֹם רֹבֹֹח! גֹם
בֹֹזֹה 1905 הֹבֹֹטֹיֹחֹבֹֹם הֹבֹֹא לֵֹחֹ לֵֹבֹֹם קֹרֹיֹ נֹבֹֹיֹח.

אֹיֹר הֹלֵֹיֹם אֹח רֹבֵֹיֹ אֹטֹר פֹֹרֹטֹם בֹֹכֹל חֹקֹם בֹֹחֹיֹר סֹחֹטֹם מֹלֵֹחֹמֹה ?
זֹכֹיֹ אֹח הֹגֹרֵֹוֹסֹיֹם הֹנֹרֹאֹיֹם וֹאֹח הֹבֹֹלֵֹיֹוֹם סֹל הֹסֹדֹיֹ אֹחֹיֹכֹם !
זֹכֹיֹ אֹח קֹיֹסֹוֹבֹֹג, אֹח הֹיֹסֹגֹ, אֹח בֹֹיֹלֵֹסֹטֹוֹק, אֹח סֹדֹלֵֹן, וֹאֹח אֹוֹטֹוֹסֹיֹדֹרֹטֹיֹם לֹסֹאֹוֹח !
זֹכֹיֹ אֹח סֹבֹֹם בֹֹיֹלֵֹיֹם וֹאֹח הֹיֹרֹצֹיֹח הֹתֹעֹוֹזֹח וֹבֹֹאֹרֹח מֹטֹטֹם הֹבֹֹטֹסֹלֵֹה נֹהֹחֹוֹק בֹֹקֹרֹב
הֹעֹם אֹח זֹלֵֹיֹוֹח אֹדֹם הֹיֹחֹעֹבֹֹה !

כֹנֹ סֹכֹר רֹבֹֹא אֹח הֹבֹֹחֹוֹר בֹֹכֹל חֹקֹם, סֹדֹבֹֹנֵֹיֹח נֹבֹֹסֹח דֹחֹק.
גֹם הֹזֹם הֹרֹיֹח לֹ בֹֹכֹח הֹרֹחֹק ! וֹאֹח הֹיֹא סֹבֹֹח הֹבֹֹנֹחֹיֹחֹאֹר.
הֹיֹחֹבֹֹם הֹקֹרֹיֹסֹה הֹיֹא בֹֹסֹח, לֹחֹאֹסֹ לֹ בֹֹכֹל חֹתֹכֹם לֹחֹוֹק אֹח דֹבֹֹר הֹסֹחֹיֹרֹה.
בֹֹו נֹחֹוֹח חֹטֹם : בֹֹצֹיֹיֹבֹֹנֹם, חֹלֵֹוֹיֹחֹבֹֹם, חֹבֹֹרֵֹוֹחֹיֹכֹם, חֹיֹיֹם לֹהֹחֹצֹב יֹחֹר נֹאֹם אֹחֹר לֹוֹצֹרֹח
הֹבֹֹוֹ הֹקֹרֵֹיֹם.

סֹ, כֹלֵֹ סֹלֹא בֹֹטֹחֹוֹ, אֹל מֹבֹֹיֹאֹ חֹלֵֹוֹ הֹקֹרֹבֹֹיֹם וֹהֹטֹוֹכֹם עֹלֵֹיֹבֹֹם !
בֹֹקֹר כֹ מֹחֹרֹה סֹחֹוֹסֹטֹ, יֹסֹוֹב סֹבֹֹך חֹקֹלֵֹיֹן !
סֹלֹ סֹלֹ צֹה חֹרֹד, לֹחֹרֹיֹד כֹלֹה אֹח הֹצֹיֹב, וֹנֹחֹבֹֹיֹא אֹח הֹיֹסֹע אֹח הֹיֹסֹע וֹאֹח הֹדֹיֹן לֹנֹסֹח נֹסֹד !

ההנהגה העליונה של צבאות גרמניה
ואוסטריה־אונגריה המאוחדים.

PLATE 13.   A German-Austrian World
War I manifesto (in Hebrew) appealing
to Polish Jews to join forces against the
Russians.   (Solomon   Anski,   *The
Destruction of the Jews of Poland, Gali-
cia and Bukovina* [Heb.], Berlin, 1929)

PLATE 14.   The exodus of Galician Jews in the wake of hostilities, 1915. (Central Archives of the Jewish People, Jerusalem)

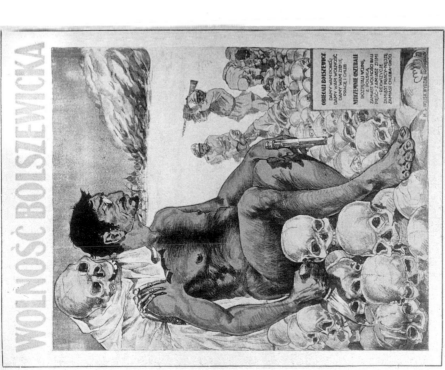

PLATE 15. Jews as symbols of Bolshevism. A Polish anti-Communist poster from the Polish-Russian War, 1920. (Eduard Fuchs, *Die Juden in der Karikatur*, Munich, 1921)

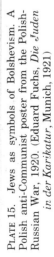

PLATE 16. An antisemitic election campaign poster issued by the Christian-Socialist Party, Austria, 1920. (Eduard Fuchs, *Die Juden in der Karikatur*, Munich, 1921)

PLATE 17.   Antisemitic vandalism in the offices of the Zionist Federation of Cluj, Transylvania, 1922. (Central Zionist Archives, Jerusalem)

PLATE 18.   Walter Rathenau, the German Foreign Minister, assassinated in Berlin by extreme right-wing militants on 24 June 1922. (Jewish National and University Library, Jerusalem)

PLATE 19.   "Spartacus" leader Rosa Luxemburg, assassinated in Berlin by para-military forces on 15 January 1919. (Deutsche Press – Agenturev GmbH, Hamburg)

PLATE 20. Antisemitic poster pasted on the wall of the Reichstag, 1920.

PLATE 21. Nazi racist propaganda against Jews.

PLATE 22.   Polish antisemitic and anti-Communist caricature of the 1930s.

PLATE 23. Posters proclaiming the boycott of Jewish shops, Berlin, 1 June 1933.
(Yad Vashem, Jerusalem)

PLATE 24. A park bench in Berlin, 1933. The sign reads: "For Aryans only." (Yad
Vashem, Jerusalem)

PLATE 25. "No place for Jews in the Army." A headline in the SS newspaper *Das Schwarze Korps*, 1935. (B. Mordecai Ansbacher Collection, Jerusalem)

PLATE 26. "Jew Perish!" Graffitti on a synagogue wall, Düsseldorf, 1933. (Yad Vashem, Jerusalem)

PLATE 27. Building the Warsaw ghetto wall, 1939. (Yad Vashem, Jerusalem)

PLATE 28. Jews waiting in line for permits to emigrate from Germany to Palestine, 1939. (Yad Vashem, Jerusalem)

ORDONANȚA

Noi, Locot. Colonel Blănaru Ioan Comandantul Garnizoanei Fălticeni, în conformitate cu ordinul No. 25007 al Armatei a 3-a și cu dispozițiile articolului 486 Cod. Justiție Militară ;

Ordonăm:

Art. 1. Populația de origine etnică evreiască de orice sex și vârstă, din întregul cuprins al județului Baia, în 48 de ore de la publicarea prezentei ordonanțe, este obligată să poarte cusut pe partea stângă a pieptului în mod vizibil, un semn distinctiv format dintr'o stea cu 6 colțuri (două triunghiuri suprapuse) din stofă sau pânză de culoare galbenă, de dimensiunile 7 cm. în diametru, aplicat pe fond negru.

Art. 2. Contravenienții dela art. 1 se vor pedepsi cu închisoare corecțională dela 1 lună la un an și cu o ámendă de lei 1000 la 10.000 lei.

Dată astăzi 18 August 1941.

Comandantul Garnizoanei Fălticeni,
Lt. Colonel, Blănaru Ioan

Tip. Românească C. Prpovici Fălticeni

PLATE 29. A Romanian military edict requiring all Jews to wear the yellow star, Moldavia, 18 August 1941. (Yad Vashem, Jerusalem)

PLATE 30. Propaganda stamp against Freemasons and Jews issued by the Serbian postal authorities, 1942. (B. Mordecai Ansbacher Collection, Jerusalem)

sidered themselves and proclaimed themselves to be loyal patriots, surrounded themselves with a bodyguard of secretaries and lectors who let nothing even slightly national enter. A professor of history had to endure the iron rod of Gabriel Monod and his Teutons or resign himself to rot in some lowly position.[34] A professor of philosophy suffered a similar fate from foreign Jews or unpatriotic Protestants. But all this would count for little had the barbarians' tyranny not attempted to reach the soul of our souls, which is the architect and mason of the idea, of art, and of action. Those barbarians and *métèques* did not satisfy themselves merely by plundering us and ruling over us. They wished to rule from *within* us, and this was their downfall. We trembled when we saw them using their insolent lordliness to impose and propagate blunt contempt or an ironic indulgence against our heritage.[35] (Girardet, 1966, p. 210)

Summary: The Heyday of Imperialism

A pronounced duality characterizes the latter part of the nineteenth century and the first part of the twentieth; the Industrial Revolution had still not staked out its claim in every country in Europe, but the revolution of electricity and steel was already under way. This was a period of transition from the dominion of the nobility, which still retained a grip on contemporary culture, to the accelerated modernization of the new century. The old liberalism had already lost much of its vitality, but faith in progress was still dominant. True, social progress was now perceived not as a gradual, harmonious process but as a turbulent struggle. Yet the future still offered hope. European rule reached every continent, and Europeans competed for global mastery. The revolutionaries believed that class war would intensify but would culminate in a just and durable solution for all social ills. National movements in the multinational empires fought for their respective rights, each believing that *it* would come out on top.

[34] Gabriel Monod (1844–1912), a member of a well-known French Protestant family, was one of the leading Dreyfusards. He also angered Maurras because of the Germanic scholarly methods he had employed as a historian. He is reprimanded here for having surrounded himself with Germans and for blocking the professional advancement of French patriots.

[35] This might appeal to readers who feel discriminated against, because of competition from minority groups, particularly from Jews. This argument is congruent with the principal accusation: that foreigners are seizing control of France, disavowing its spirit, and corrupting its culture.

Duality also marked the situation of the Jews: in Eastern Europe they suffered from a semi-official antisemitism, but elsewhere the antisemitic tide was ebbing. At the same time, the diversity amongst the Jews themselves was constantly growing. The integration into the surrounding nations undercut their sense of solidarity, the gap between the Jews of Eastern Europe and Western Jewry growing in particular. Counter to the assimilationist hopes generally harbored by the Jews, the Jewish national movement arose and sought to redirect the course of events.

On the face of it, antisemitism seemed to be in recession during *la belle époque* but nevertheless continued to leave its mark. "National" organizations bearing the cast of a conservative or radical Right took up places in the public arena in various countries. These organizations fused their hostility toward the Jews with a wide range of political, economic and social programs, but antisemitism was the hallmark common to them all. The characteristic of nationalism as a combative movement was equally applicable to antisemitism; despite emancipation and assimilation (and at times precisely because of them), Jews continued to attract hostile or unfavorable attention in various countries of Europe.

5

The First World War and Its Aftermath

The Defeated German Reich

The twentieth century, it is sometimes said, actually begins in 1914 with the outbreak of the "Great War," for that event brought to light certain characteristics which became dominant during this century:

- "Reason of State" as a supreme value;
- Modern technology used for destructive purposes;
- Total warfare directed indiscriminately against strategic and civilian targets; and
- The manipulation of the masses by means of propaganda.

The First World War changed the face of the world. It brought about the disappearance of the old multinational empires—the Austro-Hungarian and the Ottoman—and *mutatis mutandis* the Russian Empire. Following the War ancient dynasties were deposed and new republics created, inspired by the Right of Self-Determination. A surging revolutionary wave threatened to remold the structure of society but was contained and ultimately swept only through Russia. These turbulent events took years to play themselves out, encompassed numerous countries, and caused death on a scale so vast as to render an accurate account impossible.

Jews were affected, as soldiers on both sides of the front or as civilians in the occupied countries suffering together with the general population from starvation and epidemics. War and revolution caused heavy fighting in areas of dense Jewish population in Eastern Europe. Whole communities were expelled or fled as war refugees. The Jews also suffered as a minority group—minorities being particularly vulnerable in periods of crisis. Frequently they were accused of disloyalty, abetting the enemy and evading military service, or of war profiteering. These charges were levelled not only in countries known for their hostility toward Jews but even in the more enlightened ones.

The Jews, for their part, generally participated enthusiastically in the war effort, seeing it as an opportunity to better integrate into society. The War pitted Jews serving in the armies of the Central Powers against Jewish soldiers of the Allied Powers. Jewish public opinion acquiesced in the situation, as Jewish solidarity gave way to national loyalties and hatred for the enemy. In the Jewish communities of England and France, like those in Germany and Austria, these positions were voiced publicly by preachers and community functionaries and were reflected in the Jewish press. The upsurge of patriotism in the Jewish community was sometimes well received by nationalist circles, which were prepared to forgo their habitual Jew-baiting in a period of emergency.

In Germany the War erupted amid an atmosphere of national unity, and Jews felt themselves making common cause with their fellow citizens. A German victory, they tended to believe, would bring about, among other things, the emancipation of Russian Jews. Instead, the military and economic difficulties accompanying the War caused a breakdown of national solidarity and a groundswell of antisemitism. The old charges of profiteering and shirking combat were levelled at the Jews. The authorities were sufficiently swayed by the incitement as to conduct a census in 1916 to ascertain the proportion of Jews in the army and more specifically on the front. Although the census was ostensibly conducted to collect data, the very fact that it was held seemed to be a *prima facie* admission that grounds for suspicion against the Jews existed. That the Jews were subjected to special scrutiny set them apart from the rest of the population and heightened the public's mistrust toward them. The military did not publish the results of the census and did not refute the allegations against the Jews, even though various studies found that Jewish participation in the war effort was no less than that of other segments of the population (Friedländer, pp. 37–38).

The looming German defeat deepened the rift in the nation and lent new momentum to the growing antisemitism. Many Germans, unable to accept their debacle, entertained the idea that Germany had not been defeated on the battlefield but had fallen prey to treachery. The German Army had been stabbed in the back, the defeated commanders maintained, and the myth of "the dagger in the back" entered Germany's political lexicon. The accusation of betrayal was hurled at the Jews and at the Left, the two often intermingled in the public imagination.

Jews played prominent roles in the period of crisis following the War, both in the leadership of the revolutionary Left and as founders of the Weimar Republic. Right-wing circles regarded the democratic republic as a wretched successor to the greatness of the German Reich, and its fate was perceived as inextricably bound up with the shameful surrender terms imposed on Germany. The adherents of the ultra-nationalist camp, incapable of facing up to their country's defeat after years of cultivating a sense of German superiority, tended to promote the myth of the betrayal, as mentioned above, and the related allegations of Jewish destructiveness. Here a phenomenon known from earlier times and other places reappears: individual Jews who held a negative attitude toward Judaism, including converts, were—against their will—identified by the public with the Jewish community. Any such person who considered himself a citizen with equal rights and obligations and a member of the German nation was nonetheless looked on as a Jew. Does the Jewish community not bear collective responsibility for its members? Racists saw this collective link as biologically determined, while others spoke of a "Jewish conspiracy." But public opinion needed no further persuasion to recognize Rosa Luxemburg[1] or Walter Rathenau[2] as Jews.

Rosa Luxemburg was murdered together with the non-Jewish Communist leader Karl Liebknecht (1871–1919); Rathenau was killed like the Catholic leader Matthias Erzberger (1875–1921) before him. Both Jews fell victim to anti-democratic terrorism because of their standing in German public life. Had they not been Jews they might have suffered the same fate, but the Jewish theme was predominant in the incitement against them. The hatred fanned by the racial Right against Rosa Luxemburg and Foreign Minister Rathenau was simultaneously directed against Jews as a group. It

---

[1] Rosa Luxemburg (1870–1919), the daughter of a well-to-do family from Poland, became a radical socialist activist, initially in Poland and then in Germany. A prominent Marxist thinker, she headed a revolutionary organization in the latter part of the War. She was murdered by right-wing assassins in Berlin. Rosa Luxemburg had long been estranged and alienated from Judaism.

[2] Walter Rathenau (1867–1922) was a German-born industrialist, writer and statesman. During the War he efficiently mobilized the German economy, afterward becoming a member of the Weimar Republic cabinet and finally Foreign Minister. He was murdered in an ambush in Berlin. Rathenau's attitude toward Judaism was on the whole quite negative.

goes without saying that the majority of the Jews did not support Rosa Luxemburg's political views. It is noteworthy that a Zionist delegation—including the renowned scientist Albert Einstein (1879–1955)—tried unsuccessfully to dissuade Rathenau from accepting the appointment as Foreign Minister. They argued that his public exposure would prove harmful to the Jews in Germany. Rathenau replied that precisely his acceptance of the portfolio would constitute the best answer to the antisemites' attempts to isolate the Jews from the German nation. He was shot down a few weeks later (Blumenfeld, 1962, pp. 142–145).

The murder of Jewish-born leaders in Germany was fraught with symbolic significance. Naturally, a distinction must be made between prominent figures in the country's political life and the situation of the Jewish population as a whole. Nevertheless, it is clear that the actions of such individuals, and their image in the eyes of society, also affected the Jews in general. The collapse of the Empire generated an eve-of-revolution atmosphere in Germany; new political forces surged to the fore. In the campaign launched by the Right against the young democracy, Jewish names served the "nationalists" as a convenient pretext for branding the Jews with the stigma of having betrayed the fatherland.

A Jewish Youth Describes the Aftermath of the German Defeat

The following is taken from the memoirs of Edwin Landau, born in 1890 in a small town in West-Prussia.[3] He lived there as a plumber and small businessman until emigrating to Palestine in 1934.

Even though the majority of the Jewish citizens gathered around the Left, one man only had the courage to show the black-red-gold colored flag[4] on all occasions. For his courage he had to pay in a concentration camp after Hitler came to power. During the election campaign, which soon commenced and which I followed assiduously, one could easily notice the difference between the republicans and their opponents.[5] I had many Catholic acquaintances and customers, with whom one occasionally talked things

[3] The town of Deutsch-Krone (Walcz in Polish) is located in the border area Posen—West Prussia, today in Poland. On the eve of the First World War, 337 Jews resided there out of a total population of 7,673.

[4] These were the colors of the Weimar Republic flag, and they are used again today in West Germany.

[5] The reference is apparently to the first election campaign for the Weimar National Assembly in January 1919.

over.[6] Nevertheless, one may not be altogether frank with these people, as you could not look into their hearts.

There was then an atmosphere of some distrust among the citizens. They were still in a state of uncertainty and many of them did not know themselves where they belonged.

One thing was certain: in case we Jewish soldiers had believed that by participating in the war we had won the love of our fellow-men, we were mistaken. Even though there was no open antisemitism, still a great many people who hated the republic were opposed to the Jews, who usually identified with the workers.[7]

It also seemed as if the economic power of these opponents of the republic was growing very strong, and they spread the word that most Jews had been shirking their military duty. As it happened in my own hometown it happened all over the Reich, and though the workers used to protect the Jews, Jewish veterans (for whom protection coming from this side was some kind of humiliation) formed an organization led by former officers: the Union of Jewish Frontier Soldiers.[8]

I myself founded a local group which soon had forty members who—according to the regulations—could prove by their military documents that they had been fighting at the front. My father did not fully agree with my activities, since he was afraid, perhaps justifiably so, that we might lose some of our customers. Among the latter were many landowners, farmers, officials, and building contractors, who even when they were not "deutsch-national" still belonged to the *Deutsche Volkspartei* or the *Stahlhelm*.[9] Soon we also heard from the *Deutschsoziale Partei* and their leader, the notorious *Knüppelkunze*. This party held an electoral meeting to which our Union and a great many workers marched. The speaker

[6] The area was predominantly Catholic, although there were also several Protestant locales. The author notes that antisemitism was more pronounced among the Protestants (apparently Lutherans).

[7] German social-democracy in this period fought against antisemitism in the working class. The Jews considered the Social-Democrats their best support against the hostility of the Right. It is noteworthy that throughout the entire memoir the relations between workers and Jews are depicted as those of allies.

[8] The author evokes a widespread wartime allegation that the Jews shirked military duty. Note that the organization accepted only former combat soldiers in order to refute the slander that the Jews had landed comfortable, rear-echelon jobs. In contrast, no mention is made here of the later, and more serious, claim that the Jews had been among those who had caused Germany's defeat.

[9] This is an interesting characterization of the social composition of the Republic's opponents, who came from the German aristocracy and bourgeoisie, in an area also containing a Polish population. The various nationalist groups mentioned here are indicative of the postwar turmoil in Germany. Some of these parties and organizations lasted until the Nazis' assumption of power.

was a certain Dr. Veit from Meiningen.[10] The speaker told such stupid lies about the Jews that I almost asked permission to retort. But my father had strongly advised me not to speak in public, so I abstained. Later on, the workers objected to the speech, as they did not believe the accusations against the Jews. Then the speaker had the audacity to say that had he not spoken the truth, at least one Jew would have spoken up to contradict him, but this had never happened during his campaign. I could not control myself any longer and I called out: "Here is one who wants to speak." At first the speaker seemed startled, but then he called, "I shall be very happy, later on," to which I retorted, "Maybe not!" After he finished his speech I pressed through the crowd to the speaker's desk, while many members of the Front Soldiers' Union and some worker acquaintances accompanied me. In a speech which lasted almost an hour, in which I limited myself to defense only, I made such an impression on my fellow-citizens through my passionate argumentation, that I knew I would win.

The opponents, especially the students from the trade school, tried to cut me short. I dealt with them easily. The workers took my side and eventually the speaker could not make his final speech, as everything turned into a big riot. My fellow citizens called out to me, "You have given it to him!" The only thing that mattered to me was that they should not call us cowards.[11]

My father did not approve of my appearance, which was mentioned in the papers the next day. But the president of the Jewish community came to thank me for my manly appearance, and I smilingly accepted. But my adversaries blacklisted me.[12] (Landau, pp. 50–51)

---

[10] The town of Meiningen in Saxonia is today located in East Germany. The movement in question operated from 1921 to 1928. Therefore this episode could not have occurred on the eve of the first election, as is implied by the overall context. The leader of the movement was called *Knüppelkunze* to signify the clubs wielded by his followers against their adversaries. He later joined the Nazi Party.

[11] Throughout the story the father's caution is presented in contrast to the stormy temper of the author, who had returned from the front as a German officer and was unwilling to let his honor be sullied. Incidentally, the father was a supporter of the Republic, whereas the son attested that he had been a monarchist and found it difficult to adapt to the change in the regime.

[12] The memoirs were written in Palestine in 1940, and the author's memory may have betrayed him at certain points. Yet it seems a reliable description of the atmosphere in a small town during the crisis that followed the collapse of the Empire, when national, religious and social conflicts erupted under the pressure of political events. The small Jewish community experienced in its own way the great events of the era: its intimate acquaintance with the local population proved salutary.

The Revolution and the Jews

Two events in 1917 thrust the "Jewish Question" on to the international stage: the Russian Revolution and the Balfour Declaration. Although not interconnected, they were linked in the public mind as two sides of the same coin—as evidence, supposedly, of the Jews' global power. The revolution which broke out in Russia in early 1917, and especially the subsequent October Revolution, were received as epoch-making events—"ten days that shook the world," as the American John Reed described the Revolution in his famous book of the same title.[13] Reports emanating from Russia stressed the Jewishness of many revolutionary leaders and depicted the upheaval as an act of vengeance by Russia's Jews against the Czar's regime after generations of oppression.

In fact, a considerable proportion of the revolutionaries were indeed Jewish. Throughout the world names of Jews resounded in the upper echelons of the new Soviet government—Lev Trotsky (1879–1940), Gregory Zinoviev (1883–1936), Lev Kamenev (1883–1936)—the ex-Menshevik leader Julius Martov (1873–1923) and the organizer of the Communist International, Karl Radek (1883–1939). These became household names to newspaper readers everywhere, and soon enough their former names—Bronstein, Radomislsky, Rosenfeld, Zederbaum, Sobelsohn—were also revealed. The aliases had been adopted for underground purposes, but the public regarded them as an attempt to deceive the world about the true origin of the revolutionaries, so as to veil the Jewish character of the Revolution.

The convulsion in Russia triggered off revolutions in Germany and Hungary. Uprisings in the Ruhr area of western Germany and in the capital, Berlin, were quickly put down, but in Bavaria the revolution struggled for several months. Initially it was led by Kurt Eisner (1867–1919), a Jew; one of his cabinet ministers, Edgar Jaffé (1866–1921), was also Jewish. In the second stage, however, nearly the entire leadership was Jewish—Gustav Landauer (1870–1919), Erich Mühsam (1878–1934), Ernst Toller (1893–1939), Eugen Leviné (1883–1919), and others. Even though most of them were German by birth, the public associated them with the revolutionary influx of Jews from the East, such as Rosa Luxemburg, Leo Jogiches (1867–1919) and Israel Helfand-Parvus (1867–1924).

As avowed internationalists, these revolutionaries had made their

---

[13] First published in England by the Communist Party of Great Britain in 1926.

way to Germany to organize the political activity in the country where, they believed, the world revolution of the proletariat would begin. Their attitude toward nationalism was fundamentally negative, and just as they gave no thought to their Jewishness, they took no account of the impression their foreignness evoked in Germany. Incidentally, a sociological analysis of fifty Jewish-born socialist leaders in Germany at the time revealed that only eight were foreign-born (and two of those came from Vienna); the vast majority were of bourgeois extraction, and over half of them espoused relatively moderate socialist views. Nevertheless, the predominant image was that of the ugly Jewish revolutionary, an outsider who was taking over Germany with ruthless extremism (Angress, pp. 309–315).

In March 1919 the Communists seized power in Hungary. Heading the revolution was a Transylvanian Jew, Béla Kun (1886–1939), who had joined the Bolsheviks while in Russian captivity during the War. Eighteen of the Revolutionary Council's twenty-nine members were of Jewish extraction. The communist regime in Hungary survived for less than half a year and took a hostile stance *vis-à-vis* the Jews, regarding them as capitalists—a non-productive social element. The government's confiscation of private property and its struggle against religion antagonized the majority of the Hungarian population. To many, Communism seemed to be a foreign import brought into the country by aliens. The historical memory of the Communist dictatorship was of a regime founded on terror and imposed on Hungary by treacherous Jews. The Communist episode was now superimposed on the myth of the Jews who caused Hungary's defeat in the War—by shirking their duty on the battlefield, engaging in war profiteering, and finally stabbing the army in the back (Mendelsohn, pp. 94–98).

In Russia, Germany and Hungary the revolution was perceived as the handiwork of the Jews, against the peoples' will and against their best interests. A connection existed between the Russian and Hungarian revolutions and to a lesser extent between the Russian and German revolutions. The revolutionary movement was seen as a scheme manipulated by some clandestine headquarters bent on shattering the social order—a kind of Jewish revolution against the nations. To counter the allegedly foreign agents of destruction, local forces emerged who sought to preserve the old and to enlist popular support by brandishing nationalist slogans. The appeal to national sentiment was generally made in the spirit of a conservative and Christian approach. The struggle against the revolution tended to shunt aside whatever smacked of moderation and to repulse any inclination toward tolerance.

That the Jews were identified with the forces to the Left of Center on the political map only aggravated the situation. Note that the crisis of liberalism in continental Europe had brought the Jews closer to the Social-Democrats, who were more sympathetic toward minorities, even if this conflicted with the Jewish voter's social and economic interests. This cast suspicion on the Jews as acting contrary to acceptable norms and as naturally inclined to subversiveness. Moreover, middle-class Jews were closer in their views to the Left than to the Conservatives. The Jewish community was basically classless in the European sense; Jews often felt alienated from their non-Jewish peers—and even Jews who had long since cast off religion may have retained some social values of the biblical tradition. It is well-known that modern thinkers have often emphasized the prophetic heritage as a source of inspiration for social justice.

At all events, once the Russian Revolution had consolidated itself, it was obvious that despite the Jews in the leadership, the revolution could in no sense be characterized as Jewish. In effect, a process of abstraction had been at work, identifying revolution with Judaism without the need to prove the Jewish origin of any Communist leader. Antisemitism embraced this identification, maintaining that the connection between Judaism and revolution was innate; moreover, the alleged "Jewish" character was not solely confined to Jews proper.

Indeed, antisemites often call even non-Jewish adversaries "Jews" and impute to them allegedly "Jewish" attributes. At the level of party polemics this is an attempt to vilify rivals; yet another, higher level is also apparent: the more sophisticated among the antisemitic ideologues were not satisfied to wage a struggle only against genuine Jews but sought to depict Judaism as the satanic obverse of virtue. Thus Judaism was portrayed as the polar opposite of the authentic national soul and could be applied to anything and anyone at will.

The Jew as International Revolutionary

The following was written by a socialist journalist himself the son of a Jewish butcher from a small town in Galicia. His work had brought him in contact with the greatest figures of the socialist movement in Europe. Here he tells about Parvus, a cosmopolitan Jewish revolutionary.

His name was Israel Helfant, a brilliant Socialist writer himself, known generally by his pseudonym "Parvus." He was born in 1867 in Beresin, Russia,[14] attended a secondary school, joined early the Russian Social Revolutionary Movement,[15] escaped to Switzerland, studied economics and philosophy at Basle University, under Professor Bücher,[16] and graduated as a Ph.D. He specialized in finance, settled in the nineties in Saxony, and wrote for the *Neue Zeit*.[17] His articles on German finance attracted the attention of Government circles. In the controversy between Reformism and Marxism[18] he took the part of the latter, and became one of the most effective and best paid Socialist writers. His acute criticism of the Reformists, as well as of the Government's financial measures, led to his expulsion from Saxony and from Prussia.[19] In 1900, he settled at Munich, and established a publishing house for the publication of works of Russian authors, particularly Gorki, with whom he finally quarrelled.[20] At the same time he employed his talents in writing leading articles for the Marxist dailies and weeklies.

At the outbreak of the Russian Revolution in 1905 Parvus hurried to Petersburg, and, together with Trotsky, was elected a

[14] His birthplace was a small town near Minsk in White Russia. In his childhood the family moved to Odessa, where he grew up.

[15] The Socialist Revolutionary Party (S.R.), established in Russia in 1901–02, was an updated version of the nineteenth-century *Narodnaya Volya*. The influence of the S.R. was felt strongly during the revolutions of 1917 in Russia, but internal splits led to the Party's disintegration. In fact, Helfand reached Switzerland as early as 1886, where he was close to the future leaders of the Russian Social-Democracy. Thus his connection with the S.R. is rather dubious.

[16] Karl Bücher (1847–1930) was a very prominent German economic historian.

[17] *Neue Zeit* was a theoretical journal edited by the Marxist leader and ideologue Karl Kautsky (1854–1938).

[18] International socialism was divided into diverse, radical and moderate trends. The controversy within the German Social-Democrats was led among others by Rosa Luxemburg from the radical wing and Eduard Bernstein from the moderate, or "revisionist" camp (both leaders were Jewish.)

[19] The German Empire had a federal structure but was actually ruled by Prussia. However, the kingdoms of Württemberg and Bavaria enjoyed a measure of autonomy, and thus Helfand could find shelter in Munich after being expelled from Dresden.

[20] The Russian writer Maxim Gorki (1868–1936) was a socialist and was arrested several times by the Czarist government. He left Russia and took up residence in Italy. In 1904 a scandal broke out: Helfand profited from a production of Gorki's *The Lower Depths* in Germany and was accused of not remunerating the author and the Party.

member of the Petersburg Soviet.[21] In December, 1905, he was arrested and sentenced to banishment to Siberia. In December, 1906, he succeeded in escaping, and returned to Germany, where he resumed Socialist journalism and pamphleteering; but he, like many of us, came to the conclusion that the German Social–Democracy was not playing the game, but was simply pacing up and down in an impasse.[22] He gave up writing, and suffered poverty rather than waste his talents on the Germans. Though impecunious, he managed to travel to Constantinople, where he ultimately got in touch with the Young Turks.[23] They were not slow in discovering and using his great financial knowledge, and made him their adviser. In 1912, during the Balkan War, they entrusted him with the Commissariat, and he supplied the Army with provisions, which he procured in Odessa.[24] In 1914–1915, the Turkish Government, in agreement with the German Embassy, entrusted him, not only with the Commissariat, but also with a secret political mission to win Bulgaria for the German-Turkish cause.[25] In the spring of 1915, Parvus turned up in Berlin. The once impecunious journalist had come back as a rich man; the revolutionary, once banished from Prussia, was naturalized within twenty-four hours as a Prussian citizen, who deserved well of his adopted country. He chartered a steamer, carried Ruhr coal to Denmark and Sweden, and brought back fat and rubber for the German forces.[26] He founded the weekly review, *Die Glocke*, for the purpose of supporting the Social Democratic majority.[27] The paper did not

[21] In the 1905 Revolution a workers council ("soviet") was formed in St. Petersburg (later Petrograd and now Leningrad) to wage the struggle from below. The Russian Social-Democracy initially objected to this initiative, although Trotsky and Helfand believed it could serve as a political instrument. Lev Trotsky (1879–1940), one of the leaders of the Russian Revolution (a Jew), was influenced by Helfand in the conception of his revolutionary theory.

[22] Here the author adds his voice to the criticism levelled by left-wing circles at the German labor movement, because of its heed to minor social achievements and its moderation with regard to the country's ruling powers.

[23] In 1908 the "Young Turks" deposed the Sultan Abdul Hamid and installed his brother, Mohammed V. Power in the Ottoman Empire gradually shifted to a collective military leadership.

[24] In 1912, Bulgaria, Serbia and Greece attacked Turkey in the wake of a dispute over control of Macedonia. The war degenerated into an armed conflict between the former allies, with the Great Powers intervening indirectly. Turkey, finding itself in an inferior position, relied increasingly on Germany.

[25] In 1915, Bulgaria, which also sustained defeat in the Balkan War, entered the War on the side of Germany, Austro-Hungary and Turkey.

[26] The second half of 1915 and the first half of 1916 saw a respite in the naval war between the Central Powers and the Allies. As a result, supplies could be shipped by sea during this period.

[27] In his paper, Helfand called for cooperation between the Left and Germany in

pay its way; but Parvus was rich, and could afford the luxury of having a paper of his own, where his articles were given the premier place. At the same time, the German Government consulted him on Russian matters. It was Parvus who advised them in 1917 to permit Bolshevik leaders to return from Switzerland through German territory in sealed wagons to Petersburg.[28]

. . . Parvus was in those years the confidential adviser of Ebert.[29] The latter was as provincial as Hitler, knowing no other language and no other nation but his own. The country house of Parvus, in the wooded parts of Berlin-West, was the meeting-place of the new dignitaries and their wives and daughters. There, much more than in the Wilhelmplatz, State affairs were discussed and settled.[30] Parvus was the power behind the shaky throne of Ebert. He liked to play the invisible Providence, and he was never obtrusively conspicuous; he did not impose himself on anybody in authority, but was rather sought out on the score of his eminent abilities. In the years 1918–1922 he spent enormous sums of money on German patriotic propaganda in foreign lands. He genuinely liked Germany, as so many Eastern European Jews do; the German language is to them the key to Western culture, a spiritual way out of the ghetto.

. . . He did not look happy; he was longing for a return to his old country and for work with the Bolsheviks. He suffered from nostalgia, and finally applied through an intermediary to Lenin for admission into the Soviet service.[31] Lenin, however, sent him— so I was told—the pungent reply: "The Soviets certainly need clever brains, but above all clean hands." (Beer, pp. 194–197 *passim*)

order to extirpate the Czarist regime in Russia. To this end he also ran a ramified network of intelligence services and political and diplomatic operations from neutral Copenhagen. His strategy conflicted with the traditional pacifism of his former comrades in the left-wing of German Social-Democracy.

[28] This was the zenith of Helfand's efforts to bring about cooperation between the revolutionaries and the German Empire. As early as 1915 he had tried unsuccessfully to win Lenin over to his viewpoint. When the revolution broke out Lenin heeded his advice, since the provisional government in Russia and its allies in the West prevented him and his colleagues from returning to Russia.

[29] Friedrich Ebert (1871–1925) was a trade union functionary who became the leader of the German Social-Democratic Party, identified with its majority right-wing faction. After the fall of the monarchy he became Chancellor and in 1919 was sworn in at Weimar as the first President of the German Republic. Ebert tried to steer a middle course between revolutionary outbursts on the Right and the Left.

[30] The main government offices were situated in the *Wilhelmplatz* in Berlin.

[31] His approach to Lenin was apparently effected through Karl Radek (a Jew, leader of the Communist International) after the Bolsheviks seized power in Russia—that is, before he settled in Germany. At all events, the picture that emerges is of a rootless personality.

The Ukraine Fighting for Independence

At the conclusion of the First World War the Ukrainian national movement saw an opportunity to establish a state of its own. The revolutions of 1917 had ignited the national aspirations of the peoples subject to the Russian Czar. Russia's new rulers advocated national liberation [Lenin even promised national self-determination to the point of separation (Cobban, pp. 194–197)], but apprehensive that nationalism would be exploited by their enemies, they continued to uphold the earlier centrist tradition. At the end of 1917 the Ukraine became a People's Republic within a Russian federative framework, and three months later it declared independence in defiance of Petrograd. This brought in its wake an invasion by the Red Army, which was repulsed with the aid of German and Austrian forces. Until its defeat Germany remained the protector of the Ukraine and for a period even placed a dictator in power there under its patronage. The same year saw the outbreak of war between the Ukraine and Poland for control of Eastern Galicia, with its mixed population. The wars waged on Ukrainian soil from 1917 to 1920 involved the forces fighting against the Russian Revolution—White Russians, Western expeditionary forces, and irregulars. They all engaged in combat against their respective enemies and at the same time caused hardship to the civilian population.

For years the Ukraine remained a battlefield. Power passed from hand to hand and various forces rampaged across the country, pillaging and looting. Once anarchy broke loose, the Jews seemed to be fair game. Bands of Cossacks and regular army units joined with peasants and other local ruffians to wreak their vengeance on the Jewish population. Jews often organized in self-defense; still, about two thousand pogroms were perpetrated, resulting in the death of some 75,000 Jews and injury to a similar number (Ettinger, 1976, p. 954).

The fight for independence in the Ukraine, with its tragic interweaving of several classical phenomena, provides an illuminating example of the *nationalism-cum-antisemitism* syndrome. While still part of the Russian polity, the Ukrainian People's Republic granted personal-national rights to the various minorities within its borders. Following the October Revolution a falling out occurred between the leadership in Kiev and the central government in Petrograd, lending vigor to the isolationists who were militating for the establishment of an independent Ukrainian state. The minorities were far from enthusiastic about the growing propensity in the Ukraine to secede from greater Russia. However, the Ukraine declared itself a sovereign state and signed a separate peace treaty with Germany. But the young republic quickly became enmeshed in a series of wars, prompting the rising influence of the military and the ultranationalist Right. Despite these developments, steps were taken to implement the national autonomy of the minorities—including the creation of a Ministry for Jewish Affairs. Nevertheless, the intensification of Ukrainian nationalism was accompanied by a heightened suspicion toward the minorities and the Jews in particular.

The authorities feared that a connection existed between the Jews and the Red Army under the command of Lev Trotsky (himself of Jewish origin). In the meantime, the Ukrainian Army was purged of foreign elements, the troops and the public in general were seized by antisemitic fervor, and the government was unable to contain the resulting wave of pogroms. In its brief life the independent Ukraine was buffeted by adversities too overwhelming for a young, still incipient national movement. Ukrainian nationalism failed to win sufficient sympathy among the peasantry, who hated the towns and the Jews, while the occupation forces exploited conflicting loyalties and interests for their own purposes. On the other hand, the war atmosphere evoked heroic motifs grounded in historical figures and events—Bohdan Chmielnicki (1595–1657), for example, the leader of the Cossack uprising in 1648 or the Haidamak revolts in the eighteenth century, both of which had been tragic periods for the Jews. For the Ukrainians these evocations proved to be an impetus toward national cohesion, but as far as the Jews were concerned they only dredged up the generations-old Jew-hatred to which that region was prone (Cf. Slutsky, 1962, pp. 19–21).

As mentioned earlier, the unfolding events brought Ukrainian nationalism into confrontation with the Soviet government in Russia and prompted a modification of the attitude toward national minorities (Jews especially). The suspicion that the Jews are sympathetic to the enemy and ready to aid him against national interests is a recurrent motif in the antisemitic trends of various national movements. Never, this contention holds, could the majority trust the Jews during a national crisis. The mistrust of the Jews derived from the role played by Jews in the Soviet leadership, and was further nourished by the affinity of the Jews for Russia and Russian culture. Until it declared its independence, the Ukraine had been an integral part of greater Russia, lacking a distinct national identity

(Cobban, pp. 214–215). Furthermore, the western Ukraine of our own day was, until the defeat of the Central Powers, subject to Austrian rule (and known as Eastern Galicia), and the Ukrainians' attempt to establish their rule there had ended in their defeat at the hands of the Poles; the two parts of the Ukraine continued to exist separately.

The establishment of the Ukrainian Republic was an adventure to which the Jews were partners at the public and political level, but the rapid pace of events precluded their full integration into the nation-building process. As antisemitism intensified among the Ukrainians, the Jews found that their erstwhile allies could not be trusted even to safeguard life and property. By contrast, the Soviet authorities did their utmost to eradicate antisemitism and forestall pogroms (Weinryb, pp. 305–306). The dynamics of the situation ultimately led the antisemites to be confirmed in the suspicion they had harbored against the Jews from the outset—namely, that their true sympathies lay with the Russian enemy. The massacres, the impotence of the moderate Ukrainians, and the open incitement of the ultra-nationalists, all combined to thrust the Jews into the opposing camp (Slutsky, 1974, pp. 131–134).

The first attempt in postwar Eastern Europe to establish a national state recognizing the national rights of the minorities ended in abysmal failure. The romanticism that glorified the heroic deeds of the Cossacks who had slaughtered Jews and Poles in centuries past became the hallmark of Ukrainian nationalism.

Petlyura and the Pogroms in the Ukraine

The following are excerpts from a proclamation against the anti-Jewish pogroms published in Ukrainian and Yiddish in August 1919. It was signed by the Ukrainian Prime Minister and his Minister for Jewish Affairs.

> *The Socialist government* which heads the Republic *is waging, together with the Ataman Petlyura, a vigorous struggle against the pogroms.*[32] To investigate all the instances of rioting, the

[32] In April 1919 a socialist government was established in the Ukraine and attempts were made to eradicate antisemitism which was threatening to stain the country's name. Semyon Petlyura(1879–1926) was one of the leaders of the Ukrainian Social-Democratic Party and, from February 1919, also supreme commander of the Army ("Ataman"). Petlyura was gunned down by an enraged Jew, Shalom Schwarzbard (1886–1938), who wanted to avenge the victims of the pogroms. Schwarzbard was acquitted by a French court in 1927.

propaganda of the riots, and to bring the guilty to trial before a special military tribunal, a special investigative commission with broad powers has been established. The commission's members include representatives of the Jewish Democracy.[33]

An important body of *government inspectors* with extensive powers has been set up in the army, and *they are vigorously combating the pogroms* and the pogromist elements in the army.

The latest meeting of the inspectors unanimously approved the proposal of the Jewish Ministry that its representatives be co-opted to the inspecting body.

The Ataman Petlyura issued a series of orders demanding to put a total end to every attempt to perpetrate pogroms, and to execute the perpetrators by firing squad.[34] He placed full responsibility for this on the representatives of the military and civilian authorities. The special military tribunal has already carried out several death sentences. Many rioters have already been put to death by shooting.

—*The Jewish population actively supports the popular Ukrainian community*. In a series of declarations all the Jewish political parties expressed their support for the full independence of the Ukraine.[35]

. . . At this time, when the idea of peace between the peoples in the Ukraine is taking growing hold in the republican army, when the army is being purged of pogromist elements, and numerous army units are showing increasing signs of revival and healing, we see, in contrast, in the Bolshevik army growing signs of demoralization and internal disintegration.[36] Recently *there were several pogroms against Jews which were perpetrated by Bolshevik army units* of one kind or another. And just as the attacks of

[33] The Jewish parties took part in the activity of the Ministry for Jewish Affairs, and at first the minister was chosen according to an inter-party agreement. As the situation in the Ukraine deteriorated, the post was held by a series of functionaries who lacked solid public backing. It is thus stressed here that the leaflet reflects the stand of the Jewish public which supports the government's operations: the implication was that the Jews were ostensibly placing their trust in the government to uproot antisemitism.

[34] The government pressed Petlyura to take action against the rioters, but he was not prompt in abiding by the government's decision to act openly against the pogroms. The mentioning of Petlyura's cooperation indicated a united front against antisemitism, and was perhaps an attempt to exert moral pressure on him in this manner.

[35] The socialist government of the Ukraine had a Western orientation and wanted to show world opinion that it enjoyed the support of the population, including the Jews.

[36] Red Army troops did riot against Jews, and entire units shifted from one side to the other during the war. The shaky Ukrainian government sought to bolster its ranks and point to anarchy in the enemy camp.

the United Republican and Galician Army—*which contain a large number of Jewish soldiers and officers*[37]—are becoming stronger, so the demoralization in the Bolshevik army is growing.

Bolshevism, with its terror and its dictatorship, destroyed and devastated the forces of the united democracy, and serves as a base for the victorious attack of the reactionary Great Russians in the form of the "Denikinszina," which holds out the danger of the return of the old Czarist regime in the full sense of the word.[38] [Emphases in the original.] (Szajkowski, May 1970, pp. 13–14)

The Balfour Declaration

On 2 November 1917, the British Foreign Secretary, Lord Arthur James Balfour (1848–1930), sent a message to Lord Walter Rothschild (1868–1937) expressing Britain's readiness to assist in the "establishment in Palestine of a national home for the Jewish people." The document was the fruit of lengthy negotiations between the Zionist leadership and the authorities in London on the eve of Britain's conquest of Palestine from the Turks.

The British move was guided by several considerations: at one stage the hope was that a pro-Zionist declaration would impel the Jews in America to spur the entry of the United States into the War alongside Britain; it was feared that Germany would be the first to issue a declaration favoring the Zionists and would thereby gain the support of world Jewry, a development which, it was perceived, would affect the War's outcome; in the competition between Britain and France over the division of the Ottoman Empire, the Zionist argument could buttress the British claim to Palestine; and the outbreak of the Russian Revolution generated the notion that the national home would attract young Jews from Russia and thus thin the ranks of the revolutionary forces. Ranking British officials offered varying evaluations concerning the benefits to be derived from Zionism.

Historians, too, disagree about the relative importance of each of these considerations, as well as the political importance of the sympathy for Zionism enjoyed among the ruling circles in Britain.

---

[37] The units recruited in Eastern Galicia differed in character from the rest of the Ukrainian Army. Quite a few Jews served in them, in support of Ukrainian independence against the mooted annexation of Galicia by Poland.

[38] The independent Ukraine was at war not only with the Bolshevik Red Army but also with the White interventionist forces (referred to here as "Great Russians"), led by General Anton Ivanovich Denikin (1872–1947).

What all these considerations had in common was their esteem for the power of the Jews as a moving factor in world diplomacy—a factor liable to cause harm to Great Britain if not won over to Britain's side. In retrospect, it seems doubtful that the Balfour Declaration was so alluring an enticement for the Jewish public as to compel the non-Zionist leadership in the various Jewish communities to take it into account.

Equally untenable is the notion that in the midst of the War the world's Jews were capable of deciding, as a single body, to pursue a concerted international policy and to wield their influence purposefully to attain common goals. (Such an attempt was subsequently undertaken by the Jewish organizations at the peace conference under entirely new conditions; see below.) The idea that the Jews could impel the United States to enter the War was far-fetched enough, but the illusion that a pro-Zionist declaration would affect the course of the Russian Revolution attests to unrealistic thinking even among supposedly clear-headed British statesmen (Almog, pp. 8–11).

Here is testimony concerning the central figure to determine British policy toward Zionism, Lord Balfour, who was, indeed, a faithful friend of the Zionist movement all his life. The Zionist leader Chaim Weizmann (1874–1952) wrote in 1914 following a meeting with Balfour: "He told me how he had once had a long talk with Cosima Wagner [1837–1930] at Bayreuth and that he shared many of her antisemitic postulates" (Stein, p. 154). This is no easy matter, as Richard Wagner's widow was to emerge as the connecting link between the antisemitism of the deceased composer and the future Nazi movement. After the War, in 1919, Balfour believed that the revolutionary movements were being largely led by Jews and that their revolutionary ardor should be channeled toward more constructive aims. Yet it also bears stressing that Balfour greatly esteemed the Jews' contribution to religion, science and philosophy (Stein, pp. 156, 161), and that once having been persuaded of Zionism's just claims, he stood by it through thick and thin.

Actually, the notion of channeling the revolutionary energies of the Jews toward a national home in Palestine was then quite widespread and was frequently made by the Zionists themselves in their efforts to win over non-Jewish support (Stein, pp. 161, 348). The idea that the Jews possessed great political power, alongside the destructive potential attributed to them, could simultaneously serve Zionists and antisemites alike. The assessment of the Zionists' importance in the political arena was based not on hard facts but on the utilization of fears and hopes harbored by the Zionists' interlocutors—politicians, diplomats and journalists—who were trying to shape the postwar world. In the atmosphere of uncertainty that signified the last stage of the War, and particularly in the absence of reliable information from Russia, expectations were nourished in large measure by rumors, unfounded suppositions, and leaks.

Supporters of Zionism in the West tended to view the Jews as a mysterious and powerful two-headed being. One head was that of the evil, elusive, ever-changeable Jew. This archetype had now resurfaced in the form of the cosmopolitan subverter who was a menace to the nations and shook society's foundations. Yet the Zionist was also depicted stereotypically as the incarnation of the good Jew seeking only a corner of his own, ready to remove himself from the sight of others. From this point of view, a kind of morality play was performed by the good Jews against the bad. Since a victory of the cosmopolitan Jews would threaten the well-being of everybody else, all people of good will were duty-bound to assist the Zionists in getting the best of the revolutionaries.

Like the Zionists themselves, the non-Jewish pro-Zionists believed that the flaws in the Jews' character could be righted through rehabilitation in their future country. Inveterate antisemites, however, denied the possibility that Jewish character could be mended. Some, indeed, saw in the Zionist idea a far greater danger: Catholic circles feared a Jewish takeover of the Holy Land under the aegis of heretical Protestant England. For the Catholics, tidings of the resurrection of Jewish life in Palestine revived the historic confrontation between Christianity and Judaism and vested the Balfour Declaration with far-reaching theological ramifications.

Moreover, the upsurge of sympathy for Zionism in England faded with the passing of the critical War years, on the one hand, and with the growing difficulties attending settlement in Palestine, on the other. Naturally, chronic antisemites had never been under any illusion: they did not believe that Jews were capable of changing for the better and saw in every Jewish undertaking an act of deception. For them Zionism was merely the scourge of world Jewry in the alleged scheme to dominate the world. A sinister connection existed in the imagination of the Jew-haters between what the friends of Zionism termed "the national Jew" and "the international Jew." Jewry, the antisemites maintained, sought to triumph over the existing world; it was tantamount to an anti-national nationalism (Almog, pp. 11–13).

Zionism versus Bolshevism

The following two passages are taken from an article published in 1920 by the British statesman Winston Churchill (1874–1965).[39]

> . . . And it may well be that this same astounding race[40] may at the present time be in the actual process of producing another system of morals and philosophy, as malevolent as Christianity was benevolent, which, if not arrested, would shatter irretrievably all that Christianity has rendered possible. It would almost seem as if the gospel of Christ and the gospel of Antichrist[41] were destined to originate among the same people; and that this mystic and mysterious race had been chosen for the supreme manifestations, both of the divine and the diabolical.
>
> . . . Zionism has already become a factor in the political convulsions of Russia, as a powerful competing influence in Bolshevik circles with the international communistic system. Nothing could be more significant than the fury with which Trotsky[42] has attacked the Zionists generally and Dr. Weissman[43] in particular. The cruel penetration of his mind leaves him in no doubt that his schemes of a world-wide communistic State under Jewish domination are directly thwarted and hindered by this new ideal, which directs the energies and hopes of Jews in every land towards a simpler, a truer, and a far more attainable goal. The struggle which is now beginning between the Zionist and Bolshevik Jews is little less than a struggle for the soul of the Jewish people. (Churchill, p. 5)

[39] Churchill was at this time Secretary of State for War and Air Minister and supported the military intervention against the Soviets.

[40] The use of the term "race" was common at the time and did not necessarily indicate a racist approach.

[41] The Antichrist is mentioned in the New Testament as challenging Jesus Christ. The term underwent further transformations in later Christian literature.

[42] Trotsky was then People's Commissar for War and Supreme Commander of the Red Army.

[43] The erroneous spelling "Dr. Weissman" appears throughout the article. Chaim Weizmann (1874–1952) was already quite well-known in Britain, but he was obviously considered an outsider; a German-sounding name such as his was difficult to pronounce.

The Protocols of the Elders of Zion

In May 1920 the respectable London *Times* published a lengthy article on the appearance of *The Protocols of the Elders of Zion* in an English translation. The book appeared under the imprint of His Majesty's Printers, and the public tended to regard this chance occurrence as an affirmation of its credibility. The *Times* article afforded some legitimization to the intense interest in the "Jewish conspiracy," offering a tentative solution to the riddle of the cataclysmic events that had recently struck the world. The *Times*, it is true, raised several questions about the so-called document, and though not confirming the accusations against the Jews, left enough room for doubts. Other papers, less cautious, competed with one another in publishing articles by Russian exiles confirming that the revolution had in fact carried out the grand design of the *Protocols*. Other events, such as rebellion in Ireland, disturbances in Egypt, and unrest in India, were cited as proof of the alleged Jewish plan of world conquest.

In England the events which affected the British Empire were presented as the product of a partnership between world Jewry and the German enemy. In France the dissemination of the *Protocols* was accompanied by the claim that the scheme of world domination had been hatched jointly by world Jewry and the Freemasons. In Germany the *Protocols* won even greater success as a justification and excuse for the country's defeat in the War and the crises that followed. Foreign Minister Rathenau was described as one of the "Elders of Zion" and was assassinated in the wake of his signing an agreement with the Soviets, as though that confirmed his connection with the "Jewish plot." In the United States the *Protocols* were circulated at the initiative of the famous industrialist Henry Ford (1863–1947), who even founded his own weekly to disseminate similar ideas. Soon enough the *Protocols* were published in numerous languages and appeared in many editions and different versions. To this day they are cited by antisemites all over the world as the classical anti-Jewish document.

The success of the *Protocols* stemmed from the difficulty of refuting them by material evidence or of contradicting them through logical reasoning. Every deviation from acknowledged facts, every internal contradiction, could be explained away by reference to the *secret* conspiracy of World Jewry. Once the reader accepted the basic accusation, he perceived every attempt to refute it as yet another malicious pretense designed to lead him astray. The fear of the unknown and the attraction to the mysterious, the combination of half-truths with a failure to grasp the nature of the changes occurring in the real world all enabled the antisemites to posit the *Protocols* as an alternative explanation. The *Protocols* served to reinforce the critique of the liberal permissiveness which had shielded the Jews—those who, supposedly, strove to destroy the existing order and establish their own world rule. According to the tale, the secret conspiracy had already been in existence for hundreds of years, but in the past the Christian rulers had kept a tight grip on the reins of power and thus prevented the Jews from executing their designs; now that the concept of freedom had gained currency, it was abetting the Jews in their sowing of anarchy. The decline of faith, the free reign given to passion and greed, sedition and subversion, the economic crisis—all were presented as tools in the hands of the Jews in their scheme to take over one position after another in the economy and the judiciary, in education and politics, and in the press, but especially through invisible modes of influence.

The important point in the present context is that in their drive for world domination the "Elders of Zion" were said to have poisoned the relations between states and to have set Christian nations at each other's throats. The explanation for the minor role accorded nationalism in the *Protocols* emerges from their paramount goal: to depict the Jews as a subversive element endangering the peace of the entire world.

Eventually the fraud was uncovered and the *Protocols* were revealed for what they are: an antisemitic forgery. Indeed, the original document was wholly unrelated to the Jews; it was a polemical essay against Napoleon III, from 1864, written by a French lawyer, Maurice Joly, in the form of an imaginary dialogue between the enlightened thinker Charles Montesquieu (1755–1789) and the political philosopher Niccolo Machiavelli (1469–1527). The case for manipulation of power and cunning is attributed to Machiavelli, who in Joly's book stands for the French emperor and his policy. The forgers foisted the argument on to the "Elders of Zion" and extended its scope from the governing of France to the conquest of the world.

The idea of a shadow-government striving to rule the world is basically not a new one. It often cropped up in writings against the Freemasons and in time was directed against the Jews as well. Antisemitic literature since the mid-nineteenth century contained several motifs which were subsequently expanded in *The Protocols of the Elders of Zion*. The propagators of the *Protocols* insisted that it was an authentic work that had been kept secret by the Jews but had now come to light and had revealed their schemes for all the world to see. The combination of ancient demonology and up-to-date references seemed to transform the work into a kind of magic key able to unlock the secrets of world politics—hence its wide popularity precisely in a period of turmoil and change (*see* Cohn, *Warrant for Genocide*).

Yet what, it could be asked, was the connection between the world-wide plot attributed to the Jews and nationalism? The Jews, so the antisemites argued, pretended to speak in the name of religion but were actually no more than a zealous tribe with subversive tentacles everywhere, a kind of *anti-national nationality*. In contrast to the violence attributed to the Jews, the Christian peoples are portrayed as innocent victims of incitement and intrigue. Remove the Jew and all the others would live in perfect harmony. True, conflicts between nations did exist, but antisemitism would open the eyes of all to see who their real enemy was. This argument was cleverly produced to make the *Protocols* common coin everywhere. Their circulation in one country drew on their earlier success in another, as though the truth of the accusations against the Jews had been proven not just locally but by well-known evidence the world over.

In August 1921 the London *Times* published a series of articles proving that the *Protocols* were a complete forgery (Graves, p. 9) One hundred and nineteen prominent public figures, headed by President Woodrow Wilson (1856–1924), protested publicly against the publication of the *Protocols* in the United States (Higham, p. 285). Unsuspecting persons who fell into the trap laid by antisemitic propaganda with the appearance of the *Protocols* in the West could be convinced now that the plot was a mere fabrication. But legal suits, public protests and various books and articles against the *Protocols* did not invalidate them in the eyes of inveterate antisemites. Indeed, the counter-claims incorporated the fight against the *Protocols* as part of the expected reaction by "world Jewry" and its lackeys. The postwar world had much use for this demonological explanation which simultaneously answered many of the questions generated by the events of the period. The *Protocols* connected all revolutionaries everywhere, the Jewish bankers, and Zionist aspirations. Many thought they had found the key to a vexing mystery.

Zionism, Judaism and the Protocols

The following is taken from the epilogue of one of the *Protocols* published in the United States under a somewhat modified title.

The first Zionist Congress was held in Basle, Switzerland, in 1897, and Theodor Herzl, a newspaper correspondent of Vienna, was foremost in its inception. This movement was the first among the Jews with international membership, since the dispersal, that possessed a distinctly political character.[44] Herzl was a Germanized Jew and received official recognition for the "return to Palestine" scheme, first from the German Government and later from the Kaiser on the visit of the latter to Palestine in 1898.[45] The nationalization of the Jewish people in a geographical sense was his open ambition. Nilus states in his introduction that the "Protocols of Zion" were first read at this Congress by Herzl, but does not give the evidence on which he bases this statement.[46] The same idea was expressed in the introduction to the German edition which was published at Charlottenburg last year, to the effect that the "Protocols" having been read from day to day at the Basle Congress, they were sent as read to Frankfort-am-Main.[47] The disclosure of them came through the infidelity of the messenger!

Herzl's point of view on many subjects is interesting. He believed in a monarchical form of government and recognized the revolutionary instinct within the Jew.[48] The Jew carries with him wher-

[44] Prior to the creation of the World Zionist Organization a similar accusation was frequently levelled at the *Alliance Israélite Universelle*.

[45] Herzl, as is known, tried to enlist the support of various governments in order to persuade the Ottoman Empire to grant Zionism an official status in Palestine. His contacts with the Kaiser and German leaders influential in Istanbul bore no fruit. He did, however, enjoy success in England.

[46] Sergei Nilus edited one of the Russian versions of the *Protocols*, first published in 1905 in St. Petersburg. The American edition is somewhat more sophisticated and takes an ostensibly critical approach to the original text.

[47] The first German edition of the *Protocols* was printed in 1919 in the fashionable Berlin suburb of Charlottenburg, but appeared only in mid-January 1920. The editor of this edition added a totally imaginary tale of his own about the way the document reached Frankfurt from Basle, with the help of a bribe paid to a Jewish messenger by a Czarist spy.

[48] There is some truth in the rendering of Herzl's preference for the future regime in the Jewish state. Europeans might have taken a favorable view of Herzl's monarchist leanings, but the American editor undoubtedly looked askance at his political philosophy. By contrast, he stresses what Herzl had to say about the tendency of Jews to support revolutionary movements—except that Herzl makes no mention of any such Jewish "instinct," referring, rather, to a reaction to anti-Jewish discrimination and repression. According to Herzl, the Zionist solution would direct the

ever he goes the seeds of anti-Semitism, and anti-Semitism to him served as a means for maintaining the international nationality of the Jewish people.[49] It was therefore a necessary corollary that anti-Semitism should exist. To him a Jew was a Jew, regardless of citizenship in the land of his adoption and sojourn.

A complicated situation has arisen as the result of the fulfilled dream of Herzl and other ardent Zionists in respect to the citizenship of the Jew. They have strongly urged the adoption of a system of citizenship of a dual nature similar to that which Germany tried in adopting the Delbruck law.[50] At present, the Palestinian Jew is ruled by England under a mandate from the League of Nations and in the appointment of Sir Herbert Samuel as High Commissioner, England has given recognition to the Zionist organization.[51] The San Remo Conference has also recognized the aspirations of the Zionists.[52] The danger of this situation from a political standpoint is evident.

. . . Jewish nationalism, than which there is no stronger on earth, is dependent upon anti-Semitism for its continued existence, a point which makes a settlement of the "Jewish question" more difficult than is usual in such struggles.

It is therefore to the interest of the Jewish leaders to stimulate

Jews' revolutionary energy into constructive channels. This was one of the arguments he used in his negotiations with government representatives in various countries.

[49] Here we find the barbed edge of the ostensibly moderate discussion of Zionism and Jewish nationalism. The article makes use of passages from Herzl to argue that antisemitism is helpful to the Jews and is particularly necessary for Zionism. Whereas Herzl saw antisemitism as a reaction to Jewish anomaly, the author ascribes to him the view that the Jews evoke antisemitism consciously and deliberately. At bottom, this is the reiteration of an ancient motif: that the Jews deliberately isolate themselves and abhor humanity, hence Jew-hatred is a completely justified response to their behavior. What is new here is the attempt to come to terms with the claim for national identity of a group that is dispersed throughout the world, by attributing to the Jews an "international nationality"—and ultimately a conspiracy.

[50] Rudolf Delbrück (1817–1903) was a German statesman who initiated liberal laws during the early Bismarck era. The reference here is to a dual nationality law, which aroused criticism in the US.

[51] The appointment of Sir Herbert Samuel as the first High Commissioner to Palestine was a British political decision. The Mandatory authorities did grant official standing to a Jewish representation—not to the World Zionist Organization as such, but to the Jewish Agency, which incorporated non-Zionists as well.

[52] The San Remo Conference (April 18–26, 1920) drafted the later peace treaty with Turkey. It also decided to grant Britain the Mandate for Palestine. The decision was preceded by the Allies' assent to incorporate the Balfour Declaration in the arrangement concerning the future of Palestine.

anti-Semitism as an influence required to maintain the integrity of the race, and in accord with the provisions to be found in Procotol IX.[53] (*The Protocols of the Wise Men of Zion*, pp. 156–158, 163)

Summary: In the Wake of the Great War

The First World War raised patriotism to the status of a supreme value. The Jews, who were divided between the two warring camps, generally blended into the belligerent atmosphere and identified with the struggle of their respective countries. The War itself dragged on beyond all expectations and claimed victims on a large scale from all sides. Once weariness set in from the protracted war effort, the population cast around for those to blame for the troubles—and frequently they found the answer in the Jews. The antisemitic reaction was especially acute in the defeated countries, particularly in Germany, which was unable to face the sense of failure. The postwar atmosphere engendered the legend of the treason which had supposedly brought about the defeat of the German Army. In the eyes of the ultra-nationalists—those loyal to the Emperor and his army—the Jews were domestic enemies with whose help the foreign powers had vanquished the German Empire.

The turning point of the War came in 1917, when the United States joined the fighting on the side of the Allied Powers, and even more strikingly in the wake of the revolutions which jolted Russia that year. The democracies held the advantage over the Central Powers, but the winds of revolution began to blow in Europe. The War caused the collapse of the multinational empires and accelerated processes of national and social change. While the victors were engaged in reshaping the political map of Europe and the Near East, civil wars, attempts at revolution, and struggles between rival national movements broke out in various locales.

The Jews suffered directly from the ravages of the War, which uprooted whole communities, and from pogroms perpetrated by army units and local rabble in Eastern Europe. The triumph of the

---

[53] Chapter IX of the *Protocols* attributes to Jewish leaders the intention to use antisemitism as a weapon to maintain internal discipline among the Jews. The American edition extends this argument well beyond the narrow tactical aspect it had in the original version: the manipulation of antisemitism is perceived not only as a means to control the internal life of the Jews, but as the central reason for their separate existence, in marked contrast to the usual assimilation process in society (the "melting pot" ethos in the United States). As will be recalled, Jewish leaders themselves are said to provoke antisemitism, since it supposedly benefits them.

Russian Revolution, which many regarded as essentially a Jewish revolution, evoked outrage and apprehension and stamped the Jews as dangerous revolutionaries. The same year saw the issuing of the Balfour Declaration, which assured the Jews an official standing in Palestine at the War's end. These two events, the Russian Revolution and the Balfour Declaration, occurred almost simultaneously and were interpreted as a victory for International Jewry. The "Jewish Question" was discussed extensively at the political level and reverberated in the press and in public life in numerous countries.

The rise of national movements, which fought for their share in the spoils of the old empires, aggravated ethnic conflicts. The Jews were caught in a web of conflicting loyalties and were frequently the targets of hostility and suspicion from all sides. Jewish nationalism admittedly gained a modicum of recognition, both in terms of Zionist hopes *vis-à-vis* Palestine and national rights for the Jewish minority in the newly independent states. At the same time, however, misconceptions grew concerning the duality in the standing of the Jews—revolutionaries and bourgeois, nationalists and cosmopolitans, Zionists and assimilationists. The world now heard more about the Jews than it had before the War, attributed great power to them, and failed to understand their motives.

In the postwar atmosphere, marked by contradictory hopes for the future, the public's gaze increasingly focused on the Jews. From the depths of prejudice which had prevailed within Christianity for untold generations there sprang a readiness to attribute to the Jew a negative role in every national and social struggle. This was an atmosphere highly congenial to the spread of *The Protocols of the Elders of Zion*, which accused the Jews of deviously hatching a secret plot for world conquest. The Russian Revolution and the turmoil that afflicted other countries in the postwar years were seen as part of the Jews' plan to exploit an emergency situation for their own ends. The famous forgery was translated into many languages, published in numerous editions and widely distributed. The allegation that resonated most strongly among the public was that the Jews were a highly cohesive national group with tentacles reaching out, octopus-like, in a struggle against other national bodies. Zionism and Revolution were seen as salient expressions of a single Jewish entity cloaked in various guises and striving to undermine the foundations of non-Jewish civilization.

6

Between the Two World Wars

The Rights of National Minorities

Following World War I official sanction was accorded to the Right of Self-Determination and bestowed upon peoples that had formerly been part of the multinational empires. Nations that had lost their independence, such as Poland, and peoples that had fought for their liberation, such as the Ukrainians, gained sovereign status. This process was attended by complex problems, as many of the territories in question were ethnically mixed and no clear-cut boundaries could be drawn between various groups. As a result, the new states were inhabited by large national minorities, notwithstanding the now dominant ideal of the *nation-state*. This contradiction was to spark friction between majority and minority groups living under the same roof and in some cases cause conflicts between neighboring states, each acting as the guardian for a minority residing beyond its borders.

The Jewish minority presented the most difficult problem. Large numbers of Jews had resided in the now defunct empires, and the majority groups in the successor states usually regarded their Jewish compatriots as constituting an alien body. However, unlike other national minorities, Jews could not turn to a neighboring state for protection. Furthermore, several of the new states, Poland in particular, saw the Jews in their midst as a vestige of their previous subjugation, which could somehow impinge on their newly won freedom.

The League of Nations, established after the War to resolve international conflicts peacefully, was to introduce a legal procedure for maintaining minority rights. Between the two World Wars international machinery was set up to protect the rights of national minorities. The new states granted the Jews civil rights and formally undertook to provide the conditions which would permit them to retain their national, cultural and religious character as a recognized national minority. Jewish organizations sprang up to oversee the fulfillment of the clauses concerning these rights and to represent local Jewish interests. There also emerged an all-Jewish organizational network, led by the *Comité des Délégations Juives auprès de la Conférence de la Paix*, beyond the jursidiction of any individual state. This was frowned upon by the nation-states and may have heightened the antagonism between the majority population and the Jewish minority (Feinberg, pp. 311–322).

Whereas in the past the Jews of the Austro-Hungarian Empire, for example, had been able to extricate themselves to some extent from the competition between rival national movements, Jews were now much more vulnerable. The friction between competing national movements was transmuted into conflicts between sovereign states. Having been made citizens of these states, the Jews owed allegiance to their new countries. The situation was particularly grave in areas disputed by numerous countries and which sometimes passed from hand to hand (Janowsky, pp. 151–152). Such was the situation that spurred the *Comité des Délégations Juives* at the peace conference to demand that the Jews be recognized as a separate national group. Although based on the actual situation of the Jewish communities, the demand was also influenced by the Jewish national idea. For some time espoused by certain Jewish groups, the national idea was now reinvigorated in view of the recognition accorded to other nations; the unfolding vistas of the postwar world seemed to offer prospects for the idea's realization.

Running parallel with the surge of Jewish national consciousness, there was also an intensification of the opposing trend, which aspired to a fuller integration of the Jews. Those supportive of the Jews' assimilation considered it their patriotic duty to gain their participation in the building of the new state. Assimilationists also believed that this was an opportune moment for the Jews to show their sincere wish to become an integral part of the nation. In practice, the assimilationists' struggle against Jewish nationalism was to abet the authorities' inclination to infringe upon minority rights.

Moreover, the primary obstacle to assimilation was the hostile attitude of the majority toward Jews: in most of the new states, traditional Jew-hatred was buttressed by political, social and economic opposition to their integration. The triumphant nationalism in Central and Eastern Europe was often narrow-minded and sought to impose a uniform identity on minority groups. At the same time, this was a nationalism incapable of the genuine receptiveness necessary for a gradual and harmonious assimilation.

The Jews presented a particularly difficult case because of religious differences and the deeply ingrained traditional Jew-hatred. Moreover widespread social changes also generated conflicts of interest between non-Jews and Jews. In countries which until recently had been predominantly agricultural, the Jews were a conspicuously urban element. Precisely the assimilationists, who were part of the *bourgeoisie* or practised the free professions, encountered enmity on the part of the parallel stratum which in this period sprang up rapidly among non-Jews.

Frequently antisemitism became the semi-official ideology of the young state, serving as the social cement for building a nation out of the feudal strata which had just entered modernity. Even where the government tried to practice liberal policies, undercurrents of antisemitism were never far below the surface.

The Jewish Question in Slovakia

Vávro Šrobár was the Minister for Slovakian Affairs in the government of Czechoslovakia.[1] He replies here to accusations levelled by Chaim Weizmann, on behalf of the World Zionist Organization,[2] at the Czechoslovak *Chargé D'Affaires* in London concerning the incitement of anti-Jewish pogroms in Slovakia in 1919.

The Jewish Question in Slovakia has an aspect and character completely divergent from that in Western countries.[3] Slovakia, which in cultural and economic respects was systematically oppressed by the Magyars, soon became an Eldorado for the most

---

[1] The author, Dr. Vávro Šrobár, a country doctor by profession, was among the leaders of the independence movement of Slovakia. He then joined the federal government of Prague as Minister for Slovak Affairs in the Federal Government, residing in Bratislava and not the capital, Prague.

[2] Weizmann's appeal followed the arrest of Zionist activists and their incarceration under harsh conditions at Terezin, the well-known Teresienstadt. The response totally ignored the request for the release of the Zionist leaders.

[3] This contention was constantly repeated by national leaders in Central and Eastern Europe in their contacts with the West, serving as a pretext for the existence of antisemitism in the newly established states.

diverse elements, who came to take advantage of the backwardness of the people.[4] Besides the Magyar nobility and the Magyar
officials I am, to my regret, bound to say that it was the Jewish
estate-owners and innkeepers who for whole decades did the most
serious harm to the Slovak people.[5]

This phenomenon is met with nowhere in Western Europe, for no
state was ever established there on the degenerate foundations
of wickedness, of plundering and stultifying the people [as in]
Hungary, the notorious "Island of Liberty."[6] The Magyar Government was astute enough to make a tool of the Jews in Slovakia to
carry out their violent policy of Magyarization, and only too often
they found them devoted helpers, informers, agents-provocate-
urs, spies and agitators against the Entente.[7] It is unfortunately
necessary to assert, and the assertion can be substantiated by
thousands of proofs, that the Jews in Slovakia became the
exponents of the most active intrigues. For this, it is to the interest of all right-minded Jews in the world that this system, which
corrupted the race, was destroyed in Austria-Hungary.[8] During
the war this hostile activity towards the Slovak people became
more violent. As the result of information lodged by the Jews,

[4] Following the constitutional reform of 1867 in the Hapsburg Empire, the autonomous administration of Hungary vigorously engaged in imposing its culture and
authority over the peoples under its jurisdiction. Many Jews in Slovakia were considered Hungarians because of the language they spoke. In this way the Jews were
ostensibly co-opted to the ruling elite and abetted government's policy. We also find
here an allusion to the socioeconomic role played by the Jews in backward Slovakia—
in industry, commerce and banking—the implication being that this amounted to
the exploitation of the local population.

[5] Ever since the Jews were permitted to acquire land in the second half of the
nineteenth century, the number of Jewish estate owners had risen. In the rural
areas the Jews also acted as brokers, innkeepers, shopkeepers, and the like, and
antisemitic incitement had been directed against them even prior to the War's outbreak.

[6] In 1868 Hungary promulgated the "law on the equality of rights of the nationalities," which in theory assured autonomous rights to the various national minorities
but was not put into practice. This may be what the author is referring to in describing Hungary's pretension to be an "Island of Liberty."

[7] While criticizing the Jews for their relations with the local Slovak population,
the author makes an insinuation of an entirely different kind: disloyalty to Western
democracy. The implicit argument is that Jewish loyalty went to the defeated Central Powers—Germany and Austro-Hungary—whereas the Slovaks are loyal to the
victors. It should be borne in mind that the exchange of letters took place between
Bratislava, Prague, and London, hence the accusation was meant to denigrate Slovak Jews in the eyes of the British.

[8] The attempt to differentiate between the local Jewish population and the Jews
in the West evidently sought to influence the latter to stop backing their brethren
in Slovakia. Incidentally, the term "race" as used in this context referred to an
ethnic group and not necessarily to a racial group in the strict sense of the word.

persons were imprisoned and executed. In return for all this they were rewarded by the Government with various concessions and privileges, to the detriment of the Slovak people.

When the revolution occurred, and the Czechoslovak nation threw off the tyrant's yoke, it was the Jews who worked as Magyar agitators against our Republic.[9] During the Bolshevist invasion of June, 1919, it was again the Slovak Jews who proved themselves an element hostile to the people and Republic, who led Bolshevist troops, showed them the way, and denounced the loyal Slovaks, so that these were then shot or tortured by the Bolshevists.[10] The Czechoslovak Government, having espoused the principle of absolute equality and liberty for its subjects, had to exert its whole influence, even at the cost of its own popularity, to prevent the people who had suffered so much injustice from avenging themselves on those who formed quite an essential factor in the system opposed to them.[11] And it is to the credit of our Republic that, with the exception of a few unimportant cases, which were immediately suppressed by the Government at the outset, justice was here dealt out by a legal course.

This order, this stability of the conditions which not even most violent and malevolent agitation succeeded in destroying, becomes especially striking when we consider that in the Ukrainian People's Republic 120,000 Jews fell as victims of pogroms. In our Republic, on the other hand, not a single Jew perished.[12]

. . . It is not the fault of the Government if in Slovakia the majority of these culprits are Jews.[13]

[9] The initial stages of Czechoslovak independence saw an attempt to establish an East-Slovak Republic under Hungarian aegis. The attempt was foiled by Czech troops, who invaded Slovakia and cooperated with the author and his colleagues.

[10] The Communist revolution in Hungary led by Béla Kun tried to restore the defeated East-Slovak Republic. Soon enough the Hungarian Army was forced to withdraw from Slovakia by order of the Western Powers. In the wake of this turmoil, the Slovak population attacked the Jews (like the "White Terror" in Hungary), but damage was generally confined to property (the "November Pillage").

[11] The united Czechoslovak government was indeed enlightened, compared with the other new states in Central and Eastern Europe. The political system led by President Masaryk was based on cooperation between the nations forming the Republic, in contrast to the chauvinist orientation of other new states. The attitude toward the Jews was also generally fair.

[12] According to the Jewish demographer Jacob Lestschinsky, approximately 75,000 persons were killed in the Ukrainian riots from 1917 to 1921, a period which extends beyond the span of the Ukraine's ephemeral independence. The far higher figure cited by the Minister also hinted at the danger Jews faced from the Slovak populace, had it not been for the government's protection.

[13] The offenses mentioned in this paragraph refer to the forgery of commercial

It will therefore be a noble task for Jewish organizations to exert a beneficial influence upon those of their co-religionists in the villages of Slovakia who have acted against their own interests.[14] (*The Jews of Czechoslovakia* pp. 226–227)

Jews in Poland

The situation of the Jews in Poland was harsher than in most other countries. Following the pogroms there at the end of the War, a number of attempts were made to probe into the nature of the Jewish problem in Poland. The authorities were aware that the complaints reaching the West were liable to adversely affect Poland's international standing. During the first years of Poland's independence, several foreign delegations visited the country to examine the situation of the Jewish population. One such delegation, which arrived in 1919, was headed by Sir Stewart Samuel (1856–1926), brother of Herbert Samuel, the first British High Commissioner of Palestine. Samuel submitted a detailed report of his findings, but his deputy, Captain Peter Wright, saw fit to submit a separate report, which took a stance far closer to the position of the Polish authorities. Wright stated, *inter alia*:

The Polish Jews are not Poles; they are Jews. The Peace Conference may make them Poles in 1919; but the Congress of Vienna in 1815 made them Russians. It is a pity they cannot always switch from one to the other to suit the decisions of statesmen, and after being good Russians for the nineteenth, become good Poles for the twentieth century, but it is excusable. The attach-

documents, hoarding of food, smuggling, and the like, as well as attempts to foment trouble between Czechs and Slovaks, Bolshevik agitation, and menacing the public order. By appending economic offenses to hostile political activity, the writer is able to impute to the Jews all the misfortunes afflicting the new state. The author maintains that the authorities arrested the offenders irrespective of religion or nationality, yet he still accuses the Jews in particular and asserts that they constitute the majority of the criminals.

[14] This is a reiteration of the self-righteous notion which had already appeared elsewhere in the letter. Despite the Czechoslovak fairness toward the Jews, a deep sediment of antisemitism is discernible in the words of the Slovak leader. As long as the Federal Republic endured, hostile feelings were shunted aside by official policy, but these feelings undoubtedly continued to fester beneath the surface. Everything stated here was transmitted by the Foreign Ministry in Prague in reply to Weizmann's appeal; the temporary *Chargé d'affaires* in the Czechoslovak legation in London conveyed the reply verbatim and appended a rather equivocal covering letter, which seemed to attach official sanction to the rather antisemitic missive of the Slovak leader.

ment of a great number of Jews in Poland to Russia is sincere, no less than the attachment of many to the soil of Poland, where they can trace their descent for centuries. But Russia is the promised land for most Jews; their material home as much as Germany is their spiritual home.

The British officer voiced what he had apparently heard from his Polish hosts: the Jews were aliens in Poland even though they had resided there for centuries; their loyalty was allegedly reserved for Poland's sworn enemies—Russia and Germany. On the old claim that the Jews had served the Czar and the concomitant suspicion that they were agents of Bolshevism, the author superimposed the accusation, dating from the War, that they were the instrument of the Germans:

> It was with the Jews that the Germans set up their organization to squeeze and drain Poland—Poles and Jews included—of everything it had; it was in concert with Jews that German officials and officers towards the end carried on business all over the country. In every department and region they were the instruments of the Germans, and poor Jews grew rich and lordly as the servants of their masters.

Wright, seeking to draw an analogy between the situations in Poland and in England, asked the reader how he would react if every second or third person in London were a Jew, a foreigner with peculiar ways, who spoke the language of the enemy (i.e. Yiddish, because of its kinship with German). The British officer claimed to have discovered what the Poles themselves had failed to discern: "The East Jews are Jews and Jews only." He himself did not regard the Jews as enemy agents, but he implied that they were devoid of any feelings of loyalty toward non-Jews. Thus, even the claim for the existence of a distinctive Jewish nation merely confirmed that the Jews were egotistical and utterly lacking in loyalty.

Appended to the delegation's two reports was an accompanying letter from the British representative in Warsaw to the Foreign Office in London. The British diplomat tried to mitigate the aspersions cast on the host government by explaining that the atrocities perpetrated against the Jews in Poland were negligible compared with what had been done to the Jews elsewhere, because of "the strong nationalist feelings everywhere aroused by the Great War" (Samuel, p. 32; Heller, pp. 84–85). The British diplomat was referring to the pogroms in the Ukraine seemingly to diminish the weight of the accusations against Poland. Nonetheless, despite his apparent cynicism, he did not deny the facts themselves.

Polish antisemitism, whose emergence has already been noted in previous chapters, became part of the national ethos and acquired a semi-official status following independence. The partisans of the nation-state looked askance at the existence of a large and highly distinctive Jewish minority consisting of a broad stratum of traditional Jews and smaller groups of a modern Jewish identity. Concurrently, the process of Jewish entry into Polish culture continued apace, and a class emerged which sought to be part of the Polish nation. Yet Polish nationalism was densely interwoven with religion. Even Poland's singularity *vis-à-vis* the surrounding states bore religious trappings: Catholic Poland lay between Orthodox Russia and Lutheran Germany. It was difficult for Poland to accept as Poles Jews who would not accept the Catholic faith, while social reservations prevailed toward the assimilationists and even converts from Judaism (Cf. Shmeruk, p. 91, n.21).

Antisemitism in Poland, then, tended to be nearly total, and it intensified with the deterioration of the political and economic situation in the interwar period. During the 1930s organized antisemitism played a growing role in Poland's political life. The authorities gave their backing to an economic boycott of the Jews and did not prevent hooligans from imposing violent terror. Bloody riots broke out from time to time in cities and towns throughout the country. Jewish students were relegated to special benches in university lecture halls, and a veritable regime of anti-Jewish discrimination made itself felt in various domains. As the situation in Poland deteriorated in the 1930s, antisemitism was co-opted into its ultranationalist policies. Although Germany's growing aggressiveness threatened Polish independence, it did not shut off Poland from ideas originating in its powerful neighbor to the west (Ringelblum, pp. 10–22).

The Polish Authorities Present the Jewish Problem

The following passages are taken from British Foreign Office reports on contacts with the Polish Foreign Minister and officials of the Ministry in 1936–1938. The Poles request assistance in expatriating Jews from Poland.[15]

---

[15] The documents quoted here indicate an exacerbation of the antisemitic atmosphere in Poland folowing the death of Marshal Józef Pilsudski (1867–1935). The

The British Ambassador in Poland Reports on his Conversation with the Polish Foreign Minister, October 23, 1936

The Polish Jews had in the past gained a livelihood as retailers in the small towns and villages, but were now rapidly losing this business owing to the growth of the co-operative movement and larger concerns having greater facilities of distribution.[16] The peasant also, both in a cultural and material sense, was improving his outlook and becoming more restive in regard to the Jewish monopoly of this business.[17] While he hoped that Jewish emigration to Palestine might be resumed on a larger scale at some future date, he felt that this was not sufficient for Jewish requirements and that some other outlets must be found for them.[18] (No. 449; [C7552/6703/55] PRO/FO 371/19964)

Memorandum of a Meeting With the Polish Embassy Staff in London; October 29, 1936

The Polish Government, he said, were "anxious to find places in which to settle some of their Jewish citizens, especially from the country districts," giving as the pretext that they were coming into the towns and threatening to take the places of the industrial workers. Mr. Wigram gave him little encouragement, replying that unemployment must be regarded as an internal problem, to be faced by each Government for itself.[19] ([C7707/6703/55] PRO/FO371/19964)

situation was aggravated even further after 1937, when government policy began to come under the sway of the newly formed camp of "National Unity," with its antisemitic and chauvinist platform. Polish authorities pressed Britain and the League of Nations to increase the immigration quota for Polish Jews to Palestine. At the same time, various plans were put forward for the settlement of Polish Jews in other countries, such as African colonies.

[16] The Polish Foreign Minister did not reveal that the anti-Jewish economic policy was initiated by powerful interests with government backing. An anti-Jewish boycott was actually in effect: public institutions did not hire Jews, while Jews were denied government credit and were discriminated against even in taxation. This policy often involved acts of violence and repression against Jews.

[17] Not even at a diplomatic meeting did the Polish statesman try to conceal his total identification with the ousting of the Jews from their traditional sources of livelihood. As becomes clear from the documents here, the Polish government had no constructive program to enable Jews who had lost their former positions to find alternative means of livelihood. The usual solution of the Polish authorities was to encourage large-scale Jewish emigration.

[18] The conversation was held after the outbreak of the riots in Palestine in 1936 and prior to the arrival there of the Royal Commission that examined the Arabs' demand for a total halt to Jewish immigration. It is noteworthy that the official Polish spokesmen are here depicted as supposedly representing the interests of Polish Jewry. This was a cynical use of the Jews' plight, which had been caused by the Polish authorities.

[19] The British memorandum expresses reservations about the argument of the

Report by the Director of the Central European Desk on Meeting the Polish Ambassador: December 9th, 1938

I met the Polish Ambassador at lunch today. . . . He made the following points about the Jewish question:

Poland's Jewish problem was much more serious than Germany's.[20] The Jewish population was proportionately much greater. The Germans were persecuting the Jews largely for reasons of doctrine; in Poland the problem was a very pressing economic one. He felt very strongly that the Polish aspect of the Jewish problem ought to be taken into consideration now, when world opinion was roused and had for the first time come to understand that a Jewish problem exists in Europe.[21] If the present opportunity was missed, nothing would be done for the Polish Jews and the problem would grow in gravity. Anti-Semitism was increasing in Europe, and he lived in dread of an outbreak of pogroms in Poland, which might very well occur unless Poland's Jewish problem was tackled at a very early date.[22] If some large scale scheme could be evolved in which the Polish Jews could share, the anti-Jewish agitation would die down and the problem could be tackled rather more at leisure.[23] Unlike the German Jews,

Polish representatives that the economic problems of Poland's Jewish citizens are an international issue to be resolved by emigration. These reservations are characteristic of a law-abiding system, such as in Britain, yet underlying them was also resistance to the Polish pressure to issue entry certificates for Palestine and to absorb Jewish immigrants in the British Empire.

[20] Diplomatic language allows for this remark to be interpreted positively—namely, that the Poles expressed compassion with regard to Germany's Jews, who suffered under the Nazi regime. The conclusion, however, indicates that this was not their intent. On the contrary, the Polish ambassador accepted the Nazi contention that Germany had a Jewish problem. This was seemingly an objective problem, generated by a foreign minority which did not belong to the national entity and evoked a negative reaction (as the human body may reject a transplanted organ).

[21] Based on the tacit assumption concerning the validity of the antisemitic case in Nazi Germany, official Poland insists that it be assisted in overcoming its even greater Jewish problem. At the same time it is insinuated that the Jews constitute a problem all over Europe and that Britain, too, should acknowledge the need to begin solving the Jewish problem.

[22] It is unclear from the report whether this was to be construed as an expression of concern that pogroms were liable to occur or was meant as an outright threat. The wave of pogroms in 1935–1936, culminating in the organized pogrom in the town of Przytyk, was followed by a new series of anti-Jewish riots in 1937–38. The ambassador's remarks can also be taken as an excuse for past disturbances and an explanation of the government's inability to cope with the situation.

[23] The emphasis here is on cooperation with representatives of the Jewish community in order to demonstrate to the world both the Polish government's good will in espousing a constructive policy of Jewish emigration and the need to obtain Jewish support for government policy. The Jewish response to the authorities' hostile policy took various forms, such as enlisting international support and organizing

the Polish Jews were labourers and artisans rather than intellectuals. They would make good colonists in such a place as Northern Rhodesia, and would be anxious to emigrate at the rate of some 100,000 per year.[24] (PRO FO 371/22540)

The Weimar Republic

For twenty years between the two World Wars Europe was driven from shortlived hopes for a better world toward a sense of decline and despair. The international setting after World War I—democratic republics based on the peace treaties and the League of Nations—proved inadequate. Brief periods of quiet and well-being were punctuated by economic crises, internal instability, and conflicts between states. Not only the vanquished, who were made to pay the price of their defeat, but the victors, too, emerged weakened from the War.

As far as the Jews were concerned, equality of rights had been further extended, and in some countries Jews had been granted recognition as a national minority, but the overall drift was to their disadvantage. Isolationist chauvinism, xenophobia, political polarization, and antisemitic feelings all intensified in this period, albeit with occasional fluctuations here and there.

The German republic established at Weimar found itself blighted from the outset by the well-known legend of the "dagger in the back" which intimated that Germany's defeat in the War had been caused by the treachery of an internal enemy. The state was unable to take the edge off the polarization within the German nation. The ultra-nationalists, enmeshed in a net of movements and clubs, looked on the Republic as a foreign body. An abyss separated the exponents of an ostensibly *authentic* nationalism from the legitimate spokesmen of the nation. Democratic freedom was exploited by extremist groups

self-defense; on the other hand, Jewish public opinion became more radical. The authorities wished to placate the Jews in order to secure their cooperation in implementing a policy that would result in their phased emigration.

[24] As early as 1936, Foreign Minister Józef Beck (1894–1944) asked French Prime Minister Léon Blum (1872–1950) to examine the possibility of having Jewish immigrants from Poland settle in the African colony of Madagascar. Emigration was also a central issue for Jewish public opinion in Poland. One should recall in this connection the storm that erupted in the wake of a comment made in 1927 in the United States by the Polish Zionist leader Yitshak Grünbaum (1879–1970) that there were a million redundant Jews in Poland. In 1936, Vladimir Jabotinsky (1880–1940) announced his "Evacuation Program" for settling 750,000 Polish Jews in Palestine within ten years—75,000 per year. By the way, the figure of 100,000 was mentioned after the War by Chaim Weizmann, regarding entry certificates for Palestine. The plan gained the support of US President Harry Truman (1884–1972) but was rejected by Britain.

on both the Right and the Left to amass strength and undermine that very democracy.

Nationalism served as a common denominator for diverse groups that refused to reconcile themselves to the existing political structure—a superannuated nobility, a *bourgeoisie* frightened by the rise of the Left, and a *petite bourgeoisie* yearning for the immutable conservatism of an earlier era. Although not all of these groups professed an active antisemitism, Jew-hatred was nonetheless a permanent feature in the so-called "national" outlook. Anyone not belonging to the Right was branded anti-national by right-wing circles: the remnant of the Liberals who had remained faithful to their creed, the Socialists and the Communists, even the Catholics—but first and foremost the Jews. x anti-national/aliens

While the political orientation of Germany's Jewish citizens was naturally not uniform, they were, generally speaking loyal to the Republic. Indeed, so widespread was this perception that the ultra-nationalists derided Weimar as "the Republic of the Jews." Just as the Republic was beginning to recover from the tribulations of its first years, it felt the effects of the Great Crash of 1929, which ushered in years of chronic unemployment. Increasingly, the middle class shifted its allegiance to right-wing parties, which were overtly antisemitic. Jew-hatred became a political rallying cry mobilizing the masses to support the forces that disdained the Republic. It is noteworthy that scholars have found the "Jewish Question" to be a secondary issue in the Weimar Republic; that is, Jews and their sworn enemies were actively preoccupied with antisemitism but not so the public at large. However, beneath the surface social and political turmoil seethed: the enemies of the regime were also Jew-haters, and as the Republic's prestige declined, the standing of the Jews became ever more precarious (Mosse, pp. 40–41).

The ultra-nationalists' attitude toward the state reveals the paradox of a nationalism at the end of its tether. The Weimar Republic was fundamentally a nation-state; after sloughing off the many restrictions imposed by the victors after the War, it became in effect an independent, sovereign state—the incarnation of the national ideal. Yet despite this, the Republic did not enjoy broad popular support; it was perceived as an artificial entity which did not express the true German spirit. That "German spirit" coveted an organic society and despised the allegedly tainted parliamentarism and the seemingly corrupt bureaucracy. A distinction was usually drawn in Germany between *civilization* as an expression of technological and material achievements often associated with the spirit of capitalism, and a deep-rooted *culture* of which the hallmark was fellowship. The juxtaposition of these two political cultures posited German nationalism as the antithesis of the Western-type state.

To the exponents of ultra-nationalist thought in Germany, the Jews were the purveyors of values which threatened to corrupt all that was original and authentic in the "German spirit"—values such as a sterile rationalism, a predatory capitalism, materialistic liberalism, and so forth. Even without race thinking, which became ever more widespread, nationalist antisemitism metamorphosed into an all-embracing worldview: "*Deutschum*" versus "Judaism." It is here that the so-called *Völkisch* ideology and Nazism became contiguous. As early as 1925, in *Mein Kampf*, Adolf Hitler (1889–1945) depicted the Jews as the incarnation of everything negative on a global and perhaps even cosmic scale. The following passage illustrates the point:

> The Jewish doctrine of Marxism rejects the aristocratic principle of Nature and replaces the eternal privilege of power and strength by the mass of numbers and their dead weight. Thus it denies the value of personality in man, contests the significance of nationality and race, and thereby withdraws from humanity the premise of its existence and its culture. As a foundation of the universe, this doctrine would bring about the end of any order intellectually conceivable to man. And as in this greatest of all recognizable organisms, the result of an application of such a flaw could only be chaos, on earth it could only be destruction for the inhabitants of this planet. If, with the help of the Marxist creed, the Jew is victorious over the other peoples of the world, his crown will be the funeral-wreath of humanity and this planet will, as it did thousands of years ago, move through the ether devoid of men. (p. 65)

Hitler's book did not attract much attention at the time; not only was the author himself quite unknown to the general public, his opinions were hardly outstanding amid the antisemitic literature that appeared in Germany during this period. After Hitler came to power in Germany, the Nazis' "racial theory" was transmuted into a revolutionary system which extended beyond the limits of *Völkisch* nationalism and antisemitism.

The term "race" was in wide use in nineteenth-century Europe, and even though scientists may have disagreed about its significance, it became a legitimate and accepted concept. Pre-Hitler antisemitism applied the notion of "race" to emphasize that the Jews were outcasts in Europe and by no means a part of the German nation. However, this concept of race differed from the Nazis' single-minded and deterministic usage. The transition from *Völkisch* anti-semitism to Nazi "racial theory" transformed the old nationalism into a mere appendage of racism and ultimately would deny the Jews even their physical existence.

German Jews on the Eve of the Nazis' Rise to Power

The following are remarks by the Zionist leader Kurt Blumenfeld (1884–1963) at a Zionist convention held in Frankfurt prior to the rise of the Nazis to power.[25]

We can relate only to those tendencies for national renewal that do not touch upon National-Socialism.[26] There is no doubt that the idea of national self-expression is now more effective than in earlier times among all the classes of the German people, and, as we Zionists know well, among other peoples as well.[27] After a period of superficial denationalization of certain classes, when it seemed as if the entire European and American world would become uniform, after the time of a flat cosmopolitan social life, one is reminded of one's innermost feelings.[28] The continuity of historical existence is being found again; national ties grow stronger. But this also bespeaks of many dangers, as we have

[25] The speech was delivered at the Conference of German Zionists held when Franz von Papen (1879–1969) was Chancellor (the "Barons' cabinet"). His government was formed in the shadow of threats by the Nazis, who in July 1932 became the largest faction in the Reichstag. The Chancellor, from the right-wing of the Catholic Center Party, had the support of conservative circles and made various concessions to the Nazis. The following day the Chancellor dissolved the Reichstag in the wake of a parliamentary impasse brought about by Hitler.

[26] The speaker stated explicitly that a key goal of Nazism was "the destruction of the Jews" (although this need not be construed as referring to extermination). Blumenfeld considered Nazism akin to a messianic movement with a quasi-religious message. He saw no room for compromise with Nazism.

[27] The growing strength of the national phenomenon in this period is lauded by the speaker, who hinted that the Jewish people also shared in this tendency. Nevertheless, Blumenfeld favored an open-minded nationalism, based on liberty, and he rejected racism and chauvinism.

[28] In the spirit of the time, the president of Germany's Zionist Federation described the universal awakening of national aspirations, depicting this in almost liberating terms. It was contrasted with the cosmopolitan spirit that had perhaps characterized the upper level of society, but could not express the deepest feelings of the people. However, his own brand of nationalism was centered on creative labor, not on struggles against other nations.

found out in a horrifying manner in National-Socialism. No doubt, however, that such an attempt at a renewal from within is seriously being made.[29]

The question is whether the general population can sufficiently appreciate the principle of national tolerance. A real German nationalism cannot fulfill its task by sticking only to the idea of a total state.[30] Germany's population is not uniform. Moreover, millions of Germans live outside of Germany. The national idea rightfully wants to embrace them all. It cannot tolerate that members of one's own people be oppressed in another state and made into second-class citizens. This is why outstanding leaders of the German minorities, convinced supporters of German Nationalism no doubt, do not favor the denial of rights of German citizens of a different background.[31]—

. . . Members of national minorities cannot be less-privileged citizens, who have to renounce their active participation in state affairs or their right to be civil servants. Should this conception be rejected, then it is quite obvious that the average Jew, out of an easily understandable opportunism (that Germans do not cherish), might demonstrate his loyalty by assimilationist declarations, producing the kind of imposture Germans always complain about.[32]

[29] Along with a negative attitude toward Nazism, the speaker emphasized the authenticity of the national phenomenon as expressed by less extreme nationalist circles in Germany. It was his belief that a certain understanding could be achieved with these groups through mutual respect for the difference between Germans and Jews.

[30] A major aspiration of the radical Right in the Weimar era was to overcome the atomization of modern society and establish a mobilized regime in which the individual would be organically integrated into society. The state was to serve as the instrument for the total mobilization of society. The liberal Blumenfeld assailed the idea of the total state which sought to obliterate all diversity in German society.

[31] This is a utilitarian argument in favor of tolerance, while also supporting the pan-German idea which seeks to unite all speakers of the German language. The primary reference was to Austria and the Sudetenland in Czechoslovakia, but minorities speaking German dialects also resided in various locales in Eastern and Southern Europe. Moreover, large groups of German-speaking immigrants had settled overseas but tried to retain their identity and German culture abroad.

[32] Blumenfeld raised an argument here that formed a point of contiguity between anti-Jewish polemics and Zionist criticism of the Jews. On the face of it, both sides held that the Jews were a separate nation residing in Germany thanks to the presumed hospitality accorded them by the German people. During the reign of liberalism, the Zionists derided the Jewish assimilationists, just as the antisemites reserved their harshest criticism for Jews with pretensions of being good Germans. With the rise of ultra-nationalism, the assimilationists were compelled to admit their failure or disavow their own past and the liberal tradition that had been theirs.

The German environment, being interested in national revival, might thus put a premium on assimilation and even on treachery. A government representing the legitimate national feelings cannot afford to make ambiguous policies. We are convinced and have reason to believe that the *present government* does not intend to curtail the rights of Jews who openly profess their national uniqueness.[33] (Blumenfeld, 1932)

A Period of Deterioration

The 1930s saw the rise of antisemitism not only in Germany but in many other countries of Europe and beyond. The Crash of 1929 had a wide and long-lasting effect: mass unemployment, a growth of radicalism on both the Left and the Right, and a lack of confidence in parliamentary government. Heightened social polarization, a confrontation between Fascism and Communism, political instability, growing chauvinism, the impotence of democratic governments, and the final collapse of the League of Nations were the hallmarks of the situation in Europe, particularly felt in the countries possessing large Jewish communities (such as Poland, Hungary, and Romania).

The year 1936 was critical: in France the Popular Front was formed; the Rome-Berlin Axis was created and the Spanish Civil War erupted; in Russia the Stalinist purges were at their height; while in Palestine, the Arab Revolt broke out. These were portents of the onrushing storm.

For the most part, these events did not relate directly to the Jews but affected them in many ways: heading the Popular Front in France was Léon Blum (1872–1950) whose Jewishness was dredged up time and again in the political arena (Lacouture, pp.249–252). The Formation of the Axis marked Italy's partnership with Germany, an alliance which ultimately engendered anti-Jewish legislation in Italy, too (Carpi, pp. 287–289). The anti-republican camp of Generalissimo Francisco Franco (1892–1975) in Spain was prone

---

[33] Zionism could still believe that an arrangement might yet be reached with German nationalism, based on a reciprocal recognition of their respective singularities. This hope was soon shattered upon the Nazis' assumption of power, but it had been rather illusory from the outset. Jewish nationalism in Germany was a mere aspiration and did not reflect a real-life situation. It was advocated only by a small fraction of German Jewry (although its influence increased after the rise of Nazism). In the first years of Hitler's rule, German Jewry did organize as a separate minority but did not possess equal rights. Ultimately, this was just a period of transition toward the dispossession and uprooting of the Jews.

to antisemitism, and Jews were prominent in the international brigades which came to the rescue of the Republic (Thomas, pp. 595, 760). In the Soviet Union the Jewish aspect was manifested in the fact that many victims of the purges carried out by Joseph Stalin (1879–1953) were Jews—and not by chance (Conquest, p. 116). And the Arab Revolt, which was aimed directly at the Zionist enterprise and the British Mandate, exercised a long-term impact on immigration policy to Palestine (*Palestine*, pp. 905–907). The Arab uprising undoubtedly influenced Britain's stand *vis-à-vis* the Jews in Europe during the Holocaust and its aftermath.

Nazi Germany not only utilized antisemitism in its internal policy but systematically disseminated it on a global scale. Hitler's rise to power had a vitiating effect, at least for some years, on liberal and democratic forces everywhere. The unbridled aggression of the Nazi leader stunned the countries of the West, and for years they shrank from confronting him. Many in the West were unable to grasp the significance of the Nazi doctrine, viewing Hitler as a vigorous leader who would merely remedy Germany's ills and set the country on a stable course.

Outside observers looked on the persecution of the Jews as an internal German affair in which foreigners should not intervene. While Nazism ostracized the Jews and did not regard them as Germans, liberals in the West saw the victims' Jewishness as a marginal issue—for did not non-Jews also suffer at the hands of the regime? Some in the West even tended to find a grain of truth in the antisemitic propaganda of the Nazis. Enlightened circles, in contrast, rejected the Nazis' discrimination of certain German citizens, with the result that they ignored the special fate of the Jews.

In England and France groups calling for understanding toward the rise of Nazism—either because they were sympathetic to the new movement or because they were apprehensive of a new war— were increasingly heeded. Indeed, antisemitic feelings surged up in the West, triggered in part by an unwillingness to join battle against Hitler for the sake of the Jews (who, it was sometimes felt, were now getting their just desserts).

France was in the grip of a protracted economic crisis, with unemployment mounting from year to year. The situation was aggravated by corruption scandals involving political leaders. The prestige of the parliamentary regime hit rock bottom; governments came and went in rapid succession. New fascist groups, most of them antisemitic, sprang up in addition to the conservative Right. In 1936 the Socialists and the Communists created the Popular Front and obtained a parliamentary majority. The enemies of the regime focused on the Jewishness of Prime Minister Léon Blum; the attacks against him in the press, in parliament and on the street were unbridled. What follows is a typical passage from a speech delivered in the French parliament by Xavier Vallat, later appointed the first Commissar for Jewish Affairs in the Vichy Government:

> Your rise to power, Mr. Prime Minister, is undoubtedly an historic date. For the first time this ancient Gallic-Roman land will be ruled by a Jew! I say it because I think so, and I am outstanding here in taking upon myself from time to time the thankless job of saying out loud what everyone else is thinking quietly; namely that France, this land-tilling nation, would be better served. . . by someone whose modest origin is lost in the intestines of our soil rather than by a subtle Talmudist. (Philippe, pp. 279–280)

According to Vallat, the Prime Minister was alien to the indigenous French nation. The speaker admitted that Blum was a clever intellectual, but he claimed that the primordial French spirit was beyond him. What France needed, Vallat maintained, was a leader who sprang from the French people and soil. Particularly noteworthy was the speaker's suggestion that many members of parliament were in tacit accord with him in their antipathy toward Léon Blum. Manifestly, Nazi propaganda capitalized on the fact that a Jew headed the French government. Furthermore, Blum enjoyed partial Communist support and this was served up as proof that "Jewish Bolshevism" was assiduously pursuing its world-conquering scheme. The Right brandished the slogan "Better Hitler than Blum" and accused Blum of trying to drag France into a Jewish war against Hitler (Rabi, pp. 381–382). Within a year Blum resigned as Prime Minister.

A crucial development in the 1930s was the gradual transition of the French Right from its traditional enmity toward Germany to understanding and even sympathy toward Nazi Germany. Two seemingly contradictory trends converged here: the Right was the standard-bearer of French chauvinism, and revanchism was its permanent feature since the French defeat in the war against Prussia in 1871. Yet suddenly voices were heard on the Right calling for understanding *vis-à-vis* Hitler and advocating cooperation with Germany and Italy—against international Communism, against the Freemasons, and against the Jews. The polarization in the international arena heightened the feelings of solidarity with the Fascist camp on the French Right, notwithstanding its traditional narrow nationalism. A Fascist international, so to speak, of ultra-nationalists was in the making against the international Left (Guillemin, pp. 269–281; Madaule, p. 226).

In England, right-wing circles also evinced an affinity for Fascism and Nazism, while the Left, for its part, was prepared to compromise with Hitler in order to avert a war. The Jews were caught between these two camps as victims of Nazism in Germany and as refugees pounding on the gates of numerous countries, but especially of Mandatory Palestine. It is difficult to determine the extent to which the Palestine issue affected the British attitudes toward the Jews in the 1930s. Antisemitic groups in England underwent a metamorphosis similar to that of their French counterparts. The growth of Hitler's influence was accompanied by a concomitant tendency to overlook the traditional hostility toward Germany and regret the humiliating terms imposed on it after the First World War. An argument frequently adduced by Hitler's admirers in England was that their countrymen were far-removed from the events on the continent and could not comprehend the gravity of the Jewish problem in Germany. They claimed that a small Jewish minority had imposed its will on Germany and that Nazism sought to liberate the German people from its Jewish oppressors.

Whether for tactical or other reasons, British antisemites usually distinguished between the "Jewish Question" in Germany and the situation of the Jews at home. The upshot was that the local Jews ostensibly received a stamp of approval: *they* were not to be regarded as an alien, aberrant body. Nevertheless, English Jews were accused of engaging in anti-German incitement out of solidarity with World Jewry but in conflict with British interests. Similarly, antisemitic groups played adroitly on the widespread fear that England would be flooded with Jewish refugees who might deprive the residents of their livelihood. British Fascists copied the Nazis' obloquies against the Jews, although they were not quite cognizant of their real implications. Other British ultra-nationalists professed to look to the continent for a lesson in how to treat the Jews so as to best protect British interests.

The strength of Fascism in Europe convinced the Right in England that an authoritarian regime was capable of coping with the socio-economic crisis and avert a Communist revolution—hence the outpouring of sympathy for Mussolini and Hitler in both England and

France. Germany skillfully influenced public opinion in the West while establishing friendly relations with the ruling circles there. In 1938, though, following the annexation of Austria and the *Kristallnacht* (countrywide organized riots against Germany's Jews), a shift was discernible in British public opinion. The Nazis' flagrant trampling of norms hitherto sacrosanct in civilized society made a great stir in Britain. Yet after a while one got used to Hitler's aberrant style, and the policy of appeasement won out again (Cf. Griffiths; Taylor, pp. 937–938).

Nazi Germany's external network also proved highly effective outside Europe, particularly on the American continent, due to a dextrous manipulation of local conditions. The prime audience for Nazi propaganda abroad consisted of immigrants of German extraction, but Nazi agitators incited local antisemitism as well. They harped on the theme that only Jews had an interest in opposing Hitler in an attempt to drag the world into a needless war against Germany. Antisemitism served the Nazis as an export commodity, which was usually adapted to the local market and often found a receptive audience in countries containing Jewish communities. By propagating antisemitism the Nazis were able to widen the narrow bounds of German nationalism and lend their movement a *supra-national* character (Carr, p. 35).

The Noose Tightens

The following passages are from the diary of Arthur Ruppin, a member of the Jewish Agency Executive, written during his travels in Europe.

Zurich, 7 August 1937[34]
While I was taking a walk yesterday, two men noticed my congress badge and, almost without my noticing, managed to put into my breast pocket a "ticket to Palestine" with an anti-Semitic inscription. I caught up with them, took them to task and for half an hour talked with them in the street about the Jewish question. They were educated people, twenty-five to thirty years old, equipped with the whole arsenal of German racial anti-Semi-

---

[34] Arthur Ruppin (1876–1943) attended the 20th Zionist Congress, in Zurich, which discussed the partition plan broached by the Peel Commission (so named for its chairman, Lord Peel). Ruppin had settled in Palestine in 1908 and held various public posts in addition to teaching Sociology of the Jews at the Hebrew University of Jerusalem.

tism.[35] They were quite polite, but I found the conversation depressing. These people were like fanatics, genuinely convinced that the Jews in Switzerland (numbering 17,000) dominate the government and direct it in their own interest. This provides dim prospects for the time when this generation is older.

Paris, 18 July 1938
I remained in Evian[36] until Thursday, 14 July, and did not wait for the closing session on 15 July, as the resolutions were already known. They express a great deal of sympathy for Jewish (and other) refugees and emphasise that Germany must leave the refugees the means to emigrate, but the emigration problem of the East European Jews is hardly mentioned. Palestine was mentioned by Lord Winterton[37] in the closing session only in order to explain that *now*, under the present political circumstances, immigration could be considered only to a very limited extent.

. . . In Paris I met Mr. Taylor,[38] the chairman of the Evian Conference: a very delightful and cordial person. He agreed with everything I said, it is his hope that the German Goverment will yet understand that to flood other countries with people, human beings, is just as wrong as dumping goods in them,[38] and that Germany will permit the emigrants to take with them the necessary means of existence.[40] (Ruppin, pp. 285–286, 294)

[35] Nazi organizations operated quite openly in neutral Switzerland, where the country's unfriendly immigration policy became even more stringent during that time. Jewish refugees seeking shelter from Nazi persecution were not welcome in Switzerland, and many of them were even sent back to Nazi Germany.

[36] The Evian Conference was convened in 1938 at the initiative of United States President Franklin D. Roosevelt (1882–1945). Thirty-eight countries participated, in order to share the burden of refugees from Germany and Austria. Ruppin represented the Jewish Agency, alongside other Jewish organizations that dispatched representatives (including delegations from Germany and Austria).

[37] Britain was represented by the anti-Zionist Lord Winterton, who was also later involved in the "Intergovernmental Committee for Refugees" established at Evian.

[38] Myron Taylor, President Roosevelt's personal envoy, chaired the Evian Conference. Taylor continued to be active in efforts to rescue refugees afterward.

[39] The original German text makes use of the English "dumping," a pejorative term used to describe an irresponsible economic policy that floods foreign markets with cheap products and thus harms local industry. An example of such German action was the illegal transfer of Jews of Polish origin across the border to Poland on October 28, 1938 (after the Evian Conference).

[40] The 1933 *Ha'avara* (Transfer) Agreement enabled Jews from Germany settling in Palestine to retain part of their assets in the form of German-made goods. In 1938 the Inter-Governmental Committee on Refugees tried to obtain German assent for a similar arrangement concerning other refugees, but its efforts ended in failure. In the meantime the anti-Jewish economic measures had become more rigorous, and those who did manage to get out of Germany and Austria generally left destitute.

Summary: The Jews' Status Undermined

In retrospect one can see how the status of Europe's Jews was gradually undermined in the interwar period—a bitterly ironical turn of events following the hopes in the initial postwar years for the improvement of their situation. The collapse of the multinational empires with their large Jewish populations and the rise of the new nation-states proved rather disadvantageous to the Jewish minorities. These states mostly failed to uphold their commitments toward the minorities, including the Jews, as regards equal rights and their status as a national group. The bloody pogroms perpetrated against the Jews in Eastern Europe during the Russian Revolution and the subsequent civil war were transmuted into popular antisemitism and governmental discrimination. It was the Jews' misfortune to be caught up in the rivalries between other national groups, without being able to derive any benefit for themselves.

Nationalism increasingly left its stamp on public life. It was often accompanied by an official policy favorable to the majority peoples in the realms of culture, economy and politics. With the encouragement of the government, new elites from the majority peoples took over key positions and pushed out the Jewish professionals and middle class. Indeed, in many countries nationalism emerged as the dominant ideology and assumed an exclusive, parochial character.

As nationalism celebrated its triumph, the Jews were increasingly denounced as an alien body, notwithstanding their thorough assimilation and patriotic loyalty, particularly in Central and Western Europe. The isolation of the Jews reached new depths in the 1930s with the growth of fascist tendencies in many European countries. Following the Nazis' ascension to power, the status of the Jews was increasingly undermined, even outside of Germany. The gradual abolition of their rights and the threat to their security in one of the major civilized countries paved the way for heightened antisemitism elsewhere. The flow of Jewish emigration from Germany and the reluctance to absorb Jewish immigrants abroad, the Nazis' antisemitic propaganda on an international scale, followed by the expansion of Nazism in Europe through annexation and conquest, all shattered the very basis for Jewish existence on the European continent.

7

Antisemitism and the Holocaust

Poland during the Nazi Occupation

While antisemitism reached new heights during World War II, disparities were still discernible between traditional antisemitism and Nazi racism. Although the Nazi racial doctrine was directed mainly at the Jews, it also affected local populations considered inferior according to the arbitrary standards of Nazism. Germany's conquest of Europe enabled it to influence the lives of numerous peoples by fostering national conflicts, suppressing local elites, and cultivating so-called desirable racial elements through a policy based on sterilization, fertilization, displacement and liquidation. The occupation authorities disseminated Nazi propaganda and utilized antisemitism to cement their relations with the subjugated countries and satellite states. By playing on Jew-hatred the Nazis gained the support of local antisemites and heightened the enmity toward Jews in the occupied countries. Understandably, antisemitism was rife in the circles that collaborated with the Nazis, but neither was it absent among the *opponents* of the foreign conquest. However, there was a marked difference between Nazi policy and the attitude of local antisemites toward the Jews, both in the goals posited and the means for their attainment.

The antisemites in the occupied countries were usually pleased with the removal of the Jews from their positions in the economy and society, and many collaborated by taking an active part in acts of violence and abuse against Jews. However, in some cases avowed antisemites in the occupied countries shrank from the total annihilation of the Jews. Religious or moral inhibitions played a part, and sometimes the local residents had reservations about the German conqueror; generally speaking, they did not even grasp the full implication of the Nazi racial doctrine. In Poland, for example, the antisemites aspired to rid Poland of the Jews. The rulers of Poland after the death of Marshal Józef Pilsudski (1867–1935) advocated the emigration of the Jews and even abetted Zionism. Similarly, until the outbreak of the War the Nazis pursued a policy of enforced emigration in regard to the Jews, even consenting to release assets of those emigrating to Palestine under certain conditions. However, once war erupted, and particularly after Germany's invasion of the Soviet Union, a change occurred in the Nazis' stand toward the Jews: enforced emigration was replaced by extermination. The Jews in Nazi-occupied Europe were rounded up and transported to the death camps set up mainly in Poland, where most of them perished. The policy of murder came as a suprise and evoked contradictory responses among the Poles.

In the Warsaw Ghetto the Jewish historian Emmanuel Ringelblum (1900–1944) wrote a comprehensive study of Poland during the Holocaust up until his death. One of his major themes was the success of Nazi propaganda, which exploited the Poles' deeply rooted hatred of the Jews. Yet Ringelblum also cited evidence of dissociation from the anti-Jewish measures on the part of prominent antisemites, stemming from Polish patriotism or opposition to the Nazis' methods. The Polish population evinced particular readiness to assist Jews converted to Christianity or Jewish children who could be baptized. The London-based Polish government-in-exile publicly deplored the anti-Jewish atrocities, but the Polish underground only made symbolic gestures toward the Jews. The anti-Nazi resistance movement was supported by diverse organizations, most of which had espoused antisemitism before the War. Nevertheless, some members of the resistance, including die-hard antisemites, risked their lives to rescue Jews (Ringelblum, p. 199).

Polish Reactions to the Murder of the Jews and to the Warsaw Ghetto Revolt

The following passages are taken from the Polish underground press during the War; they reflect the views of different Polish groups.

450,000 People in Warsaw Await Death:[1]
There are still among us scoundrels who accept this fact with an
idiotic smile, or a shrug, saying, "Oh, well, they're just Jews."[2]
We cannot leave it at that.[3] We must remember that after the
Jews will come the Poles' turn to be evacuated to the east.[4] Thus
even now, we are all obligated to oppose these murders. . . . The
Polish population, including the farmers in the villages, must
extend aid to those who escape, conceal them, and provide them
with food. The Poles must see that the brisk rate at which Hitler
is being allowed to destroy the Jews will [only] speed up the murder of our people, the Poles. Thus the Jews who are actively resist-
ing are also fighting for the lives of the Polish population, because
they are causing the disorganization and debilitation of the abom-
inable murder machine.[5] (Gutman, p. 259)

Around the Burning Ghetto:[6]
The last time the Jews fought was 1800 years ago. With valor,
though in vain, they defended Jerusalem against Titus's legions.

[1] The article appeared in an underground paper for farmers published by the
P.P.R.—the Polish Worker's Party—established by the Communists in 1942. The
paper was reacting to the major German *Aktion* launched in July 1942, during which
over a quarter of a million Jews perished.

[2] The writers are under no illusions about the mood of the Polish population in
the face of the murder of the Jews. It is clear to them that everyone is aware of the
fate of the Jews, transported from the Warsaw Ghetto to the Treblinka death camp.
Nevertheless, mention is made of the malicious pleasure expressed at the plight of
the victims.

[3] The appeal to the population does not attempt to evoke compassion or sympathy
toward these Polish citizens (mostly Jews, but also converts from Judaism), who are
being murdered by the Nazi enemy. Perhaps an appeal to conscience would not have
generated an appropriate response, or it might have been counterproductive. It is
possible that the writers themselves had no compassion for the Jewish victims.

[4] The Nazi forces conducted a policy of brutal repression in Poland, with the aim
of making the Poles a servile, submissive population. Vast numbers of people were
uprooted and German settlers were resettled in their stead, in areas earmarked
for Nazi *Lebensraum*. The Poles' legal standing was undermined by the occupying
authorities. Many were imprisoned and were sent to forced labor. The Polish people
suffered heavy casualties in World War II, but there was no systematic extermination of Poles.

[5] A connection indeed existed between the persecution of the Poles and the
destruction of the Jews: as long as the Nazis were preoccupied with the Jews, they
were less involved in harassing the Poles. The struggle of the Jews was expedient
for the Polish population and for the underground, but it could hardly change the
course of events. We find here not only a realistic appraisal of Polish interests but
also a call for solidarity. Note that emphasis was placed not on the *annihilation* of
the Jews but on their *resistance* (which prompted a respectful attitude on the part
of the Poles).

[6] This passage appeared in the illegal organ of the Catholic youth in the wake of
the Warsaw Ghetto uprising.

That was the last accord for the existence of the state and the honor of the people—the short-lived revolt of Bar-Kochba[7]— For the first time in eighteen centuries, they have risen from their humiliation.[8] This is a momentous time. Who knows whether the spirit of Israel will not rise out of the ashes of Warsaw, out of its ruins and its fallen? Who knows whether the Jews will not emerge from the fire purified; if the wandering, parasitical, dangerous Jews will not return to being a normal people that will embark upon an independent, creative life wherever they may be.[9] The Warsaw ghetto may not be an end but a beginning; whoever dies as a human being has not perished in vain.[10] (*Ibid.*, pp. 405–406)

The Resistance in the Ghetto in Its Proper Light:[11] The Jewish resistance at the time of the final liquidation of the Warsaw ghetto was not, as some of the underground press reported it, collective resistance that proved a change in attitude among the surviving Jews.[12] If the overwhelming majority of Europe's Jews were murdered as they remained completely passive, the remnant, in their racial materialism, lacked any motivation to resist.[13] Only a tiny

[7] The "Great Revolt" against Rome occurred in 66–70 C.E. and culminated in the conquest of Jerusalem and razing of the Temple by Titus (39–81). The Bar-Kochba uprising took place in 132–135 C.E., during the reign of the Emperor Hadrian (76–138). Mention of the ancient Jewish rebellions accorded with the Polish national tradition, which revered the heroic, even desperate revolt.

[8] Here the Polish national tradition is congruent with the Christian conception of the Jews' fate after the appearance of Jesus—they were said to have fallen from grace. In the eyes of the author, the Warsaw Ghetto revolt enabled the Jews to arise from the ancient state of degradation.

[9] We find here a polar dichotomy between the negative attributes imputed to the Jews and the sudden prospect now open to them, precisely in the hour of the revolt, to undergo purification and become a paragon of virtue.

[10] Redemption through agony and death is a basic motif in Christian martyrdom. Furthermore, Polish nationalism saw itself as the "messianic nation." These traditions were posited as the criteria by which the deeds of the Jews should be gauged, and hence the Jews were found to be praiseworthy following the outbreak of the revolt in the ghetto.

[11] The following appeared in an organ published clandestinely by the intelligence service of the right-wing underground in Poland on May 15, 1943, in the midst of the ghetto revolt.

[12] In order to detract from the importance of an event which had generated sympathy for the Jews, the avowed antisemitic circles maintain that the revolt did not signify a change for the better among *all* Jews. It is noteworthy, however, that not even the extremists among the ultra-nationalists in Poland identified with the Nazis (in contrast to the behavior of the radical Right in many other countries).

[13] The authors suggest that a lack of self-respect is a typical Jewish trait and paint a picture of the Jews' readiness to accommodate the Nazi enemy. It will be recalled that these comments appeared in the midst of the revolt in the ghetto, when the Polish underground was still rather passive, and the aid proffered the Jewish resistance was all but negligible.

proportion of the few thousand Jews remaining in Warsaw (about 10 per cent) engaged in the struggle—and with support from the Communist camp at that.[14] It was the nonregistered Jews who rebelled, the "wildcat" residents in the ghetto. On the other hand, the Jews who were registered and turned up for work did not take part in the action. They capitulated by the hundreds to the Germans, who led them by the [same] old methods to the new place of slaughter, at Majdanek.[15] The resistance and supply of weapons to a public encompassing tens of thousands . . . was organized and effected by the Bund and the Communists.[16] It is precisely among that element that a mood of hostility towards the Poles has been evident throughout the occupation, and they have trained themselves in the framework of Communist organizations for a bloody battle against the Poles during the decisive transition period.[17] (*Ibid.*, p. 409)

Italy and Bulgaria

Italy was well disposed toward the Jews from the outset. The rise to power of Fascism in 1922 stamped Italy with a saliently nationalist imprint. The Jews, however, were considered part of the nation and generally supported the regime. Naturally, there were anti-Fascists among Jews, as there were among non-Jews, such as the liberal intelligentsia and the Socialists and Communists. In 1938 Italy unexpectedly promulgated anti-Jewish racial laws. Nonetheless, Italians—Germany's wartime allies—aided Jews in the occupied countries to escape the Nazis.

Italy's behavior was quite complex. Its anti-Jewish legislation was less extreme than Germany's, and it would not be wrong to say that Italians were generally unreceptive to the Nazi racial doctrine. One

[14] The Jewish Combat Organization formed friendly relations with the Polish Communist underground, but the latter, itself weak and unarmed, was unable to supply the Jewish fighters with the weapons they needed.

[15] The camp at Majdanek, near Lublin, became operative in the summer of 1942. Most of the prisoners were immediately put to death in the gas chambers, with a small percentage left alive in the adjacent concentration camp.

[16] The Jewish Combat Organization was set up at the initiative of the Zionist youth movements and encompassed the Bund and the Jewish Communists. Paradoxically, the authors of the document tried to associate the uprising precisely with these two groups, whom they loathed for being both Jews and leftists.

[17] The right-wing underground in Poland was engaged in a struggle against the Nazis but also feared a Soviet conquest. The Jews were looked upon as potential allies of the Communists, and word spread of a Jewish-Communist plot against Polish interests. Even though the actual events underscored the Jewish tragedy, these circles persisted in their traditional allegations notwithstanding the facts.

reason for this may have been the Nazis' notions of Nordic–German superiority *vis-à-vis* Italy, which viewed itself as the heir of the Roman Empire (with its perception of the Germanic tribes as barbarians). As the progenitor of Fascism, Italy was not satisfied with the role of Hitler's junior partner. Moreover, Italy and Germany competed for spheres of influence and the Duce, Benito Mussolini (1883–1945), was bent on preserving his freedom of action. The Italians for the most part looked askance at the Nazis' brutal methods and iron discipline and were moved by the plight of the Jews. Even after the advent of anti-Jewish discrimination in Italy, Nazism remained alien to the Italian people. Notwithstanding that from 1938 antisemitism was incorporated into the official ideology, Italy maintained a more humane attitude, thereby accentuating the difference between the two regimes (Michaelis, pp. 7–32; Carpi, pp. 283–284).

The situation was somewhat similar in Bulgaria, where the Jews had previously enjoyed amicable relations with the rest of the population. The 1930s witnessed the emergence of fascist and antisemitic groups in Bulgaria, under the impact of similar tendencies then prevailing in Europe. During the War Bulgaria joined the Axis Powers but did not declare war on the Soviet Union because of its historical ties with Russia. Bulgarian public opinion was not won over by Nazi racism. The attempt in 1943 by agents of Adolf Eichmann (1906–1962) to send the Jews to the death camps in Poland met with resistance among the Bulgarians. The deputy speaker of the House of Representatives, Dimiter Peshev, initiated a petition in favor of the Jews and prevented the expulsion of Jews who had held Bulgarian citizenship before the War. Jews from areas annexed to Bulgaria in 1941 were less fortunate, however, and were transported to the camps. When the German Army began to suffer reverses on the Russian Front, Bulgarian policy underwent a shift and in 1944 it changed for the better regarding the Jews.

Bulgaria was a German ally and during the War was ruled by antisemitic politicians, yet public intercession brought about a halt in the extermination of the Jews. Nazi racism did not strike roots in the public mind, and German pressure regarding the Jews aroused the opposition of the Church, the intelligentsia, and even of King Boris III (1894–1943), who determined Bulgarian policy (Oren, pp. 83–106). Both Bulgaria and Italy had relatively small Jewish populations that were not particularly distinctive, in socioeconomic terms, and were considered a legitimate part of the nation (Fein, p. 85).

Bulgarian Members of Parliament Petition to Aid the Jews

The following is the text of a memorandum sent on 17 March 1943 by 42 members of the Bulgarian House of Representatives to the Prime Minister.[18]

It is our abiding loyalty to the policies of the present regime, as well as our desire to contribute to the best of our abilities to their crowning success, that inspires us with the courage to address you.[19] . . . Given the nature of the times in which we live, we could not and would not oppose the measures prompted by national security considerations, because we realize that in this crucial period anybody directly or indirectly impeding the state's or the nation's supreme efforts must be rendered harmless. It is the success of policies conducted by the government with our approval and cooperation, policies in which we have consciously and proudly invested all our prestige and capital, that is at stake.[20] . . . We cannot conceive, however, that the Bulgarian government would expel the Jews from Bulgaria, as a vile rumor would have it.[21] Such a measure would stain Bulgaria's reputation and place an unmerited blemish on her brow. Not only would it weigh on her morally, it would invalidate all her political arguments which will undoubtedly be needed in her future international relations.[22] Small countries cannot afford the luxury of ignoring

---

[18] The petition was drawn up at the initiative of the Deputy Speaker of the House of Representatives. Dimiter Peshev, who was convinced that the extension of the expulsion order regarding Bulgarian Jewry, over and above the residents of the areas annexed in 1941, was in violation of the law. He was later removed from his post.

[19] Most of the signatories were from the majority faction in the *Sobranje*, including some known for their pro-German sympathies.

[20] It is clear from the petition's formulation that the signatories were not objecting to the general thrust of government policy and would be prepared to approve it even with regard to the deportation of Jews, were this required for "Reasons of State."

[21] The petition was sent following the temporary intercession of the Deputy Speaker with the Interior Minister, after the deportation orders had already begun to be implemented. Notwithstanding this, the petition spoke of a *rumor* only, no doubt to keep up appearances and avoid the impression of an unconventional intervention in an officially approved operation.

[22] As they signed the petition, the Bulgarian politicians were already in doubt about the War's outcome, following the defeats sustained by the Axis Powers in the Soviet Union and North Africa.

such arguments because—regardless of what the future may bring—these arguments will always remain one of the strongest weapons, possibly the strongest one, at the nation's disposal. This particularly applies to us, because, as you will remember, not so long ago we suffered grave moral and political consequences for deviating from certain human and ethical standards.[23] What Bulgarian government would be willing to take such a responsibility *vis-à-vis* the future? (Tamir, p. 201)

Persecution and Rescue of Romanian Jews

I now turn to events in Romania, which as a German ally in World War II, was able to thwart, to a large extent, the Nazis' extermination policy. Germany's influence made itself felt in Romania following Hitler's assumption of power, and the Führer made use of antisemitic organizations to strengthen his control of that country. With German support the right-wing forces became preponderant in local politics and were able to shift the foreign policy of Romania from its Western orientation toward the German-Italian Axis. In 1937 King Carol II (1893–1953) brought the antisemitic Right to power in order to neutralize the Fascist opposition of the Iron Guard. A year later the King assumed power, hoping to maintain Romania's independence under German protection while concurrently fighting against the attempts of the pro-Nazi Iron Guard to seize power.

In 1940 King Carol was forced to abdicate in favor of his son, Michael (b. 1927, abdicated 1947), while actual power resided with a Regent, Marshal Ion Antonescu (1882–1946). Antonescu established a Fascist dictatorship in Romania and ruled with the aid of the Iron Guard, which unleashed a reign of terror. A year later the dictator deposed the Iron Guard leaders and formed a military government. In 1941 Romania entered the War against the Soviet Union and systematic pogroms were perpetrated against Jews, most notably in the restituted territories of Bessarabia and Bukovina. German-commanded Romanian and German units took part in the massacre of Jews during their expulsion from the border areas.

Nonetheless, Romania's ruler and his henchmen showed some consideration for petitions submitted by the Jews and protests by various neutral parties. They tried to steer a course between Nazi

[23] The allusion here is evidently to the deportation of the Jews of Macedonia and Thracia—the areas annexed by Bulgaria from Serbia and Greece—under an agreement between Eichmann's envoy and the Commissar for Jewish Affairs in the Bulgarian government, signed on 22 February 1943.

pressures and opposing currents. Groups of Jews embarked for Palestine from Romanian ports with the assent of the local authorities. With the deterioration of the German positions on the Russian Front, resistance to Nazi pressures increased: now the Romanian authorities sought to prevent deportations of Jews, viewing this as an infringement of Romanian sovereignty. Romanian leaders tried to establish closer ties with the Allies by making some gestures of goodwill towards the Jews. In November 1943, Marshal Antonescu declared that he would not be a party to the extermination of Jews. The following March the Regent permitted the return of Jews who had been deported to the Transnistria region in the Ukraine. Throughout this period Germans (particularly Eichmann's agents) operated in the country, endeavoring to influence Romanian policy against the Jews. As the tide of the War turned, Antonescu was arrested in August 1944 and Romania joined the Allies (Fischer-Galati, pp. 166–168).

Wartime Romania demonstrates the profound difference that obtained between traditional antisemitism and Nazi racism. The efforts by Eichmann and his aides to bring about the total destruction of the Jews clashed with the notions of the local antisemites and ran into evasion and dilatory tactics on the part of the Romanian government. By the time the Romanians grasped the true nature of Nazism, they were already committed. At this stage, moral inhibitions, Romanian patriotism, and utilitarian politics combined to save a large part of Romanian Jewry (Lavi, pp. 177–186).

The Attitude of Romanian Leaders toward the Jews

Iron Guard leader Corneliu Codreanu (1899–1938) in 1938:[24]

> The Jews, the Jews, they are our curse. They poison our state, our life, our people. They demoralize our nation. They destroy our youth. They are the archenemies. You talk of the Jewish problem; you are right. The Jews are our greatest problem, the most important, the most urgent, the most pressing problem for Romania.[25]

[24] Codreanu's remarks were made to a British journalist in 1938 after his Party finished third in the parliamentary elections at the end of the previous year. The King despised Codreanu, who was too independent for his liking, preferring instead the leaders of the conservative Right. In that same year Codreanu was arrested and later found dead along with thirteen of his followers.

[25] Antisemitism intensified in Romania during the 1930s, particularly on economic grounds, and was directed against both Jews in key positions and Jews in the villages, such as property-owners, shopkeepers, innkeepers, and the like. Jew-

The Jews scheme and plot and plan to ruin our national life. We shall not allow this to happen. We, the Iron Guard, will stand in the way of such devilry. We shall destroy the Jews before they can destroy us. There are influences, important influences on the side of the Jews. We shall destroy them, too.[26]

King Carol on the Jews in January 1938:[27]

The question of the Jews in Romania is the principal factor in the situation. It cannot be denied that there is a strong anti-Semitic feeling in the country. That is an old question in our history.[28]

The measure to be taken to deal with it is on the principle of revision of citizenship for those Jews who entered the country after the war.[29]

What happened was something in the nature of an invasion of Galician and Russian Jews who came in illegally. Their number has been exaggerated; some say as many as 800,000, but the maximum was about 250,000, who invaded the villages and are not a good element.[30]

hatred was prevalent in various political groups, but Codreanu stood out by making antisemitism the linchpin of a revolutionary fascist worldview. His fascism was centered on mystical nationalism and the creation of a new man—energetic, decent and responsible—in contrast to the depraved character he attributed to the government and its lackeys, the Jews and their allies.

[26] The allusion here is unmistakably to court circles, to King Carol's mistress, Madame Lupescu, and his millionaire friend Max Auschnitt, both of Jewish origin, who would supposedly persuade the King to support the Jews.

[27] A month later the King staged a coup: parliamentary democracy was abolished and a new constitution introduced; power was placed in the hands of the monarchy. Carol's remarks in this context are thus particularly significant for the future position of the Jews in Romania.

[28] In the nineteenth century Romania was considered the cradle of antisemitism and joined Czarist Russia in refusing to recognize the Jews as citizens with equal rights. The claim that the Jews were foreigners in Romania had also been advanced in the past as an excuse for their subordinate status—this despite the fact that the Congress of Berlin in 1878 had obligated the authorities to grant equal rights to "religious minorities."

[29] Under the peace agreements following World War I, Romania undertook to recognize the civil rights of those who had lacked rights, but in practice a procedure was introduced diminishing the possibility of implementing these rights. Here the King intended to further reduce the number of Jews who enjoyed Romanian citizenship. On 22 January 1938, a law for the examination of citizenship was promulgated, and one-third of Romania's Jews were deprived of their civil rights.

[30] Following World War I, Bessarabia, Bukovina and Transylvania were annexed by Romania; all these areas contained Jewish communities that were not Romanian-speaking. In the wake of the pogroms a stream of immigrants from the Ukraine also poured into Romania, although the majority did not settle in the country but proceeded to the United States or Palestine. On the other hand, some Romanian Jews also emigrated. Even the lower figure cited by the King is improbable; more-

Can people be regarded as good citizens who entered the country by fraud? Those Jews who lived in Romania before the war are without legal rights, except as refugees. About them we shall consider what to do.[31]

(Quoted in Mendelsohn, pp. 204–205)

Hungary under Horthy

The course of events in Hungary bore a similarity to that in Romania insofar as the Nazis' assumption of power bolstered local Fascist elements, heightening the cooperation between Hungary and Nazi Germany. Austria's annexation by the Reich created a common border between Germany and Hungary, and the latter effectively became a satellite of Nazi Germany. In 1938, notwithstanding the objections of the opposition, anti-Jewish laws were for the first time promulgated formally and openly in Hungary. This legislation was applied to the "members of the Mosaic faith" and was not initially based on racial principles. The legalized anti-Jewish discrimination also gained the support of various Church leaders in Hungary. A year later the anti-Jewish legislation was extended to encompass certain converts to Christianity and their offspring.

These laws were rigidly enforced in the areas annexed from Czechoslovakia and Romania, under the claim that the Jews there were not loyal to Hungary. Prior to World War I these areas had been part of the Hungarian Monarchy within the Dual Empire. For twenty years, independent Hungary had aspired to return to its historic borders but looked askance at the Jews residing in the outlying districts, even though they were generally immersed in Magyar culture.

As a German ally, Hungary enjoyed a large measure of independence, and thus Jewish refugees were able to find shelter there, in

over, the number of Jews in Greater Romania at the end of World War I exceeded their number in the 1930 census. The notion of a Jewish "invasion" of the villages echoes the typical Romanian antisemitic allegation dating back to the peasants' revolt of 1907, when antisemitic politicians incited the rebels against the Jews.

[31] During King Carol's dictatorship, from February 1938 until his ouster in September 1940, previous antisemitic policies continued. The government, under pressure from both the Iron Guard and the Germans, tried to preserve some maneuverability in political matters precisely by adopting an antisemitic line. King Carol's Cabinet comprised ministers of an antisemitic background, and the enmity toward the Jews did not abate. The antisemitic policy was convenient for the government and did not offend public opinion.

some cases with the consent of the local authorities. Jews continued to serve in the Hungarian Army, while others were conscripted to special Labor Units comprising members of the national minorities. In 1941 the anti-Jewish legislation was exacerbated and more rigorous use was made of the racial clause. Jews were deported from the border areas, many of them perishing at the hands of SS units aided by Hungarian military personnel.

Hungarian policy during the War fluctuated between collaboration with the Nazis and clandestine attempts to negotiate with the Allies. This flexible posture was also reflected in the authorities' attitude toward the Jews. The German embassy in Budapest complained to the Foreign Office in Berlin about the Hungarian public's friendly attitude toward the Jews, including incoming Jewish refugees. Mounting pressure was exerted on the Hungarian leaders, by Nazi officials and by Hitler personally, to cooperate in the implementation of the "Final Solution" policy against the Jews. On several occasions the Hungarian Regent, Admiral Miklós Horthy (1868–1957), was summoned to Hitler and told in no uncertain terms to cooperate in the deportation of the Jews to the death camps.

The Hungarians desisted; when the German armed forces invaded Hungary in March 1944, the Germans seized all the strongholds in Hungary and Eichmann established his headquarters in Budapest. Hungarian Jewry was speedily processed for the "Final Solution" through expropriation, confinement, enforcement of the "Yellow Star," regulation, and the imposition of *Judenräte*. All these were stages toward destruction devised according to the experience the Nazis had accumulated elsewhere in Europe. The Catholic Church was outraged, since the German edicts also applied to the many converts in Hungary, including clergymen of Jewish extraction. April witnessed the first transport of Jews to the Auschwitz death camp, and a month later mass expulsions were carried out in the border areas. Horthy again tried to foil the transport of Jews to death camps.

After conducting negotiations with the Allies, in October 1944 Horthy publicly called for an armistice, condemning, *inter alia*, the Gestapo's policy toward the Jews. His move failed, however, and he and his family were arrested by the Germans. The reins of government were handed over to Ferenc Szálasi (1897–1946), leader of the Hungarian Nazi organization, the "Arrow Cross." The organization's militants tortured their victims and helped the

Germans round up Jews as part of the extermination plan. Seventy percent of the Jews of Greater Hungary perished in the Holocaust (Hilberg, pp. 510–554; Ránki, pp. 77–92).

Only an external similarity exists between the events in Hungary and Romania, since in Hungary the Nazis were largely successful in carrying out their designs—doing so, moreover, in the final year of the War. Paradoxically, the close relations between Hungary and Nazi Germany were beneficial to the Jews almost until the end. On the other hand, even though Germany's defeat was a foregone conclusion during the last year of the War, and despite the lessons that they could have learned from the bitter experience in other countries, Hungary's Jews promptly fell into the Nazis' net. The Holocaust in Hungary can be seen as a total failure of Jewish emancipation, since it was in Hungary that the Jews were deeply integrated into the nation and excelled in their Magyar patriotism (Braham, pp. 177–190).

In Hungary as in Romania, the Jews in the annexed areas suffered far more than the Jewish citizens of long standing. Evidently the authorities and the population at large were more inclined to intervene on behalf of fellow citizens and neighbors while turning their back on Jews who had only recently come under Hungarian rule. Similarly, while there was satisfaction at the Jew's loss of status, a sense of uneasiness was felt when it became apparent that the Germans were bent on the total annihilation of the Jews. That objective, and the means chosen for its implementation, were alien to the local antisemitic traditions. Both countries retained some of the old norms while cooperating with Nazi Germany. Conservative politicians often viewed their collaboration with Nazi Germany as the means to ensure their country's national interests. They were more willing to comply with the policy dictated by the Nazis, as long as the Germans enjoyed superiority on the European continent. All the same, delaying tactics were employed to thwart the Nazis' demand for cooperation in the annihilation of the Jews. Yet Hungary's opportunistic policy could not withstand the events of the War's final year, when the Germans took over the country while being defeated on the military front. At this point the most extreme wing came to the fore and was prepared to join Nazism wholeheartedly in its all-out war against the Jews.

Hungarian Jewry's Outcry[32]

The following is the verbatim text of a memorandum in English by the Budapest Jewish community concerning the condition of the Jews in Hungary on the eve of the War.

The Hungarian Government published in the evening of the 22nd December the full text of the Second Anti-Jewish Bill, and on the next day the 23 December 1938 a university professor, one of the most famous occulists—who in addition was born as a Christian—committed suicide;[33] and on the same day one of the most prominent barristers of Budapest, the director of the Board of the legal advising office of the Jewish Church Community committed equally suicide. The reason for both suicides was the anti-Jewish Bill.

These two suicides with their symptom-like character enlighten better than any sentimental comments the present and future position of Hungarian Jewry. The first two shots were already fired, and further 500,000 Hungarian Jews and about 100,000 Christians who according to the new regulations[34] are to be regarded as Jews are facing coming weeks and months of bottomless despair. They are deprived of all hopes and can await no other assistance but that of their happy and free co-religionists.[35]

Further restrictions to be expected: It is almost impossible to stop on this way, it cannot be expected that this second anti-Jewish Bill which followed in less than half a year the passing of the first [Law] would make an end to this problem.[36] The disclosed reasons do not bivouac [i.e. are unequivocal]. They say clearly that Hun-

[32] The passages are contained in a memorandum of the Budapest Jewish community, which reached the Board of Deputies of British Jews near the end of February 1939.

[33] According to Katzburg, the reference is to Leo Liebermann, whose father had converted to Christianity and been titled.

[34] The Second Anti-Jewish Bill applied to anyone who had converted to Christianity after the age of seven and to converts who had one non-Christian parent before 1 January 1939 (provided their ancestors did not reside in Hungary before 1849). The law did not affect Liebermann personally.

[35] The appeal to Western Jewry, based on all-Jewish solidarity, takes no account of the paradox entailed in the use of the term "co-religionists" in reference to converts to Christianity.

[36] The First Anti-Jewish Law was passed in May 1938, and the second bill was submitted to Parliament on 23 December of that year, but took effect only in May 1939. The suicides occurred immediately after it was learned of the intention to toughen the law; the memorandum, too, speaks of "less than half a year" between the two laws.

gary surrounded by a bloc of two hundreds millions of people having an anti-Jewish legislation, Hungary is forced to follow their example, because left behind in this competition, Jews would overflow the country still to a greater extent than up to now.[37] In consequence, if Germany adopts new restrictions, they will be introduced here too, and so—alas—the "arrow-cross" member of Parliament was perfectly right when he exclaimed at the introduction of the Bill in the House of Parliament: "The third one will come too".[38]

The Government has to face a strong opposition in respect of the solution of the Jewish problem. This opposition is—unfortunately—composed, but in a small proportion of the opponents of the anti-Jewish Law, and its majority of the so called "arrownists", the national socialist opposition of the Government, who are claiming more severe anti-Jewish provisions.[39] Thus Jews are constantly menaced that the political attack which has already driven the Government to the extreme Right will claim further concessions. What future awaits Jewry after all these concessions?[40] (Quoted in Katzburg, 1981, pp. 266–267)

[37] Anti-Jewish legislation was already in force in Greater Germany (which encompassed Austria and a part of Czechoslovakia) and to a certain degree in Italy and Romania as well. Not long afterward, this legislation was extended to various other countries that surrendered to Germany or joined the Axis. The justification for the antisemitic legislation was said to be the more convenient conditions that still prevailed in Hungary and the danger that the country would be flooded with refugees. This is hardly a very convincing pretext: the blow was aimed at Jews and converts whose Magyar origins went back generations, not just at refugees.

[38] Indeed, the third law also went through, as the author of the memorandum had feared, and as the member of parliament from the Hungarian-Nazi Arrow Cross Party had hoped. On 30 June 1944, the government submitted a thoroughly racist bill, which took effect less than two months later.

[39] The memorandum took note of an emerging process in Hungarian politics: the government found itself under the dual pressure of the radical opposition and of Nazi Germany. The pressure with regard to the Jews was generally one-sided: the opponents of the anti-Jewish legislation were becoming increasingly intimidated, while the government tried to placate the maximalists. As Nazi Germany won victory after victory, Hungarian opportunists tended to align themselves all the more with it.

[40] The authors could not have been thinking about the wholesale murder of the Jews, as subsequently occurred. They were at the beginning of a long road and feared the consequences of the anti-Jewish policy. However, with a prophetic sense they pointed out the slope down which Hungarian Jewry was beginning to slide.

Vichy France

The government established in Vichy under Marshal Philippe Pétain (1856–1951) collaborated with Nazi Germany, and its policy toward the Jews was similar to that of Hungary and Romania. The Vichy Government also tried to display a measure of independence *vis-à-vis* the occupation forces, while minor political changes occurred from time to time. Here, too, the authorities regarded foreign Jews as expendable but made efforts to restrain the Nazis when they trained their sights on the French Jews.

Unlike Germany's allies, the Vichy Government, established after the fall of France, ruled in only part of the country. Other parts were administered directly by the Germans or the Italians, with the latter attempting to prevent the Nazis from deporting Jews to Poland. Consequently there were substantial disparities in behavior toward the Jews in the different zones of France. As in other countries, the readiness of the French to resist the Nazis increased gradually, corresponding with Germany's deteriorating military situation.

The Vichy Government's policy toward the Jews was shaped in the spirit of the old French antisemitism, and those responsible for its implementation were veteran antisemites. Even so, the French authorities did not see eye to eye with the occupation forces, following the divergent interpretations adduced by each side for its particular type of antisemitism. By late 1940 the Vichy Government had already promulgated a law to remove Jewish influence from public and cultural life. This was followed by restrictions of various kinds on Jews, particularly those of foreign nationality. By contrast, better treatment was accorded Jews who had demonstrated their loyalty to France, and the Church opposed the Nazis' race laws because it could not acquiesce in the application of anti-Jewish measures to converts to Christianity.

Political leaders and intellectuals in occupied Paris, who favored closer collaboration with the Nazis, assailed the Vichy Government for its apparently moderate policies. To one degree or another these pro-Nazi groups supported Hitler's "New Order" in Europe and distanced themselves from the traditional stance of conservative French nationalism. Together with a willingness to welcome Nazism as a system bridging the differences between the French and the Germans, these circles also professed racial antisemitism. Yet on the other hand, there were Frenchmen who had been antisemitic in the past, but were now ready to help Jews, motivated by their opposition to the Germans (Paxton, pp. 173–180; Philippe, pp. 289ff).

The German occupation threw France into a moral crisis: the cradle of the Revolution and of The Declaration of the Rights of Man and of the Citizen had suffered not only a military defeat but a social and intellectual upheaval. The nationalistic and antisemitic Right broke up: one camp identified with the Nazis and their racial antisemitism; another camp preferred to fight Germany and abandoned active antisemitism; while the Vichy regime tried to steer a course between traditional anti-German nationalism and total submission to the conqueror with its attendant acquiescence in the destruction of the Jews. France's defeat challenged the French people and its elites and exposed the innate weaknesses of a country which had claimed the cultural leadership of Europe. The more self-confident elements on both sides determined the opposing courses that were taken: while some chose to resist the Nazis and aid persecuted Jews, others identified closely with the Germans and the anti-Jewish policy. Most Frenchmen followed the line of least resistance, tended to overlook the gravity of the situation forced on them, and made do with nationalist rhetoric justifying the opportunistic policy of collaboration with Nazism (Marrus and Paxton, pp. 343–372).

A French Antisemite's Remorse

From a letter written by the French writer Georges Bernanos (1888–1948) in May 1944.[41]

I have received several extremely moving letters from certain Jewish compatriots[42] who reproached me for having written that the Jewish and German spirits had a profound affinity for each other.[43] I am sorry to have caused them any pain, but that is all I can say. To detract any further would misconstrue my thoughts. I prefer to state it again precisely today, even at the risk of aggravating the misunderstanding, for I respect the sincerity of my dear opponents too much to sacrifice my own.

[41] The author was a well-known French writer from the Catholic antisemitic camp but later changed his political orientation, was critical of Franco's Spain and, after the signing of the Munich Agreement (1938), emigrated to Brazil. During the War he supported General De Gaulle's Free French.

[42] In the original, *compatriotes*—that is, the author wishes to stress the part of the Jews in the common homeland, France.

[43] The allegation that the Jews represented the detested spirit of Germany was a standard motif in French antisemitism.

A Jewish Question exists. It is not I who say so: the facts prove it. After two thousand years, the Jewish racial and national sentiment is so obvious to all that none found it remarkable that in 1918, the victorious Allies intended to give them back a homeland.[44]Does this not suffice to demonstrate that Titus's capture of Jerusalem and the dispersion of the vanquished Jews had not solved the problem?[45]

Whoever so speaks, is liable to be called an antisemite. This word horrifies me more and more. Hitler has dishonored it once and for all.[46] (Bernanos, pp. 437–438)

Summary: War and Holocaust

The nationalist radicalization in the 1930s, and particularly the spread of Nazism, rendered antisemitism the official or semi-official policy in many European countries and undermined the status of the Jews. The respectability accorded antisemitism in the 1930s was so extensive that Jew-hatred was almost congruous with nationalism. No one doubted of course that the position of the Jews was worsening. In some quarters warnings were voiced of an impending calamity. Yet not even the most pessimistic observers could imagine the catastrophe that lay only a few years ahead. The Holocaust is unexampled in the course of human history, which has witnessed innumerable massacres, or for that matter in comparison with the persecution experienced by the Jews themselves in the past. Furthermore, we do not know enough about the decision-making pro-

[44] In 1918, at the end of World War I, the Zionist Commission which visited Palestine included a representative of French Jewry. Thus a quarter of a century later the author could recall the decision of the "victorious Allies"—the Western powers—to support Zionist aspirations in Palestine. France, as is known, was quite reserved about Zionism, but appended its formal support to the Balfour Declaration.

[45] In other words, the Jews had not assimilated into the nations, as they had been expected to do since the destruction of the Temple; hence they constitute a problem to this day. This well-known historical motif in Jew-hatred leads here to an affirmation of the Jewish national solution.

[46] He had initially considered the term "antisemite" as perfectly respectable. It signified no more than an acknowledgement of the Jews' distinctiveness as an ethno-cultural group. Now that Hitler had sullied this word, a decent antisemite could no longer identify with it. The antisemitic position was sound, but the appellation should no longer be used because of its external corruption. His stand could thus be summed up by saying that a Frenchman had to choose between his nation and antisemitism. Since Hitler, and most especially after the German occupation of France, it was no longer possible simultaneously to be a French nationalist and an antisemite, for antisemitism went hand-in-glove with national treason; it was tantamount to collaboration with the Nazis.

cess that led to the extermination of the Jews; indeed, there is no indication that the "Final Solution" was planned prior to the outbreak of the War (and perhaps not even before the German invasion of the Soviet Union in 1941).

Thus no one could predict the reaction of the antisemitic collaborators to the Nazi demand that the Jews be rounded up and sent to the East to be murdered there. These antisemitic leaders were motivated by a mixture of short-term considerations and deep-rooted Jew-hatred, as against moral inhibitions and the desire to preserve their country's sovereignty. There may seem to be no clear-cut difference between the regimes that collaborated with the Nazis and the perpetrators of the "Final Solution" themselves, still a dividing line must nevertheless be drawn between the nationalistic leaderships of the satellite countries and Nazi Germany. It is doubtful whether the former had absorbed the racial ideology of their masters or were as obsessed as the Nazis with an all-out war against the Jews. Their behavior, on the whole, was cruel, cynical and opportunistic, whether they persecuted Jews, turned them in, or even helped them escape. Nonetheless, they were part of a less dogmatic climate than that of the Nazis. They were driven by complex considerations of utility, loyalty, honor, perhaps even by Christian conscience and a sense of guilt and shame. Such antisemites hated the Jews and wanted to remove them from positions of power, to expel them and even to kill. They saw in the Jews a national enemy but not a cosmic enemy, as Hitler did.

Their maneuverings, mixed feelings and complex motives sometimes brought about a slowdown in the workings of the Nazis' death machine. A substantive difference undoubtedly existed between politicians who operated in a pervasively antisemitic atmosphere and those in countries where Jews had been more or less integrated. During the War changes occurred rapidly: yesterday's extremists could be tomorrow's moderates—either they were eclipsed by more rabid extremists or the time for extremism seemed to be over. So many different factors contributed to the emerging pattern that any generalizations would be quite hazardous.

Finally, it can be said that the nationalist collaborators of Germany did not constitute a stable ally. Hence the Nazis could not rely upon them, even where the Jews were concerned. Nationalism fulfilled a dialectical role during the Holocaust: the Nazis encouraged the national separatism of underprivileged ethnic groups and broke up former federal states, such as Czechoslovakia and Yugoslavia. On the other hand, national feelings worked against the Nazi invaders. Antisemitism was also enmeshed in this diversified texture: in general it was consonant with local nationalism and bolstered collaboration with the Nazis. In some cases, antisemites opposed the murder of the Jews for patriotic reasons, or because they had reservations about the Nazis' methods and were unreceptive to their racial theory.

Epilogue

A Hundred and Thirty Years of Nationalism and Antisemitism

An attempt to isolate a single strand in the tangled historical fabric presents difficulties. Ideas, feelings and events are often elusive and defy abstract categories. Classification will always be more circumscribed and static than the living reality. Thus, when referring to different types of antisemitism, I may fail to draw a clear line of demarcation between them. The phenomena in question are overlapping even mixed; the tortuous boundaries between them surface and vanish again and again. Furthermore, not only are the events highly complex, even the words we use to describe them assume new meanings from time to time.

What has been said so far about the different phenomena of antisemitism is also applicable to other, related, subjects. Can Jew-hatred be shorn from the broader relations between Jews and non-Jews and be considered in isolation, as though it were completely distinct? Doesn't the very use of the term antisemitism dictate a certain attitude toward the relationship between Jews and Gentiles? Add to this the problem of historical continuity; does such continuity actually exist within the history of antisemitism, what impact does it have on the nature of the relations between Jews and non-Jews, and how is that impact to be measured? Finally, the very term "anti-semitism" is anachronistic and rather dubious, yet we apply it knowingly following an established convention. Furthermore, perhaps disentangling the thread of Jewish history from the loom of human history might single it out beyond measure or place it beyond the

weave of relations of all men, peoples and religions—a weave thick
with tensions, hatreds and struggles.

On the other hand, consideration must also be given to the significance of nationalism as a point of departure. "People," "nationality," "nation," "state"—these are not synonyms but diverse concepts
charged with a broad range of meanings; indeed, it is no accident
that their translation from one language to another presents difficulties. True, nationalism is characterized by the distinctiveness of
each and every nation, yet the aspiration for uniqueness recurs time
and again in *every* nation. In other words, this is a phenomenon
which seems to be at one and the same time hermetic and universal.
This is apparently an internal contradiction. However, no one will
deny today the vast importance of nationalism in history, particularly in the modern age.

Let us then acknowledge the contradictions of reality and the
obstacles raised by language and tread our way carefully to reach
the junction at which nationalism and antisemitism meet. Their
encounter sometimes engendered mutual interplay, while in other
cases it was only an ephemeral, chance meeting. At all events, such
connections grew increasingly closer as the nineteenth century gave
way to the twentieth.

Modern antisemitism often dredged up the accusations levelled at
the Jews in earlier times, but its principal allegation was that the
Jews do not belong to the majority peoples. That allegation is
directly related to the emancipation of the Jews and the emergence
of a society in which all—Jews included—are equal before the law.
This type of society was an innovation of the American and French
revolutions on the one hand, and of a gradual development throughout Europe on the other. Opposition to Jewish emancipation frequently originated in conservative circles, which were apprehensive
of any change in society. These reactionaries were soon joined by
other critics who were disappointed in the change that had actually
occurred, or felt that bourgeois equality was not sufficiently far-
reaching. For the conservatives, equal status granted to the Jews
signified the overthrow of the Old Regime and foreshadowed the
collapse of the social order. In contrast, some Socialists saw the Jews
as a symbol of the bourgeois society which paid lip service to formal
equality but perpetuated social inequity. These were expressions of
two different responses to the Jews' entry into society and the role
played by them in the rise of capitalism.

Nationalism was originally a revolutionary slogan intent upon replacing the feudal modes of life with an egalitarian society. The idea of the nation was associated with a more open society—more open than the pre-revolutionary system. The concept "nation" was consistent with the equality of rights, freedom of opinion, *laissez-faire* liberalism—and the emancipation of the Jews. Subsequently the dark side of nationalism made itself felt in the form of the nation as an insular group struggling against liberal trends and fighting against other nations. German nationalism, steeled in the struggle against the Napoleonic conquest, was bound up with a rejection of the French spirit. Even then it showed incipient signs of what would typify it after "the Peoples' Spring"—exclusivist particularity, national isolationism, a romantic *Weltanschauung*, resentment toward modernization and enmity against Jews. These traits evolved as a counterweight to industrialization, urbanization, secularization, capitalism and liberalism. Modernization in Germany did not cause the influences of the Old Regime to vanish. Moreover, romantic nationalism spread from Germany to other countries where modernization was still lagging behind. Eventually, romantic nationalism became the dominant mode of European nationalism.

Concurrently the "Jewish Question" also rose to the fore—the Jews having evinced great adaptability to modernization. Certain traditional characteristics now served the Jews in their desire to prove themselves and gain recognition, much like other discriminated minorities. The Western capitalist countries enabled the Jews to integrate into economic and political life, whereas in Central Europe the restrictive tendency was more pronounced. The Jew was often considered alien to the nation's spirit, an agent of modernization threatening traditional society, or even a revolutionary dedicated to undermining the regime. According to the antisemites, the emancipation of the Jews presented an opportunity by which the Jews became part of the social fabric and destroyed it from within, whether as capitalists or as socialists. Antisemites saw the Jews as an alien body penetrating the national organism in order to erode it—in the economy and society, in politics and culture. A distinct connection is discernible between radical conservatism and romantic nationalism, and between both of them and enmity toward the Jews.

In the pre-modern period the Jews were an alien body that existed on the outskirts of Christian society, but at that time society as a whole was divided into classes. When the classes were ostensibly dissolved in favor of the all-embracing nation, the Jews were conspicuous as outsiders. Romanticism looked upon nationalism not as a functional association but as a living organism all of whose parts were interconnected. The organic approach was based on a common origin, temperament and heritage, on the love of one's country, and on the mutual affinity between members of the same body politic. Jews did not belong to such nationalism—they had a separate tradition, even if it was rapidly disintegrating under the process of modernization. Romantic nationalists encountered Jews who were rationalists and liberals, who had discarded any connection with the past. At times Jews who were most assimilated drew upon themselves the greatest anger. Sometimes the traditional Jew or national Jew were easier to accommodate than the more assimilated Jew, for they reaffirmed that a Jew could not integrate; since he was part of a different national organism himself and all nations were said to be hostile to each other. Zionism thus sometimes evoked a certain sympathy among antisemites, as it seemed to prove their case and to offer a prospect of solving the "Jewish Question" outside their own country

Antisemitic nationalism tended to place the emphasis on a secular interpretation of Jew-hatred. But Christian motifs were also utilized, as they offered a powerful source of hostile symbolism that stressed the Jews' alienation from the popular tradition underlying nationalism. The Jews, for their part, usually favored a liberal orientation that regarded national affiliation as a voluntary act. Many Jews favored a liberal system of government and economy, which was anathema to the typical romantic nationalist. There was a certain correlation between various traits that characterized the Jews culturally and socially, in contradistinction to the essence of romantic nationalism. Furthermore, Jewish immigration was also a disturbing factor, since it tended to impede the smooth integration of the long-established Jewish residents.

As the process of Jewish emancipation intensified, individual Jews increasingly perceived it as a right to participate in public life as they saw fit. Frequently Jews stood out as extreme innovaters, which vexed conservative circles. Non-Jews tended to regard these Jews as representing Jewish opinion, rather than as ordinary citizens merely exercising their civil rights. Over and above the letter of the law, society was particularly sensitive to the behavior of Jews, and even of converted Jews. A deep gulf separated the self-perception of these people from the impression their behavior evoked in the public mind. The Jewish community no longer exercised any authority over Jews who disregarded their Jewish ties; and even those who maintained their connection with the community were under no obligation to account for their actions. Obviously, the Jewish establishment had no authority and could not wield any moral influence on estranged Jews.

Romantic nationalism also saw in Jewry an organism all of whose parts were interlocked. Thus criminal acts involving Jews were imputed to the entire Jewish community; scathing opinions voiced by Jews were regarded as typically Jewish; wealthy Jews were perceived as representatives of Jewish capitalism; Jewish radicals were taken to be the instruments of an allegedly destructive and disintegrating Judaism. This tendency also produced the image of a "Jewish conspiracy" in which the actors seemingly played roles, such as members of the bourgeoisie or revolutionaries, but which actually concealed, as antisemitic legend had it, a Jewish scheme to destroy the existing order and conquer the world. The plot attributed to the Jews explained away the internal contradictions in the antisemitic argument and invented a common denominator for unrelated phenomena.

Antisemitism purposefully ignored the actual results of both emancipation and assimilation on Jewish life. The proviso that the Jews be accepted into society as individuals only was gradually being realized (in any event, this principle was generally adopted by the Jews themselves), whereas antisemites interpreted Judaism as signifying a wilful collective isolation. From here the argument followed that Jewish survival was not voluntary at all but a biological-racial manifestation. Incidentally, the racial motif was quite widespread in the second half of the nineteenth and early twentieth century and enjoyed an ostensibly scientific stamp of approval. Racial explanations were increasingly adduced in various domains, and antisemitism, too, made use of racial arguments.

Such racial notions were then developed by the Nazis as underpinnings for their struggle between the races and the Aryan-Semitic polarization. Nazism was the culmination of a process originally made up of diverse and even contradictory tendencies. Different types of antisemitism had coexisted and exercised reciprocal influences: antisemitic nationalism affected one country after another, sometimes overriding hostility between nations; traditional Jew-hatred made its contribution to secular antisemitism and indirectly even nourished anti-Christian antisemitism; opposition to capitalism fed the antagonism toward Jews among aristocrats on the one hand, and among Socialists and radicals, on the other. Also noteworthy are the differences between a casual use of anti-Jewish feelings or political antisemitism, which organized regular campaigns against the Jews. Similarly, distinctions must be drawn between the different shades of opposition to Jewish influence in society, in the economy, in politics and culture.

There were two particular points of interaction between antisemitism and nationalism:

— in shaping the national consciousness of peoples in Central and Eastern Europe; and

— in the struggles between rival national movements in the multinational empires and between the successor states.

The national awakening in Central and Eastern Europe came after the consolidation of the nation-states in Western Europe. Nationalism also sought to overcome a relative backwardness and free itself from a sense of inferiority with regard to the more advanced countries. The sense of honor called for an upgrading of one's national entity and a liberation from foreign influences. National consciousness extolled the nations' past and its distinctiveness, while rejecting the foreigner. The Jews were cast in the role of the stranger, even when they had contributed much to the country's development and the shaping of the national culture. Moreover, following the upward mobility of elites from within the majority, these groups looked askance at the influence of the Jewish intelligentsia and middle class. Jews were suspected of an absence of loyalty to the nation, whether because of their history and heritage, their outside connections, or even their particular desire to demonstrate their sense of belonging. This phenomenon occurred in Germany and Austria-Hungary (including the rival national movements within the Hapsburg Empire) and even more acutely in the new states established after World War I.

Following Hitler's assumption of power, Nazi Germany became a lodestone for sympathizers in the chauvinist states that arose on the ruins of the multinational empires. In these countries filled with frustration, fanatical nationalism combined with traditional Jew-hatred helped the Nazis gain influence and power. Nazi Germany bound the leaders of the satellite states through an imperial policy of "divide and rule" and through antisemitic ideology. Still, the Holocaust period made plain the difference between a narrow-minded nationalism and racist Nazism itself, between murderous antisemites and the total and absolute "Final Solution."

Finally, it must be said that the hopes the Jews and their benefactors had once placed on emancipation increasingly receded as European society became a "Europe of nations" and the national movements fought against each other. For generations the Jews had been excoriated by their critics for excessive *isolationism*. The history of the Jews combined the unusual phenomenon of a highly distinct people bearing a universal message. This combination was unconventional even in the ancient world, when a universal Helenism could reconcile itself to the full panoply of local cults—but not to the Jews with their universal claim. This dichotomy was further aggravated by Christianity, which spoke on behalf of universal salvation and suffered in its midst one single oddity—the Jews, who were destined to attest that they no longer bore the universal message.

The era of nationalism witnessed a complete reversal concerning universalism, yet Jews continued to cleave to it, while trying to integrate into national life; the result was that they were denounced as an "anti-national nation." Once again, Jews did not blend with their surroundings to the point of no return, as might have been expected of them. Finally, in the era of nationalism the Jews were ejected from Europe in an unprecedented manner. The alternative proposed by Jewish nationalism could not offer an effective solution for the majority of European Jews. No doubt the Holocaust was a watershed in history, and decades of research have not yet revealed all its secrets. Certainly no definitive evaluation can be made to date about the part played by nationalism in the Holocaust. Nationalism was but one factor, yet we could hardly omit reference to it when accounting for the developments that took place in Europe between the two World Wars, including the rise of Nazism and the dissemination of antisemitism in the world.

Bibliography

Akzin, Benjamin. *State and Nation*. London, 1964.

Almog, Shmuel. "Antisemitism as a Dynamic Phenomenon, The Development of the 'Jewish Question' in England at the End of World War I," *Patterns of Prejudice* **21**, 4 (1987).

Angress, Werner T. "Juden im politischen Leben der Revolutionszeit." In Mosse, Werner E., and Arnold Paucker (eds.). *Deutsches Judentum in Krieg und Revolution, 1916–1923.* Tübingen, 1971.

Ascher, Saul. *Germanomanie, Skizze zu einem Zeitbild*. Berlin, 1815.

Barany, George. "Magyar Jew or Jewish Magyar? Reflections on the Question of Assimilation." In Vago, Bela, and George L. Mosse (eds.). *Jews and Non-Jews in Eastern Europe*. New York, Toronto & Jerusalem, 1974.

Baron, Salo W. "Nationalism and Intolerance," *The Menorah Journal* **16** (1920a); **17** (1920b).

Baron, Salo W. *A Social and Religious History of the Jews*, Vol. XI. New York & London, 1967.

Bartyś, Julian. "Grand Duchy of Poznań under Prussian Rule," *Leo Baeck Institute Year Book* **17** (1972).

Beer, Max. *Fifty Years of International Socialism*. London, 1935.

Berger, David. "Anti-Semitism; An Overview." In Berger, David (ed.). *History and Hate—The Dimensions of Anti-Semitism*. Philadelphia, New York & Jerusalem, 1986.

Bernanos, Georges. *La Grande peur des bien-pensants*. Paris, 1969.

Bernstein-Cohen, Miriam, and Yitzhak Korn (eds.). *The Book of Bernstein-Cohen*. Tel Aviv, 1946 (Hebrew).

Billington, James H. *The Icon and the Axe: An Interpretative History of Russian Culture*. New York, 1970.

Bloch, Josef Samuel. *Der nationale Zwist und die Juden in Oesterreich*. Vienna, 1886.

Blumenfeld, Kurt. 'Referat,' *Jüdische Rundschau*, 16 September 1932.

Blumenfeld, Kurt. *Erlebte Judenfrage: Ein Vierteljahrhundert deutscher Zionismus*. Stuttgart, 1962.

Boehlich, Walter (ed.). *Der Berliner Antisemitismusstreit*. Frankfurt, 1965.

Braham, Randolph L. "The Uniqueness of the Holocaust in Hungary." In Braham, Randolph, and Bela Vago (eds.). *The Holocaust in Hungary, Forty Years Later*. New York, 1985.

Braudel, Fernand. *The Mediterranean and the Mediterranean World in the Age of Philip II*, Vol. II. London, 1982.

Carpi, Daniel. "The Origins and Development of Fascist Antisemitism in Italy (1922–1945)." In Gutman, Yisrael, and Livia Rothkirchen (eds.). *The Catastrophe of European Jewry—Antecedents, History, Reflection*. Jerusalem, 1976.

Carr, Edward Hallett. *Nationalism and After*. London, 1968.

Červinka, František. "The Hilsner Affair," *Leo Baeck Institute Year Book* **13** (1968).

Chapman, Guy, *The Dreyfus Affair*. New York, 1972.

Churchill, Winston. "Zionism versus Bolshevism, A Struggle for the Soul of the Jewish People," *Illustrated Sunday Herald*, 8 February 1920.

Cobban, Alfred. *The Nation State and National Self-Determination*. London & Glasgow, 1969.

Cohn, Norman. *Warrant for Genocide: the Myth of the Jewish World-Wide Conspiracy and the Protocols of the Elders of Zion*. London, 1957.

Conquest, Robert. *The Great Terror*. New York, 1973.

Davies, Norman. *God's Playground—A History of Poland*, Vol. II. Oxford, 1983.

Delpech, François. "De 1815 à 1894." In Blumenkranz, Bernhard (ed.). *Histoire des Juifs en France*. Toulouse, 1972.

Dictionary of the History of Ideas. Studies of Selected Pivotal Ideas, Vol. IV. New York, 1973.

Dostoyevsky, Fyodor Mikhailovich. *The Diary of a Writer*, Vol. II (trans. by Boris Brasol). London, 1949.

Duroselle, Jean-Baptiste. "L'Antisémitisme en France de 1886 à 1914," *Cahiers Paul Claudel* **7** (1968).

Encyclopaedia Britannica, Vol. XIX. Chicago & London, 1973.

Encyclopedia Judaica, Vol. VIII. Jerusalem, 1971.

Ettinger, Shmuel. "Introduction." In Tal, Uriel. *Christians and Jews in Germany: Religion, Politics and Ideology in the Second Reich, 1870–1914*. Ithaca, 1975.

Ettinger, Shmuel. "The Modern Period." In Ben-Sasson, Haim Hillel (ed.). *A History of the Jewish People*. Cambridge, Mass, 1976.

Ettinger, Shmuel. "Jew-Hatred in its Historical Context." In Almog, Shmuel (ed.). *Antisemitism Through the Ages*. Oxford, 1988.

Fein, Helen. *Accounting for Genocide: National Responses and Jewish Victimization During the Holocaust*. Chicago, 1984.

Feinberg, Nathan. *Studies in International Law*. Jerusalem, 1979.

Fischer-Galati, Stephen. "Fascism, Communism and the Jewish Question in Romania." In Vago, Bela, and George L. Mosse (eds.). *Jews and Non-Jews in Eastern Europe*. Jerusalem, 1974.

Friedländer, Saul. "Die politischen Veränderungen der Kriegszeit und ihre Auswirkungen auf die Judenfrage." In Mosse, Werner E., and Arnold Paucker (eds.). *Deutsches Judentum in Krieg und Revolution, 1916–1923*. Tübingen, 1971.

Garntsarska-Kadary, Bina. "The Jews and the Factors in the Development and Location of Industry in Warsaw." *Gal-Ed: On the History of the Jews in Poland* **2** (1975) (Hebrew).

Garntsarska-Kadary, Bina. *The Role of the Jews in the Development of Industry in Warsaw, 1816/20–1914*. Tel Aviv, 1985 (Hebrew).

Girardet, Raoul. *Le Nationalisme français*. Paris, 1966.

Glatzer, Nahum N. "Leopold Zunz and the Revolution of 1848," *Leo Baeck Institute Year Book* **5** (1960).

Gleason, Abbot. *Young Russia: The Genesis of Russian Radicalism in the 1860s*. Chicago & London, 1983.

Goldstücker, Eduard. "Jews Between Czechs and Germans Around 1848," *Leo Baeck Institute Year Book* **17** (1972).

Graves, Philip. "Jewish World Plot, An Exposure," *Times*, 16 August 1921.

Greenberg, Louis. *The Jews in Russia—The Struggle for Emancipation*, Vol. II. New York, 1976.
Greive, Hermann. *Geschichte des modernen Antisemitismus in Deutschland*. Darmstadt, 1983.
Griffiths, Richard. *Fellow Travellers of the Right*. Oxford, 1983.
Guillemin, Henri (ed.). *Nationalistes et "nationaux" (1870–1914)*. Paris, 1974.
Gutman, Yisrael. *The Jews of Warsaw, 1939–1943: Ghetto, Underground, Revolt*. Bloomington, 1982.
Halasz, Nicholas. *Captain Dreyfus—The Story of a Mass Hysteria*. New York, 1955.
Harcave, Sidney. *The Russian Revolution of 1905*. Toronto, 1970.
Harris, André, and Alain de Sédouy. *Juifs et Français*. Paris, 1979.
Haumann, Heiko. "Das Jüdische Prag 1850–1914." In Martin, Bernd, and Ernst Schulin (eds.). *Die Juden als Minderheit in der Geschichte*. Munich, 1981.
Heller, Celia S. *On the Edge of Destruction—Jews of Poland between the Two World Wars*. New York, 1980.
Herzl, Theodor. *The Complete Diaries of Theodor Herzl* (ed. by Raphael Patai), Vol. IV. New York, 1960.
Higham, John. *Strangers in the Land*. New York, 1966.
Hilberg, Raoul. *The Destruction of the European Jews*. New York, 1979.
Hitler, Adolf. *Mein Kampf (My Struggle)* (trans. by Ralph Mannheim). Boston, 1943.
Holmes, Colin. *Anti-Semitism in British Society, 1876–1939*. New York, 1979.
Janowsky, Oscar I. *Nationalism and National Minorities (With Special Reference to East-Central Europe)*. New York, 1945.
The Jews of Czechoslovakia: Historical Studies and Surveys, Vol. I. Philadelphia, 1968.
Jastrow, Marcus. 'Memoirs,' *He'avar: A Quarterly for the History of Jews and Judaism in Russia* **13** (1966) (Hebrew).
Jersch-Wentzel, Stefi. "German Jews in the Rural Economy." In Mosse, Werner E., Arnold Paucker and Reinhard Rürup (eds.). *Revolution and Evolution, 1848 in German-Jewish History*. Tübingen, 1981.
Katz, Jacob. *From Prejudice to Destruction: Anti-Semitism 1700–1933*. Cambridge, Mass., 1980.
Katzburg, Nathaniel. "The Tradition of Antisemitism in Hungary." In Braham, Randolph L., and Bela Vago (eds.). *The Holocaust in Hungary, Forty Years Later*. New York, 1985.
Katzburg, Nathaniel. *Hungary and the Jews 1920–1943*. Ramat Gan, 1981.
Kohn, Hans. *The Idea of Nationalism*. Toronto, 1969.
Lacouture, Jean. *Léon Blum*. Paris, 1977.
Landau, Edwin. "Mein Leben," *Mitteilungen des Verbandes der ehemaligen Breslauer und Schlesier in Israel* **46–47** (1979).
Laqueur, Walter. *Germany and Russia: Century of Conflict*. Boston, 1965.
Lavi, Theodor. "The Background to the Rescue of Romanian Jewry During the Period of the Holocaust." In Vago, Bela, and George L. Mosse (eds.). *Jews and Non-Jews in Eastern Europe*. Jerusalem, 1974.
Leroy-Beaulieu, Anatole. *Israël chez les nations (Israel Among the Nations)*. Paris, 1893 (French edn.) and New York, 1904.
Leslie, R.F. (ed.). *The History of Poland Since 1863*. Cambridge, 1987.
Levin, Ya'akov Halevi. *The Jews in the Polish Revolution: Memoirs of Ya'akov Halevi Levin from the Polish Revolution of 1830–1831* (ed. by N. M. Gelber). Jerusalem, 1953 (Hebrew).
Low, Alfred D. *Jews in the Eyes of the Germans, From the Enlightenment to Imperial Germany*. Philadelphia, 1979.
Madaule, Jacques. *Histoire de France*, Vol. III. Paris, 1966.

152 Bibliography

Marr, William. "The Victory of Judaism over Germandom." In Mendes-Flohr, Paul R., and Jehuda Reinharz (eds.). *The Jew in the Modern World: A Documentary History*. New York, 1980.

Marrus, Michael R. *The Politics of Assimilation—The French Jewish Community at the Time of the Dreyfus Affair*. Oxford, 1980.

Marrus, Michael R. and Robert Paxton. *Vichy France and the Jews*. New York, 1983.

Melzer, Emanuel. "Polish Diplomacy and Jewish Emigration during 1935–1939," *Gal-Ed: On the History of the Jews in Poland* 1 (1973) (Hebrew).

Mendelsohn, Ezra. *The Jews of East Central Europe between the World Wars*. Bloomington, 1983.

Mendes-Flohr, Paul R., and Jehuda Reinharz (eds.). *The Jew in the Modern World. A Documentary History*. New York & Oxford, 1980.

Michaelis, Meir. "The 'Duce' and the Jews: an Assessment of the Literature on Italian Jewry under Fascism, 1922–1945," *Yad Vashem Studies* 11 (1976).

Mosse, Werner E. "Der Niedergang der Republik und die Juden." In Mosse, Werner E., and Arnold Paucker (eds.). *Entscheidungsjahr 1932*. Tübingen, 1966.

Na'aman, Shlomo. *The Birth of a Civilization: The First Millenium of Latin Europe*. Tel Aviv, 1975 (Hebrew).

Oren, Nissan. "The Bulgarian Exception: a Reassessment of the Salvation of the Jewish Community," *Yad Vashem Studies* 7 (1968).

Palestine—A Study of Jewish, Arab and British Policies, Vol. II. New Haven, 1947.

Paxton, Robert. *Vichy France*. New York, 1982.

Peterseil, Jacob, Zev Abramovitch and Jacob Zerubavel (eds.). *Poalei Zion: Selected Papers (Yalkutei Poalei Zion)*. Tel Aviv, 1946 (Hebrew).

Philippe, Béatrice. *Être Juif dans la société française*. Paris, 1979.

Poliakov, Léon. *The History of Antisemitism*, Vol. IV. New York, 1985.

The Protocols of the Wise Men of Zion. New York, 1920.

Pulzer, Peter G. J. *The Rise of Political Antisemitism in Germany and Austria*. London, 1988.

Rabi, Wladimir. "De 1906 à 1939." In Blumenkranz, Bernhard (ed.). *Histoire des Juifs en France*. Toulouse, 1972.

Ránki, György. "The Germans and the Destruction of Hungarian Jewry." In Braham, Randolph, and Bela Vago (eds.). *The Holocaust in Hungary, Forty Years Later*. New York, 1985.

Reden gegen den Antisemitismus, gehalten in den Sitzuugen des österreichischen Abgeordretenhauses (1890), Central Archives of the Jewish People, Jerusalem, Archive of the Vienna Community, A/W 315.

Reed, John. *Ten Days that Shook the World*. Harmondsworth, 1966.

Ringelblum, Emmanuel. *Polish-Jewish Relations During the Second World War*. New York, 1976.

Rogger, Hans. *Jewish Policies and Right-Wing Politics in Imperial Russia*. Oxford, 1986.

Rogger, Hans. *Russia in the Age of Modernisation and Revolution, 1881–1917*. London, 1983.

Rosensaft, Menachem Z. "Jews and Antisemites in Austria at the End of the Nineteenth Century, *"Leo Baeck Institute Year Book* 21 (1976).

Ruppin, Arthur. *Memoirs, Diaries, Letters* (ed. by Alex Bein). London, 1971.

Rürup, Reinhard. *Emanzipation und Antisemitismus—Studien zur 'Judenfrage' der bürgerlichen Gesellschaft*. Göttingen, 1975.

Samuel, Maurice. *Blood Accusation. The Strange History of the Beiliss Case*. Philadelphia, 1966.

Samuel, Sir Stuart. 'Report,' *Jewish Chronicle*, 9 July 1920.

Schenk, Hans G. *The Mind of the European Romantics*. Oxford & New York, 1979.

Shafer, Boyd C. *Faces of Nationalism*. New York & London, 1974.

Shatzky, Jacob. "The Jews in Poland from 1772 to 1914." In *The Jews of Poland*, Vol. I. New York, 1946 (Yiddish).

Sheehan, James J. *German Liberalism in the Nineteenth Century*. London, 1982.

Shmeruk, Chone. *The Esterke Story in Yiddish and Polish Literature*. Jerusalem, 1985.

Slutsky, Yehuda. "The Geography of the Pogroms," *Heawar* 9 (1962) (Hebrew).

Slutsky, Ychuda. "Pogroms." In *Anti-Semitism*, Israel Pocket Library, *Encyclopedia Judaica*. Jerusalem, 1974.

Slutsky, Yehuda. "The Year 1905 and Russian Jews," *Heawar* 22 (1976) (Hebrew).

Smith, Anthony D. *Nationalism in the Twentieth Century*. Oxford, 1979.

Stein, Leonard. *The Balfour Declaration*. London, 1961.

Sternhell, Zeev. "Fascist Ideology." In Laqueur, Walter (ed.), *Fascism*. Harmondsworth, 1979.

Strauss, Herbert A. "Formen des modernen Antisemitismus und Probleme seiner Abwehr," *International Review of Social History* 30, 3 (1985).

Szajkowski, Zoza. "Anti-Jewish Riots During the Revolutions of 1789, 1830, 1848," *Zion* 20 (1955) (Hebrew).

Szajkowski, Zoza. "The Petlyura Affair," *Heawar* 17 (May, 1970) (Hebrew).

Szajkowski, Zoza. *Jews and the French Revolutions of 1789, 1830 and 1848*. New York, 1970.

Tamir, Vicki. *Bulgaria and Her Jews, The History of a Dubious Symbiosis*. New York, 1979.

Talmon, Jacob L. *Romanticism and Revolt: Europe 1815–1848*. London, 1967.

Taylor, Telford. *Munich*. New York, 1980.

Thomas, Hugh. *The Spanish Civil War*. Harmondsworth, 1977.

Toury, Jacob. *Die Politischen Orientierungen der Juden in Deutschland*. Tübingen, 1966.

Wagner, Richard. *Judaism in Music*. London, 1910.

Weber, Eugen. "Romania." In Rogger, Hans, and Eugen Weber (eds.). *The European Right*. Berkeley & Los Angeles, 1965.

Weinryb, Bernard D. "Antisemitism in Soviet Russia." In Kochan, Lionel (ed.). *The Jews in Soviet Russia since 1917*. Oxford, London & New York, 1978.

Weltsch, Robert. "Introduction," *Leo Baeck Institute Year Book* 7 (1962).

Wilson, Stephen. *Ideology and Experience, Antisemitism in France at the Time of the Dreyfus Affair*. London & Toronto, 1982.

Wistrich, Robert. *Socialism and the Jews, The Dilemmas of Assimilation in Germany and Austria-Hungary*. East Brunswick, NJ, 1982.

Yerushalmi, Yosef Haim. *Assimilation and Racial Anti-Semitism, The Iberian and German Models* (The Leo Baeck Memorial Lecture). New York, 1982.

Index